Interdisciplinary Contributions to Archaeology

Series Editor
Jelmer Eerkens, University of California, Davis, USA

Editorial Board Members
Canan Çakırlar, University of Groningen, Groningen, The Netherlands
Fumie Iizuka, University of Wisconsin–Madison, Madison, WI, USA
Krish Seetah, Stanford University, Stanford, USA
Nuria Sugranes, Instituto de Evolución, Ecología Histórica y Ambiente, San Rafael, Argentina
Shannon Tushingham, California Academy of Sciences, San Francisco, USA
Chris Wilson, Flinders University, Bedford Park, Australia

Archaeology stands alone among the sciences in its attempt to enlighten us about the entire record of humankind. To cover such a broad range of time and space, archaeologists must ensure that their findings are integrated into broader spheres of scientific knowledge. The IDCA series aims to highlight the collaborative and interdisciplinary nature of contemporary archaeological research.

Topics the series has covered include:

- Paleoecology
- Archaeological Landscapes
- Statistical Approaches
- Laboratory Methods
- Human Biological and Cultural Evolution
- Human Nutrition
- Emergence of Agriculture and Pastoralism

For a copy of the proposal form, please contact Christi Lue (christi.lue@springer.com). Initial proposals can be sent to the Series Editor, Jelmer Eerkens (jweerkens@ucdavis.edu). Proposals should include:

- A short synopsis of the work or the introduction chapter
- The proposed Table of Contents
- The CV of the lead author(s)
- If available: one sample chapter

We aim to make a first decision within 1 month of submission. In case of a positive first decision the work will be provisionally contracted: the final decision about publication will depend upon the result of the anonymous peer review of the complete manuscript. We aim to have the complete work peer-reviewed within 3 months of submission.

This book series is indexed in SCOPUS.

For more information, please contact the Series Editor at (jweerkens@ucdavis.edu).

Francesca Coletti • Christina Margariti
Vanessa Forte • Stella Spantidaki
Editors

Multidisciplinary Approaches for the Investigation of Textiles and Fibres in the Archaeological Field

Editors
Francesca Coletti
Department of Science of Antiquities
Sapienza University of Rome
Rome, Italy

Vanessa Forte
Department of Science of Antiquities
Sapienza University of Rome
Roma, Italy

Christina Margariti
Applied Research Department, Directorate
of Conservation of Ancient & Modern
Monuments
Hellenic Ministry of Culture
Athens, Greece

Stella Spantidaki
Hellenic Centre for Research and
Conservation of Archaeological
Textiles (ARTEX)
Athens, Greece

ISSN 1568-2722   ISSN 2730-6984 (electronic)
Interdisciplinary Contributions to Archaeology
ISBN 978-3-031-73811-1   ISBN 978-3-031-73812-8 (eBook)
https://doi.org/10.1007/978-3-031-73812-8

© The Editor(s) (if applicable) and The Author(s), under exclusive license to Springer Nature Switzerland AG 2024

Chapter 6 is licensed under the terms of the Creative Commons Attribution 4.0 International License (http://creativecommons.org/licenses/by/4.0/). For further details see license information in the chapter.
This work is subject to copyright. All rights are solely and exclusively licensed by the Publisher, whether the whole or part of the material is concerned, specifically the rights of translation, reprinting, reuse of illustrations, recitation, broadcasting, reproduction on microfilms or in any other physical way, and transmission or information storage and retrieval, electronic adaptation, computer software, or by similar or dissimilar methodology now known or hereafter developed.
The use of general descriptive names, registered names, trademarks, service marks, etc. in this publication does not imply, even in the absence of a specific statement, that such names are exempt from the relevant protective laws and regulations and therefore free for general use.
The publisher, the authors and the editors are safe to assume that the advice and information in this book are believed to be true and accurate at the date of publication. Neither the publisher nor the authors or the editors give a warranty, expressed or implied, with respect to the material contained herein or for any errors or omissions that may have been made. The publisher remains neutral with regard to jurisdictional claims in published maps and institutional affiliations.

Cover illustration: SEM micrograph of a tabby weave made of bast fibres. (Dr. Francesca Coletti. A3Tex, Sapienza Research Centre).

This Springer imprint is published by the registered company Springer Nature Switzerland AG
The registered company address is: Gewerbestrasse 11, 6330 Cham, Switzerland

If disposing of this product, please recycle the paper.

Contents

1 **Introduction: Towards Multidisciplinary Trajectories for the Study of Ancient Textiles and Fibres**.................... 1
Francesca Coletti, Vanessa Forte, Christina Margariti, and Stella Spantidaki

2 **Using Scanning Electron Microscopy for the Study of Mineralised Textiles: The Case of Roman *Venetia***............. 11
Margarita Gleba and Maria Stella Busana

3 **A Button, a Hook and a Rug Paper Wrapping: Identifying Plant Fibre Finds from Hailuoto, Finland**............ 25
Jenni A. Suomela and Sanna Lipkin

4 **The Effects of Carbonisation on the Morphology of Textile Fibres: Comparison Between Modern and Ancient Materials—The Example of Pompeii**................ 43
Francesca Coletti and Christina Margariti

5 **Multi-analytical Approach for the Characterisation of Ancient Mineral Fibres: Tracing the Use of Asbestos in the Italic Peninsula**........................... 57
Francesca Coletti, Alessandro Ciccola, and Paolo Postorino

6 **Revealing the Unknown: How Multi-technical Approach Can Be Crucial in Identification of Dyes and Protein in Archeological Remains**...................................... 71
Ilaria Serafini, Alessandro Ciccola, Roberta Curini, Gabriele Favero, Gwénaëlle M. Kavich, Timothy P. Cleland, and Caroline Solazzo

7 **Radiocarbon for the Dating of Fibres and Textiles: The Case Study of a Silk Knitted Fabric from Pompeii**........... 123
Mariaelena Fedi, Serena Barone, Francesca Coletti, and Lucia Liccioli

8	**Which Tool for Which Fiber? Experimental Spinning Tests Using Bone, Glass and Amber Instruments** 139
	Maria Stella Busana, Denis Francisci, and Agnese Lena
9	**Residues of Activities: Towards an Analytical Protocol for Studying Residues on Textile Tools** 159
	Vanessa Forte, Francesca Coletti, Carlo Virili, Alessandro M. Jaia, and Cristina Lemorini
10	**Resolving the Mystery of the 2000-Year-Old Net Found in the "Cave of Letters"** 171
	Reuven Yosef, Lee Perry-Gal, and Naama Sukenik

Index 187

About the Editors

Francesca Coletti is a classical archaeologist specialised in textile and fibre analysis. She is a research fellow at Sapienza University of Rome with the project "Archaeology, Archaeometry, and Digitalisation of Archaeological Textiles from Herculaneum" (position obtained thanks to the European Seal of Excellence 2023). Since 2018, she has taught the "Archaeology and Archaeometry of Textiles" course at Sapienza University, and she has been involved in several interdisciplinary projects focused on textiles from Greece, Italy, and Turkey. In 2020, she received her PhD, in co-tutorship at Heidelberg and Sapienza Universities, with the thesis "The Textiles of Pompeii: Materials, Techniques and Contexts", investigating the fabrics and textile imprints on human plaster casts. Thanks to recent national and international grants, Coletti is currently engaged in two collaborative research projects in the framework of the interdepartmental research centre at Sapienza "A3Tex. Archaeology and Archaeometry of Ancient Textile": TEXTaiLES (HORIZON-CL2-2023-HERITAGE-ECCCH-01-02, Innovative Tools for Digitising Cultural Heritage) and ADigText ("Archaeology, Archaeometry and Digitalisation of Ancient Textile. From Pompeii to the Roman Empire") (PRIN 2022. PI Prof. M. Galli, Co-PI Prof. M. Gleba).

Christina Margariti is trained as a textile conservator. She received an MA in Textile Conservation from the Textile Conservation Centre/University of Southampton, where she also completed her PhD on the analysis of excavated textiles. She was an MSCA Fellow at the University of Copenhagen (project FIBRANET) and is part of the EU program TEXTaiLES (HORIZON-CL2-2023-HERITAGE-ECCCH-01-02, Innovative Tools for Digitising Cultural Heritage). She is the Head of the Applied Research Department of the Directorate of Conservation/Hellenic Ministry of Culture and has taught textile conservation and analysis at the Technological Educational Institute of Athens, and the Centre for Textile Research/SAXO Institute, University of Copenhagen.

Vanessa Forte is a prehistoric archaeologist at Sapienza University of Rome, specialising in ancient technology and use-wear analysis on ceramics and clay objects. After earning her PhD from Sapienza University, she was a Marie Skłodowska-Curie Fellow at the McDonald Institute for Archaeological Research at Cambridge University (UK), focusing on craft specialisation. She later worked as a postdoctoral researcher at the Universities of Pisa and Padova, collaborating with international research groups. She integrates archaeometric analyses, technological traces, use-wear studies, and experimental archaeology to reconstruct and investigate the socio-cultural dynamics of ancient societies

Stella Spantidaki is a classical archaeologist specialised in textile archaeology of ancient Greece. In her PhD, conducted at the Universities of the Sorbonne and the Heidelberg University, she focused on textile production in Classical Athens. In her research, she uses interdisciplinary methodology and studies all available sources for textile production and consumption in antiquity. Since 2015 she has been the Director of ARTEX, a research centre in Athens specialising in the study and scientific analyses of archaeological textiles. Currently she is the PI of the Project FAROS, "The Fabric of Kings: Funerary Textiles from Mycenae and the early Mycenaean textile production", hosted at the University of the Peloponnese and funded by the Hellenic Foundation for Research and Innovation (HFRI, pr. no. 7354, 2023–2025).

Chapter 1
Introduction: Towards Multidisciplinary Trajectories for the Study of Ancient Textiles and Fibres

Francesca Coletti, Vanessa Forte, Christina Margariti, and Stella Spantidaki

Abstract The investigation of textiles, a central element of ancient cultures, has recently gained momentum in Europe (mainly in the twenty-first century) manifested by a multidisciplinary approach. Advancements in analytical techniques have revitalized the field, enabling more scientific examinations of textiles and their production contexts. Key initiatives that lead to the establishment of international research centres and various EU projects, have fostered interdisciplinary collaborations, expanding the study of textiles within archaeology and beyond. Recent methodological advancements highlight how fabrics and textile tools can provide critical insights into complex archaeological questions regarding resource interaction, craft, technology, societal dynamics, and cultural identity. In this scenario, scientific approaches integrating humanities and natural sciences are essential to interpret the archaeological evidence. This volume, titled "Multidisciplinary Approaches for the Investigation of Textiles and Fibres in the Archaeological Field", compiles research from various scholars, thus contributing to this rapidly evolving discipline encompassing traditional and novel analytical techniques. The book, serving archaeologists, conservators, scientists, and historians, is structured into three main sections: microscopy and morphometric approaches, multi-technical and archaeometric methodologies, and experimental approaches, providing a comprehensive overview of current research in textile studies.

F. Coletti (✉) · V. Forte
Department of Science of Antiquities, Sapienza University of Rome, Rome, Italy
e-mail: francesca.coletti@uniroma1.it

C. Margariti
Applied Research Department, Directorate of Conservation of Ancient & Modern Monuments, Hellenic Ministry of Culture, Athens, Greece

S. Spantidaki
Hellenic Centre for Research and Conservation of Archaeological Textiles (ARTEX), Athens, Greece

Department of History, Archaeology and Cultural Resources Management, University of Peloponnese, Kalamata, Greece

© The Author(s), under exclusive license to Springer Nature Switzerland AG 2024
F. Coletti et al. (eds.), *Multidisciplinary Approaches for the Investigation of Textiles and Fibres in the Archaeological Field*, Interdisciplinary Contributions to Archaeology, https://doi.org/10.1007/978-3-031-73812-8_1

Keywords Textiles and Fibers · Multidisciplinarity · Scientific analyses · Analytical protocols · Experimental archaeology

Textile production and consumption were one of the most significant expressions of ancient cultures. Despite the centrality of textiles in the ancient world, their scientific investigation in Europe has been limited until the twenty-first century, when the multidisciplinary approach to textile research became a fast-growing scientific practice. Many past contributions in the research field are related to the investigation of indirect archaeological evidence such as literary sources, iconography, textile tools, and production contexts. This approach has been favoured due to the general scarcity of textile remains in archaeological contexts or their poor preservation. However, the advancement of analytical techniques has led to a growing interest in textile studies and the application of more scientific and interdisciplinary approaches to archaeological and historical textiles as well as the development of experimental protocols for the investigation of textile technology and the associated tools.

Pioneering in this development has been the activity and research held by the Danish National Research Foundation's Centre for Textile Research (CTR) at the University of Copenhagen (since 2005). The establishment and spread of interdisciplinary clusters of excellence across Europe is a testimony of the recent growth in textile research fostered by systematic efforts in building a new and interdisciplinary scientific discipline focusing on ancient textiles, namely: the EU-Project DressID-Clothing and Identities in the Roman Empire (2007–2012); the ERC PROCON project (2013–2018) that has provided an important baseline for the study of pre-Roman societies through textiles; the formation of international fora (Purpureae Vestes) and networks (EuroWeb-Europe through Textiles) which have opened up the discipline to non-specialists. Lastly, the newly established research centre for Archaeometry and Archaeology of Ancient Textile (A3Tex) at the Sapienza University of Rome leads interdisciplinary research in a cross-disciplinary collaboration between humanities and natural sciences, highlighting the great potential in the application of scientific methods to textile materials and related artefacts.

In this context, the recent science-based methodological advancements have contributed to generating a renewed awareness of how fabrics can inform us about craft and technology, as well as chronological, social and identity aspects of past societies (Gleba et al., 2008; Michael & Nosch, 2010; Gleba & Mannering, 2012; Bender Jørgensen, 2012; Nosch et al., 2013; Engelhardt Mathiassen et al., 2014; Harlow & Nosch, 2014; Andersson Strand & Nosch, 2015; Rast-Eicher, 2016; Fanfani et al., 2016; Grömer, 2016; Spantidaki, 2016; Gaspa et al., 2017; Siennicka et al., 2018; Galli et al., 2020; Coletti, 2020, forthcoming; Coletti et al., 2023; Margariti et al., 2024). In fact, as recently demonstrated, the tradition of using specific techniques, raw materials and dyes, as well using specific tools for spinning and weaving activities in the ancient world, involved cultural choices expressing self or group identities.

Therefore, the scientific examination of ancient fabrics and textile tools is a key element for acquiring important information about the interaction between resources, technology, and society that cannot be extrapolated by other sources. This complex framework of materials, actions and agents required a diversified and interrelated scientific approach which involved humanities and science-based methods. Novel interdisciplinary approaches allow for the investigation and exploration of broad archaeological questions, providing a solid interpretative ground (Andersson Strand et al., 2010). Continuous testing and improvement of analytical protocols and techniques progress the discipline of textile studies by better defining and enlarging it to become a strong and highly interdisciplinary field of research within the scientific community.

With the common aim to contribute to the textile research field, scholars with different backgrounds and expertise met at the online session organised by the EAA conference in 2020 (Coletti et al., 2020). The remarkable presentations and interesting exchanges led to the idea of collecting research articles in a thematic volume to contribute to the development of this fast-growing field of research by bringing together traditional and novel analytical approaches in a cross-collaboration between humanities and science. The aim is to contribute to the recent development in the field, by the presentation of case studies and different research methods

The book "*Multidisciplinary approaches for the investigation of textiles and fibres in the archaeological field*" is aimed to archaeologists, conservators, scientists, historians and anyone interested in textile research and the scientific approaches applied to the investigation of textiles and related artefacts. The volume is far from being comprehensive of the broad approaches available nowadays, but it sheds light on key studies applications of more conventional analytical techniques and multiple of the newly emerging ones, as well as presenting unpublished archaeological materials.

The book is divided into three main sessions: (1) Microscopy and morphometric approaches; (2) Multi-technical and archaeometric approaches; (3) Experimental approaches, residue and wear analysis. The papers provide an overview of a variety of scientific approaches to investigate textiles, fibre remains and textile tools, but also summarise recent research. The overview is systematically organised based on the methodological approach used, and each chapter is related to a different scientific technique or key study application.

1.1 Section 1: Microscopy and Morphometric Approaches

Textiles are notably intricate products obtained by a complex *chaîne opératoire*, requiring diversified knowledge and a huge variety of tools in each step of processing (Andersson Strand, 2012). In particular, the study of textile construction techniques (woven and non-woven) and decoration/decorative elements reveal key information on the artefacts' production, such as cross-cultural and technical traditions, craft specialisation and standardisation of patterns, provenience, trade routes, and technological transfer. The scientific analyses play a pivotal role in investigating and reconstructing the above-mentioned aspects, providing solid data to trace wider theoretical reconstructions (Margariti et al., 2022) Archaeological evidence suggests that the fibres used in ancient societies derived from multiple sources of animal (wool and hair, silk), vegetable (lime bast, flax, nettle, cotton, esparto) and mineral origin (asbestos) fibres. Availability, intrinsic properties, and the desired function of the final fabric drove their selection in the different chronological periods and sociocultural contexts.

The conventional approach to the fabrics and fibre characterisation comprises microscopic investigation using Optical microscopy and Scanning Electron Microscope (SEM). The latter allows the investigation of fibres offering higher magnification and resolution as well as a large depth of field, offering a rather three-dimensional viewing experience of the artefacts in different preservation conditions (Tamburini et al., 2023; Klisińska-Kopacz, 2022; Margariti, 2019a; Rast-Eicher, 2016). Therefore, SEM is nowadays a widely used instrument for the identification of fibres and the assessment of their condition.

Although considered a traditional approach, microscopy still plays a crucial role as a primary diagnostic approach in textile research (Lukesova & Holst, 2024; Sien nicka et al., 2018) for technological analysis of the textile and the morphological analysis of the fibres, as well as an essential step in the selection of further analytical procedures and protocols.

The chapters in this section provide examples of microscopy applications to archaeological and historical textiles. In each case study, a suitable analytical device was selected based on the research aim and the state of preservation of the objects.

In the second chapter, M. Gleba and M. S. Busana (University of Padua), discuss the application of conventional textile analytical methods and Scanning Electron Microscopy (SEM) to the analysis of textile remains preserved by mineralisation. Their study, focusing on textile samples from funerary contexts in urban and rural cemeteries of the Roman Veneto region (North-East Italy), offers new data on the rituals and the artefacts produced in the area. The application of microscopic methods on textiles found in contact with metal objects is also the focus of the third chapter proposed by J. Suomela (University of Helsinki) and S. Lipkin (University of Oulu). The authors further explore the applicability of optical microscopy aiming at distinguishing between vegetable fibre types/species. The covered topic appeared in line with the recent research interests and debates about the more effective and accurate techniques and procedures for the discrimination of archaeological and historical bast fibres. Using a three-stage procedure based on the observations of the fibre longitudinal surface characteristics and cross sections, combined with a Modified Herzog test, the authors analyse plant fibre samples, dated between 1620 and 1756, found in burials and the ground soil underneath the Hailuoto Church (Finland). The state of fibre preservation, how to address it and how to interpret the resulting data from the archaeological point of view is one of the emerging topics and methodological challenges in textile research.

In the fourth chapter F. Coletti (Sapienza University of Rome) and C. Margariti (Directorate of Conservation/Hellenic Ministry of Culture) discuss the effects of thermal degradation on the morphology of textile structure and natural fibres from the ancient city of Pompeii. The authors combined microscopic analysis of carbonised textiles from archaeological context along with the available data in literature and experimentation on cellulosic and proteinaceous contemporary textile samples artificially carbonised in a limited oxygen environment.

1.2 Section 2: Multi-technical and Archaeometric Approaches

The role of a scientific multi-technique approach based on laboratory analyses and the use of highly sensitive analytical techniques is nowadays essential to collect data otherwise difficult to obtain with basic approaches. This section shows how a multi-technique approach is crucial in characterising various components of textiles, like dyes and fibres, and interpreting their archaeological and historical significance.

Nevertheless, the state of preservation of fibres may present challenges and limitations in their study and analysis, as in the case of mineralised (e.g. Margariti, 2019b; Gillard et al., 1994) or carbonised textiles (e.g. Margariti, 2020; Styring et al., 2013; Huisman et al., 2012), or in the case of severely decayed organic matter resulting in faint fibre residues without morphology (Osanna et al., 2021). In the cultural heritage sector as well as in the textile research field, non-destructive analytical methods are required, especially when dealing with small and unique samples. A promising path down the analysis and characterisation of archaeological textiles, aimed at research and conservation, consists of spectroscopic techniques, often combined with microscopy and experiments on the artificial ageing of textiles. Fourier-transform infrared spectroscopy (FTIR) in transmitted and attenuated total reflection (ATR) modes is widely explored for the investigation of excavated fibre-based materials. The recent efforts in assessing their value and limitations led to the proliferation of successful research applications aiming to increase the quality of the data obtained and the protocols and procedures to adopt (Coletti et al., 2021; Caggia et al., 2021; Margariti, 2019b). Conversely, when used for discriminating historical and archaeological organic fibres, Raman spectroscopy shows strong luminescence effects difficult to overcome, often precluding the proper interpretation of the spectra.[1] This technique proved to be advantageous for the characterisation of dyes (Coletti et al., 2023; Ciccola et al., 2020)[2] and mineral fibres used in textile-making, and its application is constantly growing and getting refined.

The fifth chapter by F. Coletti, I. Ciccola, and P. Postorino (Sapienza University of Rome) explores the advantages of combining morphological analysis and spectroscopic methods for the characterisation of fibre-based materials using the case of ancient asbestos fibres from the Italic Peninsula. Because it is a portable and

---

[1] Fourier-Transformed Raman Spectroscopy (FT-Raman) allows acquiring spectra with a lower fluorescence to result in high-quality spectra. Although less explored, FT-Raman proved to be especially successful in the characterisation of proteinaceous fibres (see Chap. 6).

[2] Among analytical spectroscopies, Fiber Optic Reflectance Spectroscopy (FORS) is another non-destructive and portable technique widely applied for dye identification (see Chap. 6).

non-destructive technique, the authors selected Raman spectroscopy as the most appropriate instrument that extends the possibilities of analysing archaeological mineral fibres, which could be difficult to manipulate. Moreover, the contribution offers new data regarding the actual use of mineral fibres for producing textiles in antiquity, for which available data are still rare.

Based on the preservation state of the fibres and to answer more complex questions related to the in-depth identification of the nature of fibres and dyes used in textile manufacturing, non-invasive methods can be combined with high-powered and micro-destructive techniques. The combination of such techniques with mass spectrometry represents an extremely powerful approach in the field of dye analysis in archaeological textiles. Advances in more sophisticated methods applied to cultural heritage objects lie in analytical chemistry. Liquid chromatography, with diode array detection or coupled with mass spectrometry, allows deciphering and interpreting complex mixtures and identifying the dye components in detail (Vanden Berghe et al., 2009; Galli et al., 2020; Ciccola et al., 2020). A detailed and extremely interesting overview of how a multi-technique approach is fundamental to the study of archaeological textile materials is offered in the chapter sixth by the group of Analytical Chemistry applied to Cultural Heritage from Sapienza University (I. Serafini, A. Ciccola, R. Curini and G. Favero) and the Proteomics and Mass spectrometry laboratory of the Smithsonian Institution's Museum Conservation Institute (T. P. Cleland, C. Solazzo and G. M Kavich), in the context of the Marie Skłodowska-Curie PARCA project. This contribution provides an overview and the potential of a multi-technical approach to identify dyes and protein in archaeological remains, focusing on wool and silk fibre artefacts, from several case studies.

Shifting to Geosciences and radiometric methods, the section ends, with a focus on the application of Accelerator Mass Spectrometry (AMS) with particular reference to radiocarbon dating. In archaeological and historical fields, in the case of missing contextual and provenience information, or in situations of uncertainty concerning chronological attributions and authenticity, dating can be established or verified with laboratory methods, thanks to which it is possible to place an object in time. The measurement of the decay of the carbon-14 isotope allows estimates of the age of carbon-based materials that originated from living organisms among which fibres of plant and animal origin. The seventh chapter, written by the research group of the Italian Institute of Nuclear Physics—INFN and the Universities of Florence (M. Fedi, S. Barone, L. Liccioli) and Sapienza University (F. Coletti), shed light on the critical application of Radiocarbon dating to ancient textiles belonging to museums collections that took shape over the course of several centuries based on objects discovered by non-scientific excavation and without context information. The authors discuss the potential and the possible issues arising from the application of this dating method when applied to archaeological textile objects, stressing the need for treatment procedures tailored to the specific material and adapted to its preservation state. In particular, the chapter focuses on the dating of one silk knitted fragment excavated in the XIX century and included in the ancient textile collection of the Vesuvian area.

1.3 Section 3: Experimental Approach, Residues and Use Wear Analysis

Experimental archaeology, use wear and residue analysis are particularly beneficial to textile studies. In addition, textile tools constitute indirect evidence of fibre processing. The discovery of such artefacts in archaeological sites allows scholars to state not only that spinning, and weaving were commonly practised, but to define, based on the tools' features (shape, weight etc.), how these activities were performed. Textile tools are particularly informative for prehistoric periods lacking written and iconographic sources. Reproducing textile tools and testing their possible use currently remains the main and most reliable approach of experimental archaeology. In the eighth chapter, M. S. Busana, A. Lena (University of Padua) and D. Francisci (Italian Ministry of Culture) focus on experimental archaeology trials to assess the functionality of three diverse tools made respectively in bone, glass and amber associated with textile activity and found in the burial contexts of the Roman Venezia (first to third century AD) in North-Eastern Italy. Through 3D scanning, the authors reproduced a replica of the tools to be used by craftspeople during sessions of experimental spinning of wool and flax. The results suggest that the tools were functional, supported also by traces of wear on the archaeological objects, and a very thin yarn was obtained by the spinning sessions. Nevertheless, reconstructing the actual use of spindle whorls and loom weights is not easy and an integrated approach that combines trace analysis, archaeometric analyses and experimental archaeology is required to understand their biography and contextualise them in the archaeological and historical context. Over the last year, a growing interest in the application of experimental archaeology led scholars to employ textile tool replicas and reconsider the functionality and performance of the tools and even their modification after use. These results can be considered very informative for interpreting the actual use of textile tools and suggest that use modifications on textile artefacts develop not only as surface wear but even as residue deposits (Belgiorno & Lentini, 2011, Forte et al., 2019, Cheval, 2021).

The establishment of an analytical protocol for the identification and study of residues left by textile activity on tools is the topic of the ninth chapter written by V. Forte, F. Coletti, C. Virili, A. M. Jaja and C. Lemorini (Sapienza University of Rome). Based on a previously published study on residues found on experimental tools, the authors perform residue analysis to an archaeological object and define the main steps of a protocol for extraction and analysis of the fibre residues deposited on tools after spinning. This approach is potentially informative providing further information to reconstruct textile tools' actual use and even collect general information about fibre processing in specific contexts, especially in the absence of textile products. The trace and residue analysis integrated with experimental archaeology guarantee new and pivotal data for the reconstruction of the craft gestures and skills. Even considering the limitations due to the altered and poorly preserved state of the fibre fragments deposited along tool surfaces, the recent advancements of scientific equipment, especially in the field of compositional and high magnification approaches, allow us to work and get information from small samples on preserved artefacts over time (Cheval, 2021).

Another example of the application of experimental archaeology, however, this time performed to understand the actual use of fibre-based objects is the tenth and final chapter of the volume authored by R. Yosef (Ben Gurion University of the Negev), L. Perry-Gal (Israel Antiquities Authority and University of Haifa) and N. Sukenik (Israel Antiquities Authority) investigate the actual use of a large net unearthed in the Cave of Letters in Nahal Hever, in the Judean Desert, dated from the time of the Bar Kokhba Revolt (132–135/6 CE). The actual function was addressed from different perspectives including archaeology, anthropology, ornithology, and archaeozoology which highlight again the multi- and interdisciplinarity of this field of research. The authors propose that the net was a walk-in trap for avian species that prefer to walk on the ground while foraging or fleeing potential predators.

1.4 Conclusion

In conclusion, the recent advancements in textile research underscore the importance of a multidisciplinary approach that bridges the humanities and natural sciences. The growing body of work, exemplified by the initiatives of dedicated research centres and the outcomes of important EU projects, highlights how innovative methodologies are revolutionizing our understanding of ancient textiles. Through detailed scientific analysis, scholars can uncover intricate narratives about craft practices, social identities, and technological advancements in past societies. By fostering collaboration across disciplines, researchers enrich our knowledge of textiles and enhance archaeological interpretations. This evolving landscape of textile studies promises to reveal even deeper insights into the cultural and historical significance of fabrics, encouraging further exploration and innovation in the field. Ultimately, integrating science and humanities in textile research offers a powerful lens through which we can better understand the complexity of ancient human societies.

Authors' Contributions Introduction: FC; Microscopy and morphometric approaches: FC, CM; Multi-technical and archaeometric approaches: FC; Experimental approach, residues and wear analysis: VF, FC, SS; Conclusion: FC, VF.

References

Andersson Strand, E. (2012). The textile *chaîne opératoire*: Using a multidisciplinary approach to textile archaeology with a focus on the Ancient Near East. *Paléorient, 38*(1–2), 21–40.

Andersson Strand, E., & Nosch, M. L. (Eds.) (2015). *Tools, Textiles and Contexts. Investigating Textile Production in the Aegean and Eastern Mediterranean Bronze Age*. Oxbow Books.

Andersson Strand, E., Frei, K. M., Gleba, M., Mannering, U., Nosch, M.-L., & Skals, I. (2010). Old textiles—New possibilities. *European Journal of Archaeology, 13*(2), 149–173.

Belgiorno, M., & Lentini, A. (2011). Origini e sviluppo dell'industria tessile a Pyrgos-Mavrorachi (Cipro), durante il II millennio a. C. In: M. P. Riccardi & E. Basso (Eds.), *Patron Editore. Atti del VI Congresso Nazionale di Archeometria "Scienza e Beni Culturali"*, Pavia 15–18 February 2010 (pp. 1–13).

Bender Jørgensen, L. (2012). Spinning faith. In M. L. S. Sørensen & K. Rebay-Salisbury (Eds.), *Embodied knowledge* (pp.128–136). Oxbow Books.

Caggia, P., Laforest, C., & Coletti, F. (2021). The Roman and the Middle-Byzantine Necropolis of St. Philip at Hierapolis of Phrygia. Asia Minor. *An International Journal of archaeology in Turkey, 1*, 119–140. https://doi.org/10.19272/202115261008

Cheval, C. (2021). The loom weight, the spindle whorl, and the sword beater–evidence of textile activity in the Early Neolithic? *Open Archaeology, 7*(1), 1458–1472.

Ciccola, A., Serafini, I., Ripanti, F., Coletti, F., Vincenti, F., Bianco, A., Galli, M., Curini, R., & Postorino, P. (2020). Dyes from the ashes: Discovering and characterizing natural dyes from mineralized textiles. *Molecules, 25*(6), 1417. https://doi.org/10.3390/molecules25061417

Coletti, F. (2020). I tessuti di Pompei: materiali, tecniche di lavorazione e contesti. PhD thesis, Sapienza University of Rome and Ruprecht Karl University of Heidelberg.

Coletti, F. (forthcoming). I reperti tessili di Pompei e d'area vesuviana. Edizioni Quasar.

Coletti, F., Forte, V., Margariti, F., & Spantidaki, S. (2020). Multidisciplinary approaches to identify and preserve fibres and textile products in the archaeological field (session 445 - 28 August 2020). *Archaeological Textile Review, 62*, 197–198.

Coletti, F., Cestelli Guidi, M., Romani, M., Ceres, G., & Zammit, U. (2021). Evaluation of microscopy techniques and ATR-FTIR spectroscopy on textile fibres from the Vesuvian area: A pilot study on degradation processes that prevent the characterization of bast fibres. *Journal of Archaeological Science: Reports, 36*, 102794. https://doi.org/10.1016/j.jasrep.2021.102794

Coletti, F., Ciccola, A., Caggia, M. P., Serafini, I., Postorino, P., Curini, R., & Nucara, A. (2023). Byzantine burials from the Sanctuary of Saint Philip at Hierapolis of Phrygia an Archaeometric Study on Ancient Textile Remains, in *Archeologia Classica LXXIV*, 871–887. https://doi.org/10.48255/2240-7839

Engelhardt Mathiassen, T., Nosch, M. L., Ringgaard, M., Toftegaard, K., & Venborg Pedersen, M. (Eds.). (2014). *Fashionable encounters. Perspectives and trends in textile and dress in the Early Modern Nordic World*. Oxbow Books.

Fanfani, G., Harlow, M., & Nosch, M. L. (Eds.). (2016). *Spinning fates and the song of the loom. The use of textiles, clothing and cloth production as metaphor, symbol and narrative device in Greek and Latin literature*. Oxbow Books.

Forte, V., Coletti, F., Ciccarelli, E., & Lemorini, C. (2019). The contribution of experimental archaeology in addressing the analysis of residues on spindle-whorls. *EXARC Journal, 4*. https://exarc.net/ark:/88735/10456

Galli, M., Coletti, F., Ciccola, A., & Serafini, I. (2020). Archeologia e archeometria del tessuto antico: un gruppo di manufatti aurei dall'area vesuviana (Pompei, Ercolano, Oplontis), in *Scienze dell'Antichità, 26.1*, 205–223. ISBN 978-88-5491-078-2; ISSN: 2284-3280.

Gaspa, S., Michel, C., & Nosch, M. L. (Eds.). (2017). *Textile terminologies from the orient to the Mediterranean and Europe, 1000 BC to 1000 AD*. Zea E-Books.

Gillard, R. D., Hardman, S. M., Thomas, R. G., & Watkinson, D. E. (1994). The mineralization of fibres in burial environments. *Studies in Conservation, 39*, 132–140.

Gleba, M., & Mannering, U. (Eds.). (2012). *Textiles and textile production in Europe: From prehistory to AD 400*. Oxbow Books.

Gleba, M., Munkholt, C., & Nosch, M. L. (Eds.). (2008). *Dressing the past*. Oxbow Books.

Grömer, K. (2016). *The art of prehistoric textile making. The development of craft traditions and clothing in Central Europe*. Natural History Museum.

Harlow, M., & Nosch, M. L. (Eds.). (2014). *Greek and Roman textiles and dress: An interdisciplinary anthology*. Oxbow Books.

Huisman, D. J., Braadbaart, F., van Wijk, I. M., & van Os, B. J. H. (2012). Ashes to ashes, charcoal to dust: Micromorphological evidence for ash-induced disintegration of charcoal in Early Neolithic (LBK) soil features in Elsloo (the Netherlands). *Journal of Archaeological Science, 39,* 994–1004.

Klisińska-Kopacz, A. (2022). Nondestructive testing of historic textiles. In J. Seiko, T. Sabu, P. Pintu, & P. Ritu (Eds.), *Handbook of museum textiles.* Wiley Online Library.

Lukesova, H., & Holst, B. (2024). Identifying plant fibres in cultural heritage with optical and electron microscopy: how to present results and avoid pitfalls. *Heritage Science, 12,* 1–14.

Margariti, C. (2019a). FIBRANET database, Centre for Textile Research/University of Copenhagen, Project funded under the EU Horizon 2020 Marie Skłodowska Curie programme under grant agreement No 745865. https://netlearning.gr/fibranet/

Margariti, C. (2019b). The application of FTIR microspectroscopy in a non-invasive and non-destructive way to the study and conservation of mineralised excavated textiles. *Heritage Science, 7*(63) Online publication. https://doi.org/10.1186/s40494-019-0304-8

Margariti, C. (2020). The effects of artificial incomplete burning on the morphology and dimensions of cellulosic and proteinaceous textiles and fibres. *Studies in Conservation, 65*(7), 388–398.

Margariti, C., Lukesova, H., Gomes, F. B. (Eds.). (2022). Advanced analytical techniques for heritage textiles. *Heritage Science Special Collections.* https://www.springeropen.com/collections/aatht, Accessed: 8/2/2024

Margariti, C., Sava, G., Vanden Berghe, I. et al. (2024). Exploring the provenance of a Byzantine excavated assemblage of textile and leather finds by the application of instrumental analysis. *Heritage Science, 12,* 132. https://doi.org/10.1186/s40494-024-01201-9

Michael, C., & Nosch, M. L. (2010). *Textile terminologies in the ancient Near East and Mediterranean from the third to the first millennnia BC.* Oxbow Books.

Nosch, M. L., Andersson Strand, E., & Koefoed, H. (Eds.). (2013). *Textile production in the ancient Near East.* Oxbow Books.

Osanna, M., Amoretti, V., Coletti, F. (2021). I nuovi calchi di Civita Giuliana. In M. Osanna, A. Capurso, S. M. Masseroli (Eds.), I calchi di Pompei da Giuseppe Fiorelli ad oggi. Collana di Studi e Ricerche del Parco Archeologico di Pompei 46, 129–148. L'Erma di Bretschneider. ISBN: 9788891321169.

Rast-Eicher, A. (2016). *Fibres: Microscopy of archaeological textiles and furs.* Archaeolingua Alapítvány.

Siennicka, M., Rahmstorf, L., & Ulanowska, A. (2018). Introduction. In M. Siennicka, L. Rahmstorf, & A. Ulanowska (Eds.), *First textiles. The beginnings of textile manufacture in Europe and the Mediterranean* (1–16). Oxbow Books.

Spantidaki, S. (2016). *Textile production in classical Athens.* Oxbow Books.

Styring, A. K., Manning, H., Fraser, R. A., Wallace, M., Jones, G., Charles, M., Heaton, T. H. E., Bogaard, A., & Evershed, R. P. (2013). The effect of charring and burial on the biochemical composition of cereal grains: Investigating the integrity of archaeological plant material. *Journal of Archaeological Science, 40,* 4767–4779.

Tamburini, D., Dyer, J., Cartwright, C., & Green, A. (2023). Changes in the production materials of Burmese textiles in the nineteenth century—Dyes, mordants and fibres of Karen garments from the British Museum's collection. Heritage. *Science, 11,* 150. https://doi.org/10.1186/s40494-023-00978-5

Vanden Berghe, I., Gleba, M., & Mannering, U. (2009). Towards the identification of dyestuffs in Early Iron Age Scandinavian peat bog textiles. *Journal of Archaeological Science, 36*(9), 1910–1921. https://doi.org/10.1016/j.jas.2009.04.019

Chapter 2
Using Scanning Electron Microscopy for the Study of Mineralised Textiles: The Case of Roman *Venetia*

Margarita Gleba and Maria Stella Busana

Abstract The paper presents the results of the analyses of about 30 mineralised textile samples from Roman Veneto region (North-East Italy), which were investigated using conventional textile analytical methods and Scanning Electron Microscopy (SEM). They were predominantly preserved on bronze or iron objects (but also on alabaster) that were found in funerary contexts in urban (the main Roman cities including Padua, Verona, Altino, Este, Aquileia), and rural cemeteries of *Venetia*. Despite the poor preservation of the textiles, SEM permitted identification of raw material in all but one sample. Textile traces examined include plant bast fibre (likely linen) and wool fabrics of various qualities. The research provides new data regarding the funerary rituals and the textile production, offering, for the first time, a picture of textiles produced in the area.

Keywords Mineralisation · Fibre · Textile · Scanning Electron Microscopy · Roman period · Venetia

2.1 Introduction

Mineralised textiles are formations in which metal corrosion products form casts of or around fibres retaining their external morphology and size almost unaltered, resulting in positive or negative casts. The mechanisms of textile mineralisation have been studied intermittently over the past four decades (Jakes & Sibley, 1984; Jakes & Howard, 1986; Janaway, 1983, 1987, 1989; Gillard et al., 1994; Chen et al., 1998; Moulhérat, 2008; Reynaud et al., 2020). The process can be summarised as follows. In an acidic environment and in the presence of water, the metal oxidises and produces metal ions which diffuse in solution. At the same time, the bacterial

---

M. Gleba (✉) · M. S. Busana
Department of Cultural Heritage, University of Padua, Padua, Italy
e-mail: margarita.gleba@unipd.it

© The Author(s), under exclusive license to Springer Nature Switzerland AG 2024
F. Coletti et al. (eds.), *Multidisciplinary Approaches for the Investigation of Textiles and Fibres in the Archaeological Field*, Interdisciplinary Contributions to Archaeology, https://doi.org/10.1007/978-3-031-73812-8_2

activity from the burial environment causes degradation both in the amorphous zones and in the crystalline zones of the fibre, eventually freeing spaces in which the metal ions can diffuse. On the surface of the fibre, the metal ions come together to form a layer of solid compounds (for example oxides, carbonates, etc.), while inside the fibre, they can form complexes and bonds with the fibre macromolecules (cellulose, protein).

In surface mineralisation, corrosion products cover the fibre which retains its physical and chemical integrity. Negative casts (negative mineralisation—Moulhérat, 2008) form when the rapid formation of corrosion products around the fibre is followed by the complete destruction of its organic matrix. If the decomposition of the fibre is faster than the deposition of the corrosion products, it is no longer identifiable. Frequently, however, the negative casts allow fibre identification. Positive casts (positive mineralisation—Moulhérat, 2008) form when the organic matter is completely replaced by the mineral matter. Positive casts (and sometimes erroneously negative ones) are often called pseudomorphs, in analogy with a geological phenomenon of pseudomorphosis, although true pseudomorphs are rare (Gillard et al., 1994, 138). First, there is a rapid deposition of the corrosion layer which then impregnates the fibre more or less completely. The fibre is thus destroyed in the process, but the mineral matter that replaces it retains its external and even internal micromorphological characteristics.

Mineralised textile traces, even when minute, can provide surprising amount of information about their structural characteristics and the nature and processing of the raw material. In this contribution we present some observations derived from a detailed SEM analysis of mineralised textiles from the Roman period burials excavated in Veneto, north-east Italy.

2.2 Case Study

In Roman times, the *Venetia* region of northern Italy was renowned for its sheep husbandry and textile crafts, and its products were famous and traded across Italy (Rome) and in the provinces (Noricum), as amply attested by the Roman written sources (Varro de r.r., 2, 3, 9–10; Colum. 7, 3; Strabo, V, 1, 12; Mart. ep., 14, 143, 152). Over the last decade the University of Padua has been involved in the study of textile production in the region (Busana et al., 2012; Busana & Basso, 2012; Busana & Tricomi, 2016, 2018; Busana et al., 2021). The project *TRAMA* (Textiles in Roman Archaeology: Methods and Analysis), carried out between 2015 and 2017, involved a systematic study of archaeological textiles from Roman *Venetia* in the collections and museums of Veneto and of Aquileia. Thirty-two objects with traces of fabric or yarn, completely or partially mineralised, have been identified from ten sites.

All the objects come from funerary contexts: most of these have been found in association with cremations, while a few come from inhumations (Busana & Gleba, 2018). Chronologically, the two earliest burials date to the second to first century BC, while the latest is dated to the fourth century AD. The most numerous objects with textile traces are iron pins or fibulae and bronze coins, but other objects such as finger rings, needles, knives and shears are also represented. In two cases, the ossuaries were dressed in fabric (Busana & Gleba, 2018, 2021). The majority of the textiles can be interpreted as ritual: (1) used to wrap the cremated bones or the entire urn; (2) used to wrap burial goods; or (3) used as a shroud to wrap the dressed deceased. These various 'wrapping' practices appear to continue in the Veneto Region during the Roman times the traditions of the wider, pan-European pre-Roman funerary rite (Gleba, 2014; Busana & Gleba, 2021). Only in two cases we may be dealing with remains of actual garments.

2.3 Methods

Textile traces were observed using digital DinoLite microscope. Digital microphotographs were taken at different magnifications (20×, 50×, 230×). The textile analysis included determination of structural parameters such as weave and thread count per cm (which is indicative of textile quality), thread twist (z—clockwise; s—counter-clockwise, i—no discernible twist), diameter and angle, presence of edges, and any other characteristic elements, such as pattern, sewing, and other features.

Twenty-five objects were sampled for fibre analysis. The samples were about 1–4 mm in size and were taken with the greatest consideration for object conservation. In fact, it was decided not to sample some of the objects in order not to compromise their integrity. Fibre analysis was carried out using Scanning Electron Microscope (SEM) in order to determine the morphological characteristics of the fibre and to acquire more detailed surface information for fibre identification. The choice of method was conditioned by the fact that all textiles examined are completely or partially mineralised and cannot be easily studied using transmitted light microscopy (Janaway, 1983; Anheuser & Roumeliotou, 2003, 23). The samples were analysed using a Hitachi TM3000 TableTop SEM. The samples were not coated. The following instrumental settings were used: analytical condition mode at 15.00 kV accelerating voltage, compositional imaging and working distance of 5–10 mm. The diameter of fibres was measured using SEM utility tool at 400× magnification.

2.4 Results

A total of 23 fabrics (in some cases the same fabric appears on two objects found closely together in the same context) and 3 threads were identified. The latter may have originally been textiles but the preservation is insufficient for a certain identification. All of the textiles are variations of plain weave or tabby, with s/s tabbies constituting more than half of the fabrics identified—13, followed by 5 z/z tabbies, 3 half-basket weaves and 2 weft-faced tabbies (Busana & Gleba, 2018).

Twenty-seven samples from 25 objects analysed were taken for fibre identification and analysis. Despite their mostly mineralised nature and at times extremely poor preservation, in all but one case fibre origin was successfully identified.

Eighteen samples presented fibre morphology consistent with plant bast fibres based on the following characteristics: smooth surface with frequent dislocations (Fig. 2.1) and somewhat polygonal cross section with occasional lumen, and diameters only rarely exceeding 20 micron (Fig. 2.2) (Cattling & Grayson, 2004; Rast-Eicher, 2016). The most likely fibre is flax (*Linum usitatissimum* L.). In nine cases, the splitting or the twisting of the fibres in S direction was observed (Fig. 2.3). While it is not yet scientifically demonstrated, the phenomenon likely reflects the

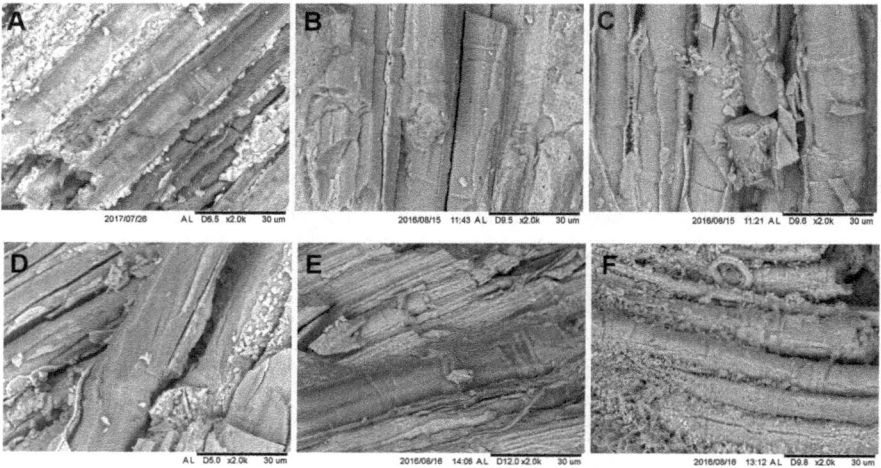

Fig. 2.1 SEMicrographs of plant fibres showing characteristic nodes or dislocations: A. Aquileia IG23061; B. Este Rebato T102 IG14212; C. Este Rebato T41 IG14092; D. Este Benvenuti T2 IG15079; E. Legnano VR60485; F. Padova Via Gradenigo T200 IG255056a (Images: M. Gleba)

Fig. 2.2 SEMicrographs of plant fibres showing polygonal cross section with lumen" A. Padova Via Gradenigo T200 IG355058; B. Sarcedo T34 IG327767; Padova Via Gradenigo T200 IG255056 (Images: M. Gleba)

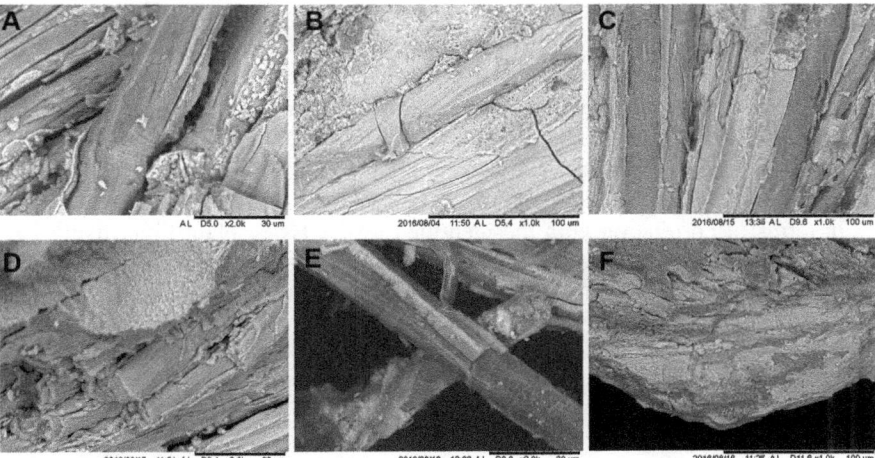

Fig. 2.3 SEMicrographs of plant fibres showing S-twisting of fibre surface: A. Este Benvenuti T2 IG15079; B. Este Rebato T64 IG14051; C. Este Rebato T47 IG14304; D. Este Rebato T102 IG14212; E. Padova Via Gradenigo T182 IG327631; F. Padova Via Gradenigo 200 IG355057 (Images: M. Gleba)

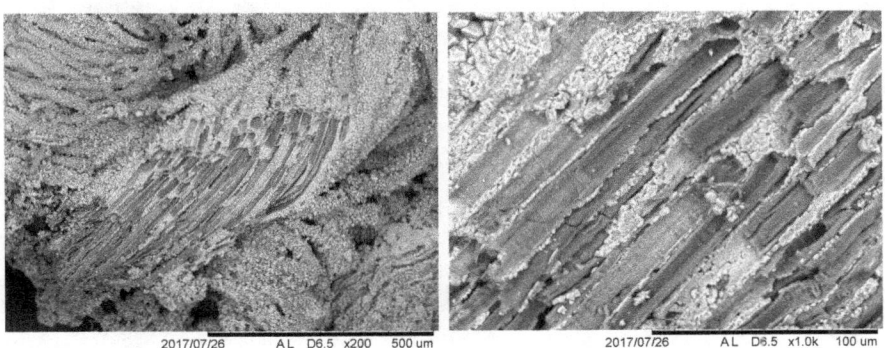

Fig. 2.4 SEMicrographs of plant fibres on the Aquileia urn IG23061 (Images: M. Gleba)

microfibrillar orientation of the cellulose chains in fibre cell cuticle. S-microfibrillar orientation is typical for flax (Bergfjord & Holst, 2010, 1193; Haugan & Holst, 2013; Lukesova, 2017), so the splitting may further confirm the species identification as flax.

Plant fibres have primarily survived as positive casts although negative casts were also observed. In some cases, only surface mineralisation is observed, with organic fibres intact under the corrosion product layer. This type of preservation is particularly interesting in the case of the alabaster urn from Aquileia, which is the only example of non-metal mineralisation in our case study. The fibres appear to be preserved under the layer of mineralisation (Fig. 2.4). This is unusual, since in other cases of textile calcification, the organic matrix of the fibre had been completely replaced with inorganic matter in a way that precludes fibre identification since fibre micromorphology did not survive.[1] This may be because, in the other cases, the calcification was most likely due to intentional addition of calcium-containing substance such as lime (Nicole Reifarth, pers. com. 10.06.2022), whereas in the case of the Aquileia urn, calcium may derive from the urn itself. However, further in-depth investigation into the calcification process is necessary.

In terms of correlation with the identified textile types, plant fibre, likely flax, was the raw material in eleven balanced s/s tabbies and four balanced z/z tabbies. It is highly probable that the balanced z/z tabby on the bronze coin from Montagnana that was not sampled is also made of plant fibre.

Five samples were identified as sheep wool based on the negative casts of cuticular scales of coronal or imbricate type (Fig. 2.5) (Mahal et al., 1951). Wool was the

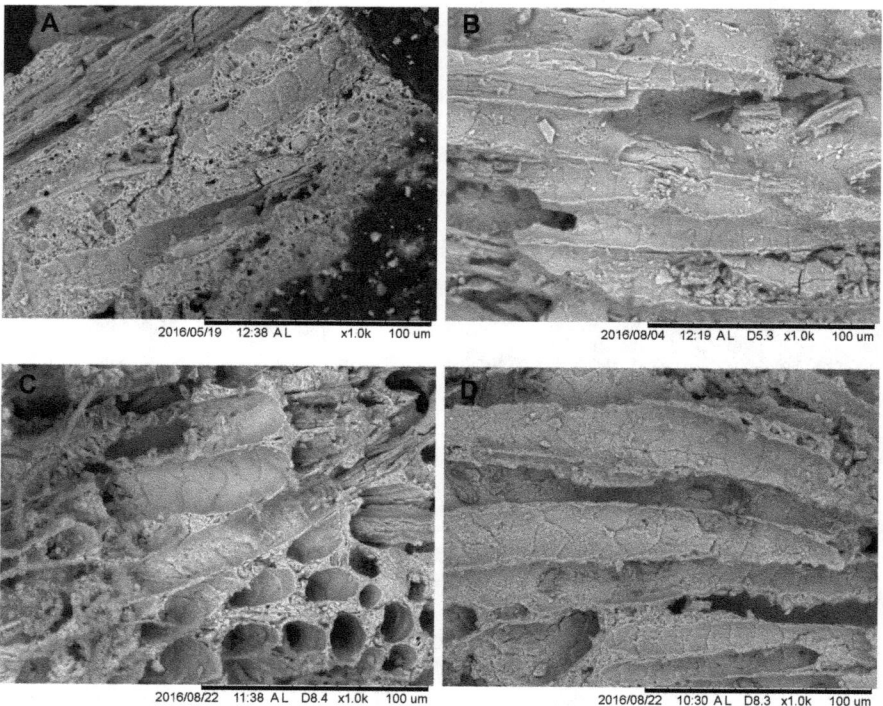

Fig. 2.5 SEMicrographs of wool fibres showing cuticular scales, which in adjacent fibres are pointing in opposing directions indicating combing: A. Altino-Albertini T1-5; B. Este-Rebato T64 IG14055; C. Verona Spianà T579 VR10096; D. Verona-Porta Palio VR18184 (Images: M. Gleba)

---

[1] Middle Bronze Age textile from Sidon in Lebanon (Gleba & Griffiths, 2011); Late Bronze age textiles from Qatna in Syria (James et al., 2009; Reifarth & Drewello, 2011) and textiles recovered from the late Etruscan travertine urns in the Perugia region of Italy (Gleba et al., 2017, 133).

raw material in the three half-basket weaves from Verona and Este and the thread from Este. Wool fibres primarily survive as negative casts (Fig. 2.5), although in one case we have a mix within the same sample, demonstrating that the preservation in iron does not always lead to negative casts (Fig. 2.6). Another aspect that could be recovered through SEM is evidence of wool fibre preparation, in particular combing, indicated by the opposing direction of cuticular scales in adjoining fibres (Rast-Eicher, 2016, 41).

In three cases, the fibre casts were sufficiently well preserved to permit wool quality analysis, which consists of measuring the diameter of approximately 100 fibres and statistical analysis resulting in a distribution histogram (Ryder, 1964; Rast-Eicher, 2008; Gleba, 2012; Skals et al., 2018). In mineralised textiles, the negative casts which formed around the fibres before they disintegrated, allow measuring the diameter of these fibres. The method was suggested by Ryder and Gabra-Sanders (Ryder & Gabra-Sanders, 1985, 133) and developed by Rast-Eicher (2008) and Moulhérat (2008). Since mineralisation has been demonstrated by the

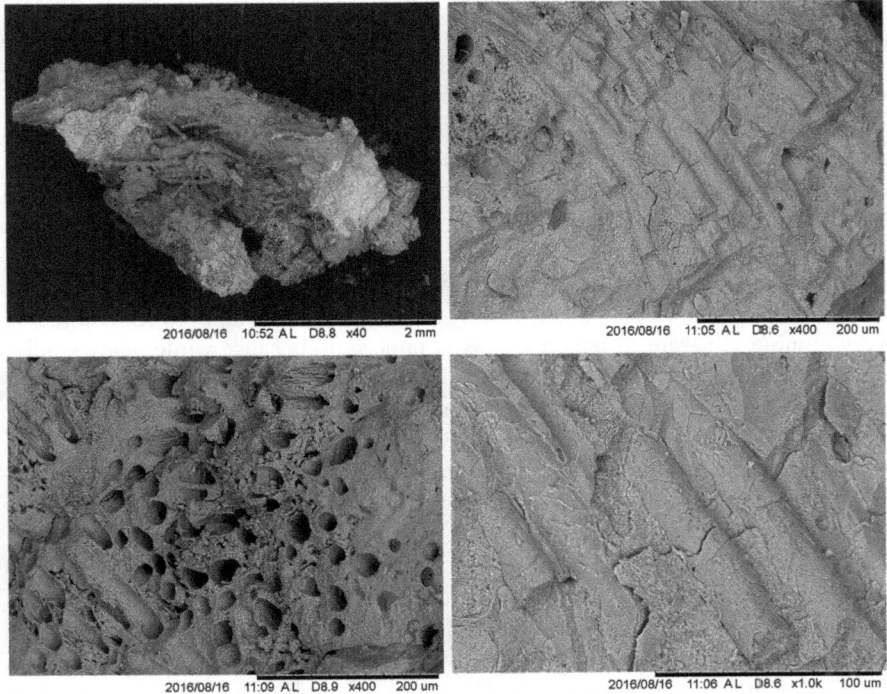

Fig. 2.6 SEMicrographs of wool fibres showing negative and positive casts in the same sample from EsteRebato T59 IG14203 (Images: M. Gleba)

experimental work to occur within the first few weeks of burial when the conditions for it are present (Gillard et al., 1994), the casts are likely to reflect the original fibre size. Therefore, the method may in fact be more reliable than measuring organically preserved fibres, which are more prone to shrinkage/swelling, flattening and biodegradation, all of which affect the diameter of the fibre.

The two half-basket weaves from Verona appear to have extremely fine wool and fall within the finest category of wool known from ancient times in both Ryder's and Rast-Eicher's wool classification systems (Busana & Gleba, 2018, 343). They may provide the first direct evidence of the raw material so highly prised by contemporary written sources, especially the famous wool of Altino (Colum. 7, 1, 2; Mart. ep., 14, 155; Plin. Jun. ep., 2, 2, 25; Tert. de pall., 3, 6; Edict. Diocl. 25, 1–6; 21, 2). The sample number is too small to draw conclusions regarding any correlation between the wool quality and the weave, but further research should be carried out on half-basket weaves elsewhere to explore this possibility.

2.5 Conclusion

We hope to have demonstrated the utility of SEM in retrieving the data on raw material, its quality and preparation in mineralised textile samples as well as their preservation. While the research on textile mineralisation has stalled in the recent decade (although see Reynaud et al., 2020), we hope that increasing number of studies on such material will reignite interest in the taphonomic processes that lead to the creation of incredibly detailed mineralised structures in archaeological contexts—such work requires interdisciplinary collaboration between archaeologists, conservators, chemists and other specialists.

Mineralised textiles allow to recover such fundamental textile data like the weave, thread twist direction and—using SEM— raw material even from arguably very humble mineralised remains. This is important, because while many studies have been devoted to Roman written, epigraphic, papyrological and literary testimonies or textile remains from the regions with environments conducive for their preservation (such as Egypt, Near East or Britain), we still know very little about textiles from the heart of the Roman empire—Italy. With the exception of the material preserved due to the volcanic eruption in the Vesuvian area, which is currently the subject of important ongoing studies (Galli et al., 2018; Coletti et al., 2021; Coletti, forthcoming), and textiles preserved in the shipwrecks of Nemi and Comacchio, also under study, textiles are assumed not to survive in Italy. Yet, as demonstrated by the *PROCON* project for pre-Roman Italy (Gleba, 2017), and the *TRAMA* project for the Roman North-Eastern Italy (Busana & Gleba, 2018), this in fact is not the case if we pay attention to the mineralised remains preserved on metal and even non-metal objects. A greater awareness by the excavators and conservators, as shown by the Veneto case, may produce sufficient data to draw important conclusions about textiles that cannot be drawn from indirect sources (Table 2.1).

Table 2.1 Contextual information and structural data of analysed textile

No. textile	Site	Necropolis	Tomb	Weave	Thread count (per cm) warp/weft	Thread twist warp/weft	Thread diameter warp/weft	Twist angle warp/weft	Fibre
T1	Ponte nelle Alpi (BL)	Piaia-Rive Alte	–	Tabby 1/1	9/9	s/s	0.6–0.8/0.6–0.8	Medium/medium	Flax
T2	Altino (VE)	via Annia	Albertini 1-5 (4)	Tabby 1/1 weft-faced	8/20	s/i-z	0.4/0.4–0.5	Hard/loose	Wool
T3	Padova	via Gradenigo	182	Tabby 1/1	22/30	z/z	0.2–0.3/0.2–0.3	Medium-hard/medium-hard	Flax
T4	Padova	via Gradenigo	200	Tabby 1/1	20/20	z/z	0.2–0.3/0.2–0.3	Medium-hard/medium-hard	Plant bast (fala?)
T5	Este (PD)	Fondo Rebato	41	Tabby 1/1	10/10	s/s	0.4–0.5/0.6–0.7	Medium/loose	Plant bast
T6	Este (PD)	Fondo Rebato	47	Tabby 1/1	9/8	s/s	0.8–1/0.6–0.8	Medium/loose-medium	Flax
T7	Este (PD)	Fondo Rebato	50	Tabby 1/1	16/16	s/s	0.3–0.5/ 0.3–0.7	Medium/medium	Plant bast
T8	Este (PD)	Fondo Rebato	50	Tabby 1/1	10/12	s/s	0.4–0.5/ 0.4–0.5	Medium-hard/medium	Flax
T9	Este (PD)	Fondo Rebato	59	Tabby 1/1	13/10	s/s	0.5–0.6/0.6	Medium/medium	Plant bast
T10	Este (PD)	Fondo Rebato	59	Thread	–	S2z	0.7	Medium	Wool
T11	Este (PD)	Fondo Rebato	64	Tabby 1/1	12/8	s/s	0.6–0.7/1	Medium/medium	Flax
T12	Este (PD)	Fondo Rebato	64	Tabby 2/1	4–5	z/z	1.2–1.5	?/medium	Wool
T13	Este (PD)	Fondo Rebato	102	Tabby 1/1	17–18/17–18	s/s	0.3–0.5/0.3–0.4	Medium/medium	Flax
T14	Este (PD)	Fondo Rebato	113	Tabby 1/1	20/20	s/s	0.3/0.3	Medium-hard/medium-hard	Plant bast
T15	Este (PD)	Benvenuti	2	Tabby 1/1	20/16	s/s	0.4–0.7/0.4–0.6	Medium/medium	Flax
T16	Este (PD)	Benvenuti	2	Thread?	–	Z?s	0.3–0.4	Medium	Flax
T17	Este (PD)	Benvenuti	6	Tabby 1/1?	ND	ND	ND	ND	NA
T18	Montagnana (PD)	Vassidii	13	Tabby 1/1	12/12	z/z	0.5–0.6/0.5–0.6	Medium/medium	NA
T19	S.M. Zevio (VR)	Lazisetta	106	Tabby 1/1	16/15	z/z	0.2–0.3/0.3	Hard/hard	Plant bast
T20	Verona	Porta Palio	708	Tabby 2/1	25/25	z/z	0.2–0.3/0.3–0.4	Hard/hard	Wool

(continued)

Table 2.1 (continued)

T21	Verona	Spianà	579	Tabby 2/1	20/30	s/z	0.2/0.4–0.5	Medium/medium	Wool
T22	Verona	Spianà	137	Tabby 1/1	12/14	z/z	0.3–0.6/0.4–0.5	Hard-medium/medium	Plant bast
T23	Sarcedo (VI)	Madonnetta	34	Tabby 1/1	20–25/25–30	s/s	0.3/0.3	Hard-medium/medium	Plant bast
T24	Aquileia	Zuccherina	recinto XV	Tabby 1/1	18–20/18–20	s/s	0.2–0.4/0.3–0.5	Medium/medium	Lino
T25	Montebelluna	via S. Maria in Colle. loc. ex Siberia	3	ND	ND	ND	ND	ND	ND
T26	Montebelluna	via S. Maria in Colle. loc. ex Siberia	3	ND	8/?	ND	0.1?/0.2?	ND	NA
T27	Montebelluna	via S. Maria in Colle. loc. ex Siberia	3	Tabby 1/1	30/20	s/s	0.3/0.3	Medium/hard	flax
T28	Montebelluna	Caonada. fondo Sernaglia	23	Thread?	–	s	0.3	Medium-hard	NA

ND not determinable, *NA* not analysed

Acknowledgements Research leading to these results has received funding from the European Research Council under the European Union's Seventh Framework Programme (project "Production and Consumption: Textile Economy and Urbanisation in Mediterranean Europe 1000-500 BCE (PROCON)", FP/2007-2013-312603, PI: M. Gleba) and from Università di Padova (Progetto di Ateneo "Textile Roman Archaeology: Methods and Analysis. Tools, technology, products (TRAMA)", CPDA142705/14, PI: M.S. Busana).

Material access kindly facilitated by: Mariolina Gamba (Polo Museale del Veneto—Museo Archeologico Nazionale di Altino); Giovanna Gambacurta (Polo Museale del Veneto—Museo Archeologico Nazionale di Este, Museo Civico di Montagnana); Elena Pettenò (Soprintendenza Archeologia, Belle Arti e Paesaggio, Veneto); Francesca Veronese (Museo Archeologico agli Eremitani di Padova); Benedetta Prosdocimi (Soprintendenza Archeologia, Belle Arti e Paesaggio, Veneto); Chiara D'Incà (Soprintendenza Archeologia, Belle Arti e Paesaggio, Veneto); Brunella Bruno (Soprintendenza Archeologia, Belle Arti e Paesaggio, Veneto); Giovanna Falezza (Soprintendenza Archeologia, Belle Arti e Paesaggio, Veneto); Gianni De Zuccato (Soprintendenza Archeologia, Belle Arti e Paesaggio, Veneto); Marta Novello (Museo Archeologico Nazionale di Aquileia). Technical and scientific support by: Denis Francisci (Università di Padova); Michele Pasqualetto (Museo Archeologico Nazionale di Altino); Stefano Buson (Museo Archeologico Nazionale di Este); Sara Emanuele (Soprintendenza Archeologia Veneto); Alessandro Ceccotto (Museo Archeologico agli Eremitani di Padova).

MG wrote Introduction, Methods and Results; MSB wrote the Case Study; both authors wrote Conclusion.

References

Anheuser, K., & Roumeliotou, M. (2003). Characterisation of mineralised archaeological textile fibres through chemical staining. *The Conservator, 27*(1), 23–33. https://doi.org/10.1080/01410096.2003.9995187

Bergfjord, C., & Holst, B. (2010). A procedure for identifying textile bast fibres using microscopy: Flax, nettle/ramie, hemp and jute. *Ultramicroscopy, 110*(9), 1192–1197.

Busana, M. S., & Basso, P. (Eds.). (2012). *La lana nella Cisalpina romana: economia e società*. Antenor.

Busana, M. S., & Gleba, M. (2018). Textile production and consumption in Roman *Venetia* (Italy): Preliminary results of the study of mineralised fibres and textiles. In M. S. Busana, M. Gleba, F. Meo, & A. Tricomi (Eds.), *Purpureae Vestes VI* (pp. 333–350). Porticos.

Busana, M. S., & Gleba, M. (2021). L'uso del tessuto nei rituali funerari del Veneto antico: continuità in età romana di una tradizione preromana. In M. Gamba, G. Gambacurta, F. Gonzato, E. Pettenò, & F. Veronese (Eds.), *Metalli, creta, una piuma d'uccello ... Studi di Archeologia per Angela Ruta Serafini* (Documenti di Archeologia 67) (pp. 187–195). SAP Società Archeologica.

Busana, M. S., & Tricomi, A. R. (2016). Textile archaeology in Roman *Venetia* (Italy). In J. Ortiz, C. Alfaro, L. Turell, & M. J. Martínez (Eds.), *Purpureae Vestes V* (pp. 111–118). Universitat de València.

Busana, M. S., & Tricomi, A. R. (2018). Archeologia tessile nella *Venetia* romana tra storia e archeologia: i casi di Altino, Padova e Verona. In M. García Sánchez & M. Gleba (Eds.), *Vetus Textrinum. Textiles in the Ancient World. Studies in Honour of Carmen Alfaro Giner* (pp. 165–176).

Busana, M. S., Cottica, D., & Basso, P. (2012). La lavorazione della lana nella *Venetia*. In M. S. Busana & P. Basso (Eds.), *La lana nella Cisalpina romana: economia e società* (pp. 383–433). Antenor.

Busana, M. S., Francisci, D., & Rossi, C. (Eds.). (2021). *Lanifica. Il ruolo della donna nella produzione tessile attraverso le evidenze funerary* (Antenor Quaderni 51). Padova University Press.

Cattling, D., & Grayson, J. (2004). *Identification of vegetable fibres*. Archetype Books.

Chen, H. L., Jakes, K. A., & Foreman, D. W. (1998). Preservation of archaeological textiles through fibre mineralization. *Journal of Archaeological Science, 25*, 1015–1021.

Coletti, F. (forthcoming). *I tessuti di Pompei: materiali, tecniche di lavorazione e contesti*. Roma.

Coletti, F., Galli, M., & Mitschke, S. (2021). I calchi per lo studio della cultura tessile a Pompei. In M. Ossana, A. Carpuso, & S. M. Masseroli (Eds.), *I calchi di Pompei da Fiorelli a oggi* (pp. 161–199).

Galli, M., Coletti, F., Lemorini, C., & Mitschke, S. (2018). The textile culture at Pompeii. In M. S. Busana, M. Gleba, F. Meo, & A. Tricomi (Eds.), *Purpureae Vestes VI* (pp. 267–285). Porticos.

Gillard, R. D., Hardman, S. M., Thomas, R. G., & Watkinson, D. E. (1994). The mineralization of fibres in burial environments. *Studies in Conservation, 39*, 132–140.

Gleba, M. (2012). From textiles to sheep: Investigating wool fibre development in pre-Roman Italy using scanning electron microscopy (SEM). *Journal of Archaeological Science, 39*, 3643–3661.

Gleba, M. (2014). Wrapped up for safe keeping: 'Wrapping' customs in Early Iron Age Europe. In S. Harris & L. Douny (Eds.), *Wrapping and unwrapping material culture: Archaeological and anthropological perspectives* (pp. 135–146). Left Coast Press.

Gleba, M. (2017) Tracing textile cultures of Italy and Greece 1000-400 BCE, *Antiquity 91*(359): 1205–1222. https://doi.org/10.15184/aqy.2017.144

Gleba, M., & Griffiths, D. (2011). Textile remains from a Middle Bronze Age burial in Sidon. *Archaeology & History in the Lebanon, 34–35*, 285–296.

Gleba, M., Vanden Berghe, I., & Cenciaioli, L. (2017). Purple for the Masses? Shellfish purple dyed textiles from the quarry workers' cemetery at Strozzacapponi (Perugia/Corciano), Italy. In H. Landenius Enegren & F. Meo (Eds.), *Treasures from the sea* (pp. 131–137). Oxbow Books.

Haugan, E., & Holst, B. (2013). Determining the fibrillary orientation of bast fibres with polarized light microscopy: The modified Herzog test (red plate test) explained. *Journal of Microscopy, 252*(2), 159–168. https://doi.org/10.1111/jmi.12079

Jakes, K. A., & Howard, J. H. (1986). Replacement of protein and cellulosic fibres by copper minerals and the formation of textile pseudomorphs. In H. L. Needles & S. H. Zeronian (Eds.), *Historic textile and paper materials: Conservation and characterisation* (Advances in chemistry series 212) (pp. 277–287). American Chemical Society.

Jakes, K. A., & Sibley, L. R. (1984). An examination of the phenomenon of textile fabric pseudomorphism. In J. B. Lambert (Ed.), *Archaeological chemistry III* (Advances in Chemistry Series 205) (pp. 403–424). American Chemical Society.

James, M. A., Reifarth, N., Mukherjee, A. J., Crump, M. P., Gates, P. J., Sandor, P., Robertson, F., Pfälzner, P., & Evershed, R. P. (2009). High prestige Royal Purple dyed textiles from the Bronze Age royal tomb at Qatna, Syria. *Antiquity, 83*(322), 1109–1118.

Janaway, R. C. (1983). Textile fibre characteristic preserved by metal corrosion: The potential of SEM studies. *The Conservator, 7*, 48–52.

Janaway, R. C. (1987). The preservation of organic materials in association with metal artefacts deposited in inhumation graves. In A. Boddington, A. N. Garland, & R. C. Janaway (Eds.), *Death, decay and reconstruction: Approaches to archaeology and forensic science* (pp. 53–85). Manchester University Press.

Janaway, R. C. (1989). Corrosion preserved textile evidence: Mechanism, bias and interpretation. In *Evidence preserved in corrosion production* (UKIC occasional papers 8) (pp. 21–29). United Kingdom Institute of Conservation.

Lukesova, H. (2017). Application of Herzog test on archaeological plant fibre textiles. Possibilities and limits of polarized light microscopy. In M. Bravermanová, H. Březinová, & J. Malcolm-Davies (Eds.), *Archaeological textiles—Links between past and present. NESAT XIII* (pp. 219–226). Liberec.

Mahal, G. S., Johnston, A., & Burns, R. H. (1951). Types and dimensions of fiber scales from the wool types of domestic sheep and wild life. *Textile Research Journal., 21*(2), 83–93. https://doi.org/10.1177/004051755102100205

Moulhérat, C. (2008). Archéologie des textiles. Une nouvelle méthodologie appliquée à l'etude des tissus minéralisés. *Nouvelles de l'Archeologié, 114*, 18–23.

Rast-Eicher, A. (2008). Textilien, Wolle, Schaffe der Eisenzeit in der Schweiz. *Antiqua* 44. Basel.

Rast-Eicher, A. (2016). *FIBRES—Microscopy of archaeological textiles and furs*. Archaeolingua Alapítvány.

Reifarth, N., & Drewello, R. (2011). Textile Spuren in der Königsgruft. Vorbericht zu ersten Ergebnissen und dem Potenzial zukünftiger Forschungen. In P. Pfälzner (Ed.), *Interdisziplinäre Studien zur Königsgruft von Qatna* (Qatna Studien Bd. 1) (pp. 469–482). Harrassowitz.

Reynaud, C., Thoury, M., Dazzi, A., Latour, G., Scheel, M., Li, J., Thomas, A., Moulhérat, C., Didier, A., & Bertrand, L. (2020). In-place molecular preservation of cellulose in 5,000-year-old archaeological textiles. *PNAS, 117*(33), 19670–19676. https://doi.org/10.1073/pnas.2004139117

Ryder, M. L. (1964). Fleece evolution in domestic sheep. *Nature, 204*(4958), 555–559.

Ryder, M. L., & Gabra-Sanders, T. (1985). The application of microscopy to textile history. *Textile History, 16*(2), 123–140.

Skals, I., Gleba, M., Taube, M., & Mannering, U. (2018). Wool textiles and archaeometry: Testing reliability of archaeological wool fibre diameter measurements. *Danish Journal of Archaeology, 7*(2), 161–179. https://doi.org/10.1080/21662282.2018.1495917

Chapter 3
A Button, a Hook and a Rug Paper Wrapping: Identifying Plant Fibre Finds from Hailuoto, Finland

Jenni A. Suomela and Sanna Lipkin

Abstract Hailuoto is an island in the Bothnian Bay in front of the city of Oulu, a local trading centre during the Post-Medieval period. Hailuoto Church, which was built in the early seventeenth century, burned down in 1968 and was excavated in the mid-1980s. Among other finds, textile remains dated to the period between 1620 and 1756 were found both in burials and the ground soil underneath the church floor.

Six (6) plant fibre samples were analysed to identify the materials. All these samples were preserved due to immediate contact with a metal object in the form of a pin, a button, a coin, or a hook. The samples were analysed using a three-stage procedure which is suitable for distinguishing flax, hemp, and nettle from each other. The procedure is based on the observations of the longitudinal surface characteristics and cross sections, combined with a Modified Herzog test that reveals the microfibrillar orientation in the S2 layer of the bast fibres.

Because of the small preservation areas and gaps in the excavation reports, the origin of some of the samples can only be speculated on. The samples attached to a button or a hook, both used in fastening clothes, are dress-related. The fragment with the pin is an example of fabric reuse for funerary attire. However, an interesting story might be told through a coin, wrapped and tied in rag paper, and deliberately dropped through the planks of the church floor.

Keywords Hailuoto Island · Plant fibres · Fibre identification · Modified Herzog test · Optical microscopy

---

J. A. Suomela (✉)
Department of Education, Craft Science, University of Helsinki, Helsinki, Finland
e-mail: jenni.suomela@helsinki.fi

S. Lipkin
Faculty of Humanities, Archaeology, University of Oulu, Oulu, Finland
e-mail: sanna.lipkin@oulu.fi

3.1 Introduction

Hailuoto is an island at the north end of the Ostrobothnia Sea, the Bothnian Bay, ca. 35 km in front of the coastal city of Oulu. Or to be exact, because the land in the Bothnian Bay is rising quite rapidly, Hailuoto was still formed of four islands in the mid-eighteenth century (Hicks, 1988, 39; Fig. 3.1). It has been inhabited since as early as 1000 AD, and from the mid-sixteenth century there are written documents of inhabitants on the island (Hicks, 1988, 65; Vahtola, 1988, 90). In the mid-seventeenth century Hailuoto already had 77 tax-paying houses. A significant loss of population occurred in the early eighteenth century during the Great Wrath (1713–1721), the Russian occupation of Finland at the time of the Great Northern War (1700–1721), when Hailuoto lost one-third of its population. (Hicks, 1988, 66–68.) In the early twentieth century, Hailuoto had little more than 2000 inhabitants (Paulaharju, [1914] 1993, 1).

The examined textile materials in this study come from burials inside a Protestant church located on the island. The church was most likely built in the 1620s and enlarged in 1686 (Paavola, 1998, 28). The church was renovated in 1756 and 1872–1873 (Paavola, 1988, 15). The last renovation took place in 1964–1966, and the church burned down just two years after that.

Local museum intendent and ethnographer Samuli Paulaharju ([1914] 1993) has made a survey based on interview material on Hailuoto Island reviewing life in the old days. Understandably, this is much later period than the scope of this paper, but it provides a good picture of what life has been like on the island. Circumstances have been harsh, as one could imagine on an island so far north—fishing has been the principal source of livelihood, with little farming and relatively close connections to the nearest city, Oulu.

Side by side with Christian beliefs, the folk belief tradition stayed strong on the island. People believed that spirits were present everywhere: in the forest, earth, trees, and rooms. There were certain evil spirits called 'manolaiset' or 'männingäiset' who were "moving around dead bones", also referred as idle, empty, or church people. When moving to a new place, the earth spirit was offered a needle or something else as sacrifice. The church spirit, aka the oldest of the church people, became the one who was buried first on church ground—in Hailuoto he was Lauri. The bell-tower spirit was Kaija; the first person for whom the death bells were tolled. Lauri even had a wooden statue of himself with a book under his arm in the church (Paulaharju, [1914] 1993, 113–114).

On the island, death was also confronted with strong folk beliefs. When death was imminent, the dying person was dressed in shabby clothes. The death bed with its linens was burned for fear of death being caught. The deceased was washed and dressed in a white shirt and old men in a pixie hat, old women with a hat with gathering at the side. Younger girls were buried with a crown made of gold paper and yarn, whereas younger boys had a wreath on their heads and a twig staff in their right hand. Both girls and boys had a flower on their chest. Sometimes the coffin was equipped with a bottle of liquor or a lunch bag. Even old, useless coins were put

3 A Button, a Hook and a Rug Paper Wrapping: Identifying Plant Fibre Finds...

Fig. 3.1 Map showing the location of Hailuoto. (CC0 1.0 Wikimedia Commons)

in the coffins "for the house to be in peace and for nothing to be demanded" (Paulaharju, [1914] 1993, 106–108).

Paulaharju's ethnographic survey shed also light on what textile materials were used and cultivated in Hailuoto. Flax was little-cultivated in Hailuoto and it is generally known that it does not thrive well in such northern latitudes (Virrankoski, 1996). Flax was imported from Häme, which was the main source of flax in Finland.

Paulaharju's survey mentions both white and yellow flax. White was used for coarser nets and fishing equipment. Yellow was stored for finer netting and clothing fabrics. Hemp again was still being cultivated and used as sack material in Hailuoto in the 1830s. Hemp stalks were retted in the coast where the sea water stays in the pits and hollows (Paulaharju, [1914] 1993, 68–70).

Archaeological excavations took place in the ruins of Hailuoto Church in 1985–1987, with the aim of finding remains of even older church from the Middle Ages. During the excavations, almost 250 burials were found below the church floor. The burials date from the 1620s to the 1750s. At that time, the modern territory of Finland was a province of Sweden. In 1756, the parish prohibited burials under the church floor. Archaeological investigations revealed that the burials were covered with sand after the tradition of the under-church-floor burials ended (Paavola, 1988, 15–16). The archaeological team led by Kirsi Paavola made plenty of metal finds—coins, pins, accessories, buttons, and mountings—and some of these had also preserved textile fragments from decaying. In addition to pins, coins were clearly a common item in the finds: ca. 400 coins were found in the excavations, which is a large number compared to other ecclesiastical excavations in Finland (Nurmi et al., 2009).

Sumptuary laws shaped dress codes during the seventeenth and eighteenth centuries. In the seventeenth century, these laws mainly concerned the clergy and burghers' estates, but at the start of the eighteenth century, they spread to concern all citizens from estates to workers (Lehtinen & Sihvo, 2005, 8–9). Restrictions were mainly placed on fancy foreign textile materials such as silks and laces to promote the domestic Swedish textile industry (Pylkkänen, 1970, 39–45). Something of the local social structure and their garments can be interpreted based on the wigmaker's register (Vilkuna, 2021). Only the highest class wore wigs as parts of their outfits. In the nearby city of Tornio, in the mid-eighteenth century, wigs were possessed by the mayor, aldermen, clerks, merchants, and even craftsmen (Vilkuna, 2019, 105). The city of Oulu did not have any wigmakers in the early eighteenth century, and only one with his apprentices in the late eighteenth century (Vilkuna, 2021, 1377). However, remains of wigs have been unearthed in burials excavated at Oulu Cathedral. Based on these, it could be quite safe to assume that the number of luxurious foreign dress wearers was quite small and did not reach the outer island of Hailuoto. The Finnish part of Sweden was at the periphery of European dress culture, where fashion trends arrived late, and a small island inhabited by fishers and farmers with rough living conditions could be considered as an extremely remote place in Europe. However, extensive research on the funerary attire found in the burials below Hailuoto Church has revealed that luxurious fabrics such as silver embroidered silks and silk bobbin laces made in European cities were after all used to embellish funerary attire (Lipkin et al., 2022).

The working class mainly dressed in wool. In males' wardrobe, only the shirt, which often had a long hem, was made of linen. Loose linen pants were also used in summertime by males (Lehtinen & Sihvo, 2005, 13–15). Women had a much larger variety of linen garments, from underwear, headgear and scarves to aprons and shirts (Lehtinen & Sihvo, 2005, 35; Pylkkänen, 1970, 222).

In the eighteenth century, buttons were used especially in gentry men's, soldiers', and service dresses. Mostly the buttons were used on jackets, vests, cloaks, shirts, and pants. In female dress, buttons were usually used only on shirts. The 1739 sumptuary law forbade importing foreign buttons to Sweden. The law also made clear that the size of the buttons in use had to be similar to *sex styver*, which is a silver coin with a diameter of 2.3 cm. Hooks were used widely in both male and female garments, such as blouses, jackets, cloaks, fur coats, and women's vests. (Kuokkanen et al., 2015.)

This paper concentrates on linen materials, so small summary of the possible textile types of that time might be in order. Printed calicos made of cotton were imported from India and European counterparts were printed on flax. Finest cotton muslin was a rarity in Finland; instead, various sorts of fine flax cloth were imported. Still, the majority of flax cloth was woven in Finland, either by professional weavers or in homes. Most of the linen lace was also locally produced (Pylkkänen, 1970, 79–84).

This paper concentrates on six plant fibre textile finds from the site. We are interested in what plant materials were used in these fragments, and based on our results, what can be speculated to be the context in the original textiles and what could be their meaning for the community.

3.2 Sample Preparation and Identification Methods

Samples were identified by analysing the fibre morphology with transmitted light microscopy methods (Suomela et al., 2018). Sample preparation was done under a stereo microscope, preparing both longitudinal and cross-sectional samples simultaneously. Fibres' longitudinal characteristics were observed from permanent glass slide mountings made using the Entellan New mounting media. Cross-sectional samples were studied from cork sheet cuttings made with Entellan New, with methodology thoroughly explained in Suomela et al. (2018). Cuttings made with a razor blade were placed on glass slides and studied as such with no mounting or cover glass. Both longitudinal and cross-sectional samples were observed using a Leica DM4500P microscope and imaged with a Leica DFC420 camera with 5-megapixel resolution. Analyses were made using the Leica application suite LAS Core 4.5.0 software.

From the longitudinal samples, typical fibre characteristics were observed to determine fibre type. These included cross-markings and dislocations (bast fibres), convolutes (cotton), or possible scales (animal fibres). In the case of bast fibres, polarised light was utilised in the microscope. Cross-markings and dislocations are more easily observable under it. In addition, the possible presence of calcium oxalate crystals was checked by rotating the sample under crossed polarised light (Bergfjord & Holst, 2010). The microfibrillar orientation of the bast fibres was observed by applying a lambda plate to the polarised light and conducting the Modified Herzog test (Haugan & Holst, 2013). The cross-sectional appearance of the fibres was studied from the cork sheet cuttings, paying attention to the fibre shape and the shape and size of the lumen. By combining these morphological attributes, bast fibres can be identified on the species level.

3.3 Materials and Results

Six plant fibre textile samples were selected for this study (Table 3.1).

3.3.1 Sample 1/KM87131:261

A tabby-woven, 16 mm long piece of cloth had survived because of a pin (Fig. 3.2). The pin was found below the church floor level but was not associated with any of the coffins. Originally the material of the pins that were abundant in the excavation finds was listed as bronze. After analyses with a Scanning Electron Microscope, the material was identified as tin-covered brass (Paavola, 1991, 35). Yarns were single-plied, Z-twisted, quite thick, and brownish-grey in colour. Over time, the structure of the yarns had flattened.

Table 3.1 Details of the textile materials sampled for this research

Sample no. / KM-inventory number	Item	Structure/ weave	Yarns	Textile material identification results
Sample 1/ KM87131:261a	Fabric preserved associated with a pin (0.9 × 1.6, 0.4–0.5 cm)	Plain weave, 15/16 yarns/cm	Z-twist, 0.5 mm thick	Flax
Sample 2/ KM87131:370b	Fabric preserved wrapped around a Queen Christina 1/6 öre, 1671	Plain weave, 20/29 yarns/cm	Z-twist, 0.3–0.4 mm thick	Flax
Samples 3 and 4/ KM86088:255	Rag paper (diameter 2.5–2.8 cm) wrapped around a Queen Christina 1/6(?) öre, 1667, and tied with yarn	Rag paper	S-twist, 0.8–1.1 mm thick	Paper: cotton, bast fibres yarn: hemp (or tree bast (willow?))
Sample 5/ KM86088:108	Two fabric fragments (0.8 × 0.6, 0.6 × 0.4 cm in size) preserved on a hook (length 1.4 cm)	Plain weave, 24 yarns/cm	Z-twist, 0.3–0.4 mm thick	Nettle
Sample 6/ KM86088:251	Four fragments (0.3 × 0.5–0.8 × 1.2 cm in size) of fabric preserved on the back of button (diameter ca. 2.2 cm)	Plain weave, 24/26 yarns/cm	Z-twist, 0.3–0.4 mm thick	Cotton

3 A Button, a Hook and a Rug Paper Wrapping: Identifying Plant Fibre Finds…

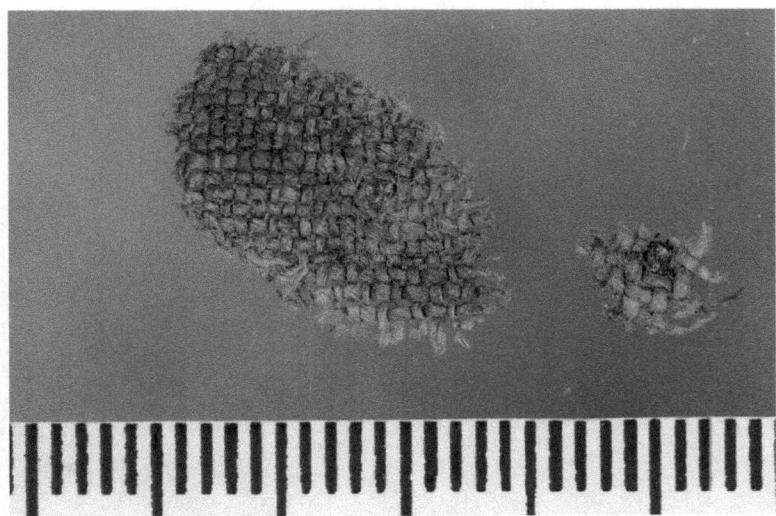

Fig. 3.2 Sample 1, KM87131:261a

The fibres were covered with greenish metallic salts, probably copper from brass (Fig. 3.3a). In addition to the metallic salts, some other organic material was present on the fibre surface, and clearly recognisable lens-shaped mould spores. At some parts, the fibres were eroded and degraded to a state where the fibres had started to break into pieces. With the Modified Herzog test, it was still possible to detect the S-twist in the microfibrillar orientation (Fig. 3.3c–d). The cross-sectional images are not that clear, but in analysis, the fibres were observable to be polygonal with a small lumen (Fig. 3.3b). All these aspects point to the identification result being flax.

3.3.2 Sample 2/KM87131:370b

A tabby-woven cloth was wrapped around a 1/6 öre copper coin from 1671 (Fig. 3.4). The eminent presence of copper had most likely worked as the preservation agent. The coin was found in the excavation of an old wooden cross not far from the actual excavation site.

The fibres were in good condition, although they had a greenish shade which was probably contamination from the coin. The twist of the sample yarn had unravelled but had been most likely Z. Individual fibres were relatively thick and cross-markings were pronounced (Fig. 3.5a). The microfibrillar orientation was S and the cross-sectional view showed a polygonal shape with a small lumen (Fig. 3.5b–d). All these attributes refer to flax.

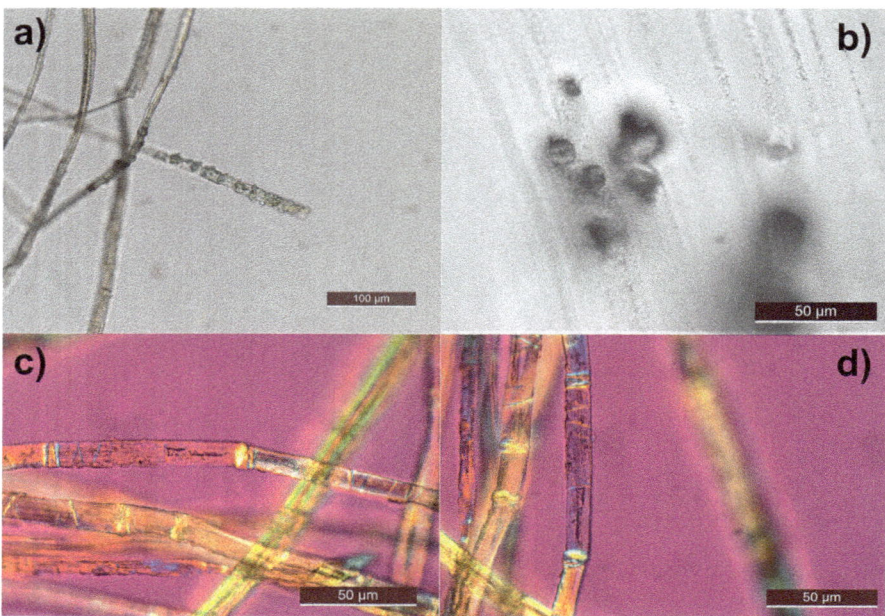

Fig. 3.3 Microscopy images of KM87131:261a. (**a**) Greenish metallic salt on fibre; (**b**) Cross-section of the fibres; (**c-d**) Results of the Modified Herzog test

Fig. 3.4 Sample 2, KM87131:370b

3   A Button, a Hook and a Rug Paper Wrapping: Identifying Plant Fibre Finds...

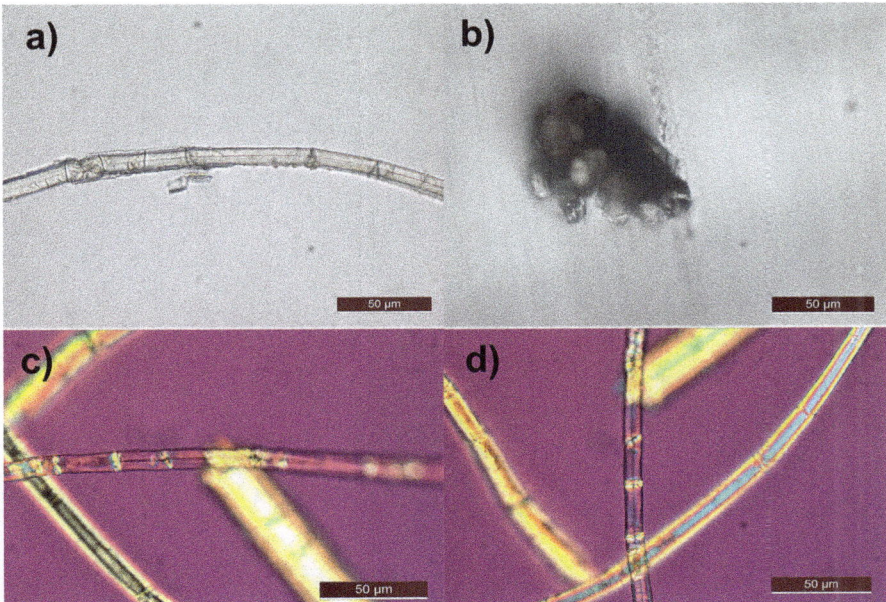

Fig. 3.5 Microscopy images of KM87131:370b. (**a**) Pronounced cross-markings; (**b**) Cross-section of the fibres; (**c-d**) Results of the Modified Herzog test

3.3.3   Sample 3/KM86088:255

The sample was taken from a piece of rag paper wrapped around a 1/6 öre copper coin from year 1667 (Fig. 3.6). The item was found below the floor level of the church. At the sample preparation stage, individual fibres were clearly visible with brownish foreign matter. In the TLM analysis it was clear that the fibres were badly decomposed, eroded and unoriented (Fig. 3.7a). Some weave structures of tabby-woven cloths that had been used as the material were still visible (Fig. 3.7b). Probably the heavy processing in paper-making had affected the fibres. With polarised light it was possible to identify cotton (Fig. 3.7c) and bast fibres with a microfibrillar orientation of S (Fig. 3.7d). Due to the unoriented positioning of the fibres, cross-sectional analysis did not give any further attributes for identification.

3.3.4   Sample 4/KM86088:255

A tying string was used for attaching rag paper around the coin. The fibres in the yarn are roughly processed, more like they were still in bark strips than individual fibres and most probably tree bast fibres. The material was so thick that polarised

Fig. 3.6 Samples 3 and 4, KM86088:255, rag paper

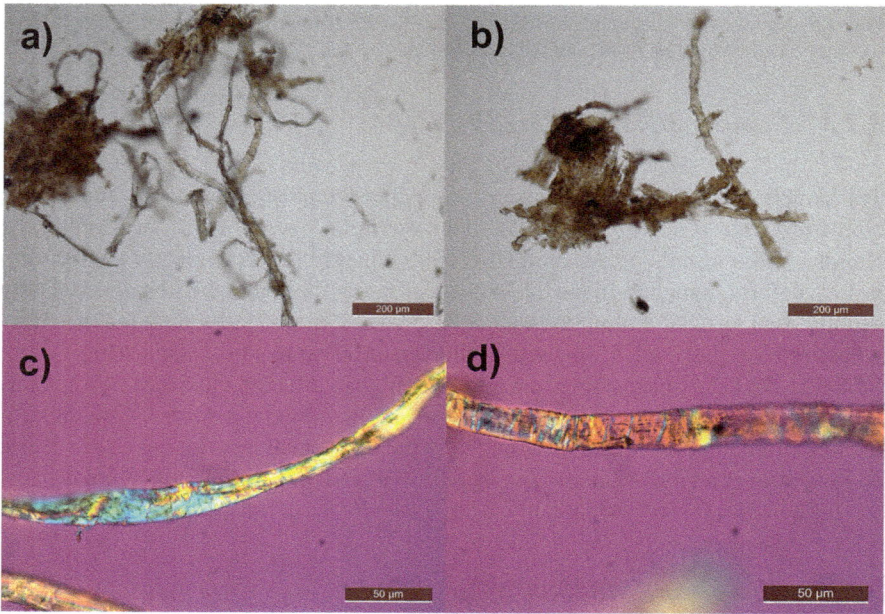

Fig. 3.7 Microscopy images of KM86088:255, rag paper. (**a**) Degraded fibres; (**b**) Fragment of the rag paper; (**c**) Cotton fibre imaged with lambda plate; (**d**) Result of the Modified Herzog test

3 A Button, a Hook and a Rug Paper Wrapping: Identifying Plant Fibre Finds…

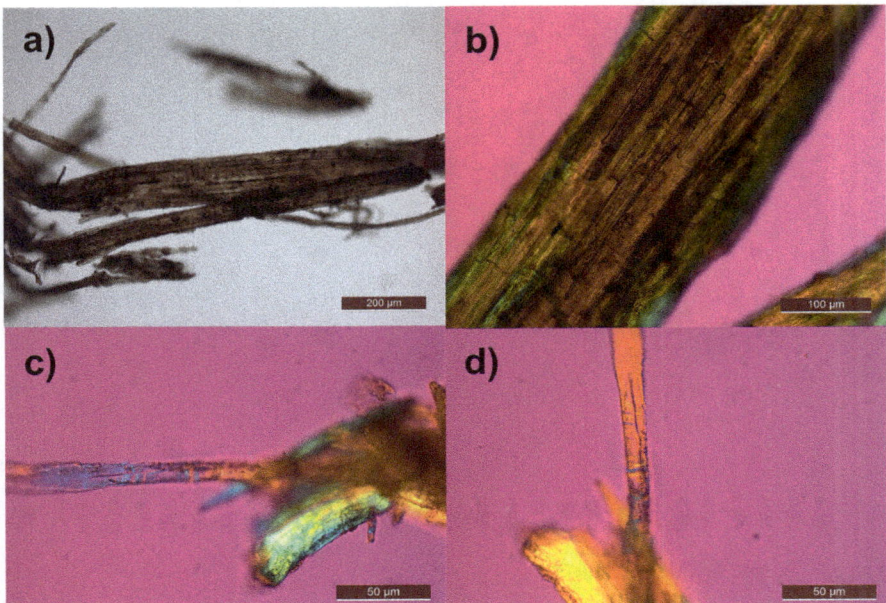

Fig. 3.8 Microscopy images of KM86088:255, tying string. (**a**) Fragment of bark strip; (**b**) Air pockets; (**c-d**) Results of the Modified Herzog test

light did not pass through it well (Fig. 3.8a) and interesting air pockets were visible here and there in the bark strips (Fig. 3.8b). It was possible to conduct the Modified Herzog test on a few individual fibre ends: the result showed a Z-twist in the microfibrils (Figs. 3.8c–d). The cross-sectional view was vague: if anything can be said, the fibres were adhering to one another and had some kind of elongated angular form. Tree basts can be identified based on three main features—rays, cell structure, and oxalate crystals (Rammo, 2021). None of these were detectable in the sample. With the lack of reference materials of tree basts, further identification was beyond our skills. Based on the results, our educated guess is the results indicate hemp, or possibly some tree bast used in the area, such as willow (*Salix*).

3.3.5 Sample 5/KM86088:108

A tabby-woven piece of cloth had survived as attached to a bronze hook (Fig. 3.9). The hook was found below the church floor level. The yellowish single-plied yarns have a Z-twist. In transmitted light analysis, the fibres appeared brownish and badly degraded (Fig. 3.10a). The fibres had started to break into pieces and were surface-eroded and full of residue. The Modified Herzog test gave an S-twist as a

Fig. 3.9 Sample 5, KM86088:108

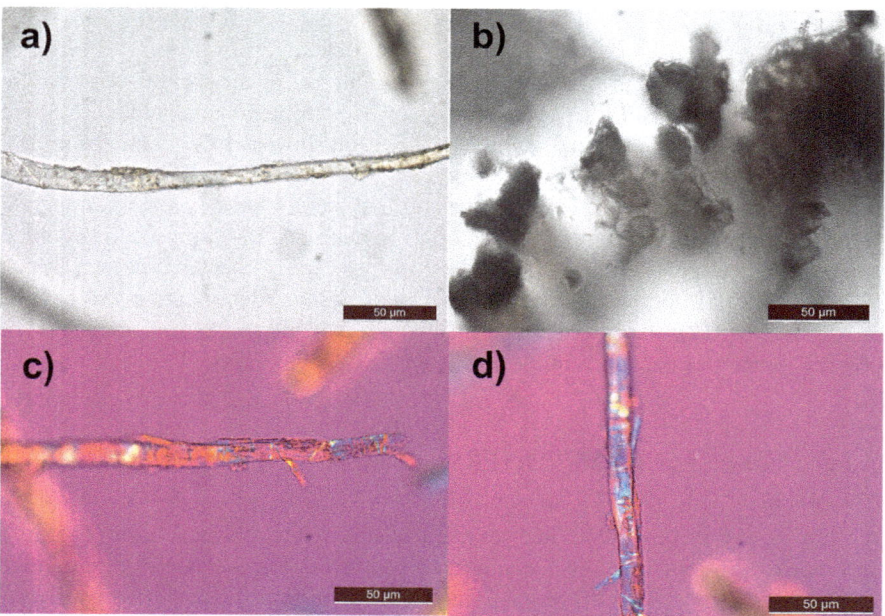

Fig. 3.10 Microscopy images of KM86088:108. (**a**) Fibre with foreign matter on the surface; (**b**) Cross-section of the fibres; (**c-d**) Results of the Modified Herzog test

Fig. 3.11 Sample 6, KM86088:251

result. The cross-sectional analysis showed a mostly kidney-shaped outline with a flattened lumen which, together with the microfibrillar orientation, points to nettle (Fig. 3.10b–d).

3.3.6 Sample 6/KM86088:251

Sample 6 was taken from a tabby-woven cloth attached to the back of a cast tin button (Fig. 3.11). The button was found below the church floor. The button has diameter of ca. 22 mm and on it the text "NORIE TINKNAP" ('Norwegian tin button') and a profile picture of a male bust. The loop socket of the button is broken. The yarns had a Z-twist and their thickness varied.

Longitudinal observation showed clear convolutions of cotton fibres (Fig. 3.12a). The fibres had much natural variation and were covered with residue (Fig. 3.12a). The cross-sectional view also showed that the fibres were in varying stages of ripeness (Moulhérat et al., 2002; Fig. 3.12b).

3.4 Discussion

First, we will discuss topics related to microscopy research methods, and then we will address issues connected to the actual findings.

The cross-cutting method with Entellan and a cork sheet was chosen on purpose. The other option, to mount the cuttings with paper glue (Rast-Eicher, 2016, 70), was dismissed in fear of losing the precious samples. PVA-based paper glues, depending

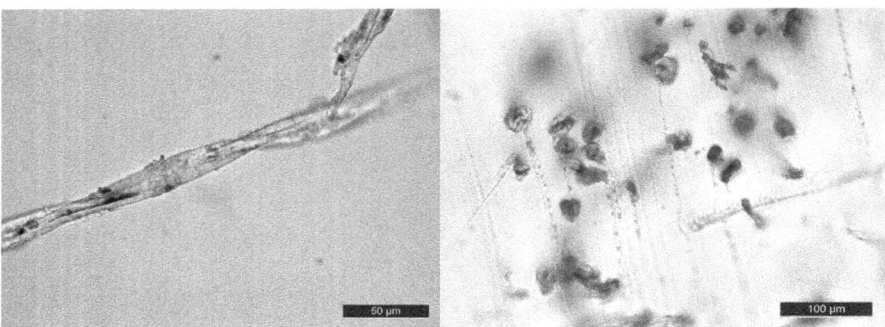

Fig. 3.12 Microscopy images of KM86088:251. (**a**) Convolutions in the fibre; (**b**) Cross-section of the fibres

on the manufacturer, tend to dry milk white and turbid in colour, which makes finding the fibres difficult. With Entellan, the optimal drying time was also monitored for cuttings, and in laboratory conditions under the fume hood it was between 7 and 10 days. In shorter time the Entellan was too soft to cut, and after 10 days it became too brittle and hard.

No calcium oxalate crystals were detected in these textile samples to clarify the identification process among the bast fibres. When it comes to the Modified Herzog test, it is important to state that in these images the lambda plate was applied to the microscope at a 225° angle instead of the usual 135°. The results of yellow and blue hues appear the opposite at this angle. The colour changes are comparable only within the research and should always be checked on the applied microscope with known reference samples.

None of the studied items were found inside the burial coffins. However, they reveal different aspects of using fabrics while constructing coffins to be buried below church floors as well as religious beliefs concerning the space and burials themselves.

During the seventeenth and eighteenth centuries, it was common to bury the deceased wearing white clothing that was often constructed on the body. The deceased could wear a shirt that was used while living or fabrics were laid and pleated on the body to resemble real clothes. Fabrics were often pinned together and attached to the interior fabrics that covered the mattress (Lipkin et al., 2021). A pin was the most common find in Hailuoto Church. Many of them were fragmentary and sometimes it is difficult to know whether pin fragments were originally from one or more pins, but at least ca. 750 pins or their fragments were found at the site. Whereas many pins were found in burials and associated with textiles, similarly to the one studied here, most were found between burials. It is likely that the linen fabric associated with the pin was from either a burial shirt or other fabrics covering the body in one of the nearby burials. In other churches, where we have been able to study coffin fabric in more detail (at Haukipudas, Köyliö, and Keminmaa), the fabrics covering the coffin edges and mattress are usually coarser than the one in Sample 1.

Pins were also used in clothing in everyday life, as were buttons and hooks. Nineteen buttons were found in the excavations (Mutka & Riutankoski, 2011). Among those was the Norwegian tin button associated with the fabric of Sample 6. Tin buttons were used on modest clothing (Pylkkänen, 1970, 92), so this gives a small hint or direction as to what kind of garment it could originally be from. Then again, Kuokkanen (2016, 72) argues that buttons made of cheaper materials like brass were also used by burghers. The button in Sample 6 was 22 mm in diameter, so it respected the sumptuary regulations. The piece of cloth that was attached to it was clearly made of white cotton tabby, which limits the possibilities for the original garment. Cotton was a rarity as a textile material until the eighteenth century, when it starts to appear in probate inventories (Suomela et al., 2023). According to our educated guess, based on the undyed cotton material, it is probably from a shirt.

Hooks were also commonly used in different kind of clothes. Circa 50 hooks were found below the floors. Based on size, the hook of Sample 5 would be suitable to be used in a vest, shirt, or skirt. Based on the cross-sectional characteristics, the material is identified as nettle. Due to natural variation and the poor quality of the images, there is a small possibility that the sample could also be flax. Because of the Modified Herzog test results for the S microfibrillar orientation, these are the only possible candidates. If not from a shirt, the fabric could be a piece of very fine quality lining.

Hooks and buttons were not found in any of the burials, and considering the traditions described in historical sources and evidence from archaeological studies, it is most likely that these items ended up below the floor for other reasons than burials. It is also impossible to say when the hooks and buttons slid there. Similarly to the coins, it is likely that they ended up there either before the renovation of the wooden floor in 1756 when the floor planks were presumably placed tighter against one another or after the late nineteenth century renovations when the occurrence of coins resumes (Nurmi et al., 2009). Nevertheless, finding hooks, buttons and coins under the church floor is likely not accidental. Instead of them of dropping there from churchgoers, it is more likely that they were placed there for magical purposes (Paulaharju, [1914] 1993, 107; Nurmi et al., 2009, 209; Lipkin, 2020). Even though it was a severe crime, bones, pieces of funerary attire, wood chips, and soil from below the church floor could be stolen and used for witchcraft (Tittonen, 2008). These could be used either for ill-natured spells or those aiming to help a household economically or healing diseases. Because taking these from the burials could disturb the deceased and the church people, they were given payment in coins (Harva, 1948, 499–500; Koski, 2011, 242). Wrapping coins, and possibly also hooks and buttons, in either fabric or paper further emphasises their magical nature (Lipkin, 2020). In addition to the items selected for sampling in this study, in Hailuoto Church there are three other coins wrapped in yarn (KM87131:64, copper 1/6 öre, 1666), plant-based fabric (KM87131:95, silver ½ öre, 1577), and rag paper (KM87131:151, silver 1 öre, 1732). The one wrapped in plant-based fabric was found on the coffin lid of an adult (Burial 155) that was laid below the floor but was not found inside any of the burial chambers. The most common coin found in the excavation was the 1/6 öre copper coin from the time of Charles XI of Sweden pressed between 1666 and 1686: 140 out of those ca. 400 coins were of this type. (Nurmi et al., 2009, 307–308). This is also the type represented by both coins in our collection. Using 1/6 öre copper coins is also in line with Paulaharju's ([1914] 1993) notion that they used "cheap and old" coins, because this was the smallest coin in value what was pressed. However, more valuable coins were also found below the floor (Mutka & Riutankoski, 2011).

According to Paulaharju ([1914] 1993, 37–38), Hailuoto had a tradition of making ropes from *Pinus* roots and *Salix* tree bast, also from hemp. All these were used for fishing purposes. The other possible three bast materials used in the Finnish peninsula are limited to *Populus* or *Tilia* (Miettinen et al., 2008). Hicks's (1988) pollen analysis verifies the presence of all the above-mentioned except *Tilia* on the island in the studied time. Still, based on our observations of a microfibrillar twist of Z and no indicative ray-structures of tree basts, our results point to hemp in Sample 4.

Rag paper was produced in Europe by fermenting old flax textiles that had been cut into small pieces. When these moistened piles of lumps developed mould on the surface, they were thought to be ready, and were then washed and stamped to form pulp for the paper. Whereas flax and cotton textiles are not always easy to distinguish by material, it is not surprising that some cotton ended up in rag paper pulp. In addition, the fermentation process explains the condition and all the additional residue, which is probably some microbial growth, in Sample 3 (Putkonen, 1997, 116–125).

3.5 Conclusion

Even though there were only six samples in this study, they represented versatile materials and contexts. This enabled a rich interpretation of their sources and meanings. It is obvious that these items did not land under the church floor by accident, but intentionally, although the textile fragments that were attached to the hook or button were probably in a secondary position. Intentional or unintentional, these metal object that prevented the textiles from decaying also enabled speculation on their context to a certain extent. It is good to acknowledge that garments are often more than just textile structures: sometimes the non-textile components can be more informative.

Acknowledgements We acknowledge the provision of facilities and technical support by Aalto University at OtaNano—Nanomicroscopy Center (Aalto-NMC).

References

Bergfjord, C., & Holst, B. (2010). A procedure for identifying textile bast fibres using microscopy: Flax, Nettle/Ramie, Hemp and Jute. *Ultramicroscopy, 110*, 1192–1197. https://doi.org/10.1016/j.ultramic.2010.04.014

Harva, U. (1948). *Suomalaisten muinaisusko*. WSOY.

Haugan, E., & Holst, B. (2013). Determining the fibrillary orientation of bast fibres with polarized light microscopy: The modified Herzog test (red plate test) explained. *Journal of Microscopy, 252*(2), 159–168. https://doi.org/10.1111/jmi.12079

Hicks, S. (1988). Siitepölytodisteita Hailuodon varhaisesta asutuksesta. In K. Julku & R. Satokangas (Eds.), *Hailuodon keskiaika* (Studia historica septentrionalia 15) (pp. 35–88). Pohjois-Suomen historiallinen yhdistys/Gummerus oy kirjapaino.

Koski, K. (2011). Uskomusperinne ja kristillinen kasvatus 1800-luvulla. *Kasvatus & Aika, 5*, 4.

Kuokkanen, T. (2016). *Vaatetuksen Luokka Ja Sukupuoli 1600–1800-lukujen Oulussa: Historiallisen Ajan Arkeologian Näkökulma*. Oulun yliopisto.

Kuokkanen, T., Mutka, K., & Ylimaunu, T. (2015). Nappeja, solkia ja asetuksia: lainsäädännön vaikutus pukeutumiseen varhaismodernissa Oulussa. *Artefactum 5*. Artefacta, Helsinki.

Lehtinen, I., & Sihvo, P. (2005). *Rahwaan puku: näkökulmia Suomen kansallismuseon kansanpukukokoelmiin = Folk costume: an owerview of the folk costume collection of the National Museum of Finland*. Museovirasto.

Lipkin, S. (2020). The clothed dead body in northern Ostrobothnian Finland between the 17th and mid-19th centuries. In T. Äikäs & S. Lipkin (Eds.), *Entangled beliefs and rituals* (MASF 8) (pp. 54–69). Archaeological Society of Finland. http://www.sarks.fi/masf/masf_8/MASF8-3-Lipkin.pdf

Lipkin, S., Ruhl, E., Vajanto, K., Trandberg, A., & Suomela, J. (2021). Textiles: Decay and preservation in seventeenth- to nineteenth-century burials in Finland. *Historical Archaeology, 55*(1), 49–64. https://doi.org/10.1007/s41636-020-00270-4

Lipkin, S., Tranberg, A., Kallio-Seppä, T., & Ruhl, E. (2022). Preparing children's burials in post-medieval Finland: Emotions awakened by sensory experiences. *Historical Archaeology, 56*(2), 184–198. https://doi.org/10.1007/s41636-022-00343-6

Miettinen, A., Sarmaja-Korjonen, K., Sonninen, E., Jungner, H., Lempiäinen, T., Ylikoski, K., Mäkiaho, J. P., & Carpelan, C. (2008). The palaeoenvironment of the 'Antrea Net Find'. *Iskos, 16*, 71–87.

Moulhérat, C., Tengberg, M., Haquet, J. F., & Mille, B. (2002). First evidence of cotton at Neolithic Mehrgarh, Pakistan: Analysis of mineralized fibres from a copper bead. *Journal of Archaeological Science, 29*(12), 1393–1401.

Mutka, K., & Riutankoski, M. (2011). Rahvaan muoti: kukkakuvioiset kansanpuvun napit Hailuodon kirkon kaivausaineistossa. In J. Ikäheimo, R. Nurmi, & R. Satokangas (Eds.), *Harmaata näkyvissä: Kirsti Paavolan juhlakirja* (pp. 137–148). Kirsti Paavolan juhlakirjatoimikunta.

Nurmi, R., Ylimaunu, T., Kuokkanen, T., & Kallio-Seppä, T. (2009). Uuden ajan alun kuparikolikot Pohjois-Suomessa – rahaa kuin roskaa? In J. Ikäheimo & S. Lipponen (Eds.), *Ei kiveäkään kääntämättä: juhlakirja Pentti Koivuselle*. Pentti Koivusen juhlakirjatoimikunta.

Paavola, K. (1988). Domus pro templo: Hailuodon kirkon varhaisvaiheet. In K. Julku & R. Satokangas (Eds.), *Hailuodon keskiaika* (Studia historica septentrionalia 15) (pp. 9–34). Pohjois-Suomen historiallinen yhdistys/Gummerus oy kirjapaino.

Paavola, K. (1991). Hailuodon kirkon arkeologiset tutkimukset vuosina 1985–1987. In J. Okkonen (Ed.), *Arkeologian tutkimusraportteja 3*. Oulun yliopisto.

Paavola, K. (1998). *Kepeät mullat: kirjallisiin ja esineellisiin lähteisiin perustuva tutkimus Pohjois-Pohjanmaan rannikon kirkkohaudoista*. Oulun yliopisto.

Paulaharju, S. ([1914] 1993). *Kuvauksia Hailuodosta* (2nd ed.) [i.e. facsimile.]. Werner Söderström.

Putkonen, V. (1997). *Paperia!: lyhyt johdatus paperin historiaan ja valmistusmenetelmiin*. Otatieto.

Pylkkänen, R. (1970). *Barokin pukumuoti Suomessa 1620–1720*. Weilin + Göös.
Rammo, R. (2021). Usage of tree bast in the Baltic Sea region based on 14th century cog finds. In M. Berihuete-Azorín, M. Martín Seijo, O. López-Bultó, & R. Piqué (Eds.), *The missing woodland resources—Archaeobotanical studies of the use of plant raw materials* (pp. 111–122). Barkhuis Publishing.
Rast-Eicher, A. (2016). *fibres: microscopy of archaeological textiles and furs*. Archaeolingua Alapítvány.
Suomela, J. A., Vajanto, K., & Räisänen, R. (2018). Seeking nettle textiles—Utilizing a combination of microscopic methods for fibre identification. *Studies in Conservation, 63*(7), 412–422. https://doi.org/10.1080/00393630.2017.1410956
Suomela, J. A., Viljanen, M., Svedström, K., Wright, K., & Lipkin, S. (2023). Research methods for heritage cotton fibres: Case studies from archaeological and historical finds in a Finnish context. *Heritage Science, 11*(1), 175. https://doi.org/10.1186/s40494-023-01022-2
Tittonen, E. (2008). "Nouse ylös vanha väki, lastujen perään!": hautausmaiden taikuus 1700-luvun lopulla. *J@rgonia, 6*(14), 1–19. Retrieved from http://urn.fi/URN:NBN:fi:jyu-20095111563
Vahtola, J. (1988). Hailuodon varhainen asutushistoria nimistön valossa. In K. Julku & R. Satokangas (Eds.), *Hailuodon keskiaika* (Studia historica septentrionalia 15) (pp. 35–88). Pohjois-Suomen historiallinen yhdistys/Gummerus oy kirjapaino.
Vilkuna, K. J. H. (2019). Peruukki, puuteri ja varhaismodernimies. In A. Turunen & A. Niiranen (Eds.), *Säädyllistä ja säädytöntä – Pukeutumisen historiaa renesanssista 2000-luvulle*. SKS.
Vilkuna, K. J. H. (2021). *Ruotsin peruukintekijät 1648–1810*. Suomen sukututkimusseuran vuosikirja, 49, part 4. Suomen sukututkimusseura.
Virrankoski, P. (1996). *Myyntiä varten harjoitettu kotiteollisuus Suomessa autonomian ajan alkupuolella (1809-noin 1865)*. Suomen historiallinen seura.

Chapter 4
The Effects of Carbonisation on the Morphology of Textile Fibres: Comparison Between Modern and Ancient Materials—The Example of Pompeii

Francesca Coletti and Christina Margariti

Abstract Archaeological textiles are usually rare finds in excavations, as they are generally made of organic material. However, special environmental conditions can cause deceleration or even stop their deterioration yielding unique textile finds. Especially, carbonisation can preserve the textile structure but might also greatly affect the morphology and physico-chemical properties of the fibres, which are the main elements used for their identification. To explore this issue, this paper focuses on the effects of carbonisation on natural fibres, through the case study of the carbonised textiles from the ancient city of Pompeii and their comparison to a set of cellulosic and proteinaceous contemporary textiles that were artificially carbonized in a limited oxygen environment at 250, 350 and 500 °C. All carbonised samples were analysed with Optical and Scanning Electron Microscopies. The research combined the analysis of excavated finds, the available data in literature and experimentation on reference samples.

The study showed that the vegetable fibers can better withstand heat, but marked effects on the dimensions of fibres after 250 °C. Conversely, the proteinaceous swatches were generally destroyed whereas the archaeological ones do not alter to an unrecognisable degree even at higher temperatures, as long as the material is preserved. This distinct effect seems related to the complete exclusion or extremely limited presence of oxygen in context.

This research contributes to a better understanding of the carbonisation process that the fibres underwent during the volcanic eruption of AD 79 in Pompeii, offering new data and conclusions concerning their different stage of carbonisation in relation to the events that occurred in their context of deposition. The investigation

F. Coletti (✉)
Department of Science of Antiquities, Sapienza University of Rome, Rome, Italy
e-mail: francesca.coletti@uniroma1.it

C. Margariti
Applied Research Department, Directorate of Conservation of Ancient & Modern Monuments, Hellenic Ministry of Culture, Athens, Greece

© The Author(s), under exclusive license to Springer Nature Switzerland AG 2024
F. Coletti et al. (eds.), *Multidisciplinary Approaches for the Investigation of Textiles and Fibres in the Archaeological Field*, Interdisciplinary Contributions to Archaeology, https://doi.org/10.1007/978-3-031-73812-8_4

related to the thermal degradation phenomena on fibres from the Vesuviana area is an important topic concerning not only textile research such as the identification of the raw materials but also the archaeological issue, currently under discussion, about the effect of the volcanic eruption on ancient artefacts caused by the natural disaster and the temperatures reached.

Keywords Textile fibres · Carbonisation · Pompeii · Thermal degradation

4.1 Introduction

The survival of ancient textiles and organic fibres requires special climatic or environmental conditions in the context of deposition. Indeed, archaeological textile finds are usually rare in excavations, since the organic matter is sensitive to aggressive post-depositional processes (Andersson Strand et al., 2010). There are cases where specific environmental conditions considerably decelerate deterioration, as they prevent microbial growth, yielding unique textile finds that preserve their structure and appearance. Exceptional conditions for textile preservation can be found in salt mines, leading to the drying out of bacteria as well as ice, which offers a combination of freezing and drying (Grömer, 2016, 24–25, 27). However, certain conditions like mineralization (Margariti, 2019; Gillard et al., 1994), waterlogging (Mannering & Skals, 2020; Gleba & Mannering, 2012) and carbonization (Margariti, 2020; Styring et al., 2013; Huisman et al., 2012) might also greatly affect the morphology and physico-chemical properties of the fibres. Both, morphology and the original organic properties of the fibres, are the main elements used for their identification.

Carbonisation, i.e. incomplete burning, is a particular condition that has been responsible for the preservation of archaeological textiles (Harris, 2015; Margariti, 2020). A study of carbonised grain material (i.e. of organic nature, like the textiles) showed, that carbonisation enhances preservation as it makes the organic material resistant to micro-organisms (Kanstrup et al., 2012, 2533). This type of preservation contributes to the survival of highly fragmented textiles, usually of an intense black colour, and with a glossy surface (Jakes et al., 2010, 329). However, it has proven to be a state of preservation that allows for the recognition of the weave and yarn structure as well as enabling other visual observations of the structure of the finds (Malmius, 2002, 63; Srinivasan & Jakes, 1997, 521–522). In fact, different shades of the black colour of carbonised textiles seem to correspond to different chemical alterations in their organic matter, and usually, the darker the colour of the finds the higher the degree of carbonisation (Jakes et al., 2010, 326). Carbonised textiles are generally extremely brittle and do not retain their flexibility (Harris, 2015, 78), making the handling and study of such finds particularly challenging. In addition, animal fibres, are considered usually more susceptible to the effects of fire than cellulosic ones (Rottoli, 2005, 66).

This research aimed to study the effects of carbonisation on the morphology and dimensions of textile fibres. To this aim, carbonised fibres from Pompeii excavations were analysed with microscopy and compared to a set of standard tests of artificially carbonised cellulosic and proteinaceous fabrics. Although both cellulosic and proteinaceous textiles had survived the volcanic eruptions, the wool and silk swatches were destroyed at temperatures above 250 °C. The carbonisation process that the textile finds from Pompeii underwent could be attributed to the combination of extreme heat with anaerobic conditions triggered by the telluric and eruption events. The eruption of Mount Vesuvius in 79 AD sealed the city of Pompeii and the surrounding areas, preserving the ancient cities and villas with a multitude of unique archaeological evidence. Among that, a wide range of organic materials has been preserved, such as vegetables, wood, leather, and textiles. Most of the textile fragments from Pompeii, of both cellulosic and proteinaceous nature, have most probably been preserved due to the high temperatures developed and, in certain cases, the exceptional micro-environmental conditions established in specific contexts because of the occurrence of fire (Galli et al., 2018, 2019; Coletti, 2020, forthcoming; Médard, 2020).

The scientific excavations recently conducted by the Archaeological Park of Pompeii provide new evidence of the effect of the volcanic eruption on architectural structures and organic artefacts, also providing detailed documentation of the investigated context.[1] The interdisciplinary and top-notch approach applied in the excavation practice allows us to interpret better not only the new finds but also the carbonised textiles found in past centuries' excavations, for most of which their find spots and contextual information are unknown. Particularly revealing for our aim was the excavation carried out in the House of Orion (V, 2, 15), where numerous textile fragments in different states of carbonisation were found in a room with three beds and wooden furnishing.[2]

4.2 Materials and Methods

4.2.1 Archaeological Material

The investigated samples are part of the old collection of carbonised textiles found in Pompeii from the nineteenth to the first half of the twentieth century. About this finding no information related to the discovery, exact context of recovery and their position in relationship with other materials are known. However, the carbonised

---

[1] Also called House of Jupiter.
[2] All the contextual information were provided by the archaeologists of the Archaeological Park of Pompeii and those who carried out the excavation.

samples showed different states of carbonisation, sometimes even within the same artefacts.

A different set of textile fragments were selected for comparison. They were found during the very recent excavation carried out by the Archaeological Park of Pompeii in the Regio V of the ancient city. For the interpretation of the analytical data, all the documentation and information about the discovery, contexts and recovery of the materials were essential. Even in this case, the carbonised samples were selected with special attention in choosing remains with different degrees of carbonisation.

All textile fragments were firstly analysed with USB digital microscope Veho VMS-004 for documenting the general appearance of the artefacts and their macroscopic alteration due to the carbonisation process. This stage also allows for collecting data about the fabric structures (type of weave, threads, borders, etc.). Scanning Electron Microscopy (SEM) was used on micro samples in order to characterise the fibre types and to investigate the effect of thermal degradation on the fibre morphology at the microscopic level. The fibres were analysed with the SEM Hitachi TM 3000 at 15 kV, without coating.

4.2.2 Reference Material

Cotton (Gossypium sp.), flax (Linum usitatissimum), hemp (Cannabis sativa), nettle (Urtica dioica), silk (Bombyx mori) and sheep wool plain weave textiles were carbonised in a Heraeus Muffle furnace MR 170E, 1300 °C, wrapped in aluminium foil to reduce oxygen and placed for 1 h (6 min for the wool samples) at 250, 300 and 500 °C (Margariti, 2020). The textile samples were studied before and after the experiments with a DINO AM413T digital stereomicroscope. Fibres from the samples were analysed with Scanning Electron Microscopy (SEM) (*JEOL* JSM-7401f FESEM and JEOL JSM-6510LV) at 15 and 20 keV, without coating.

4.3 Results and Discussion

4.3.1 Archaeological Material

The carbonisation of the Pompeian textiles contributes to the survival of highly fragmented textiles, usually of intense black colour, but in a relatively good state of preservation, allowing the recognition of the weave and yarn structure as well as other visual observations.

The SEM analyses allowed the study of the surface morphology of the fibres, enabling the identification of the fibre types, like bast and wool fibres, and, in some cases, the recognition of specific diagnostic features related to combing for preparing the fibres for the spinning activity and surface ware damages.

Concerning the bast fibres, the comparison with contemporary non-carbonised ones revealed their exceptionally good state of preservation.

Generally, their microscopic structure survived without great alterations: their characteristic shape, nodes and dislocations were recognisable. In particular, the carbonisation process did not seem to have had any significant effect on the fibre diameters, like shrinking. However, in a few cases, the effects of high temperature appeared to have affected the fibres' condition to what seemed a stage of degradation before complete melting (Fig. 4.1). At this final stage of thermal degradation, the fibres were fused and merged and had lost their original morphology. This effect was also visible to the naked eye as a kind of vitrification. In fact, in the areas where the highly degraded fibres were located, the fabrics appear shiny and with irregular structures.

In the case of carbonised wool, it was possible to obtain quite interesting results. Indeed, the fibers showed different degrees of preservation, most likely correlated to their quality and the different temperatures they were exposed to (Fig. 4.2).

In the case of medullated wool fibres, those from Pompeii with diameters between 20 and 40 μm, different stages of thermal degradation could be detected and seemed to have occurred progressively (Fig. 4.3): (1) None or limited alteration of the cuticle scales; (2) Initial disappearance of the medulla (leading to what has been described as the "micro-tube" effect); (3) Enlargement of the internal hole from the medulla to the cortex and partial disappearance of the scales; (4) The empty space of the hollow tube increases to the degree of totally consuming the medulla and cortex and additionally the loss of the scales; (5) Breakage of the fibres,

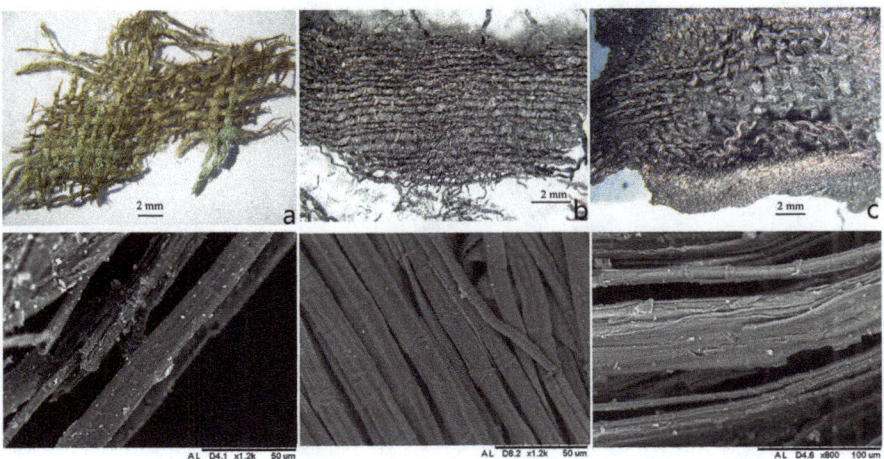

Fig. 4.1 Bast fibres and textiles showing different state of preservation: (**a**) non-carbonised; (**b**) carbonised without great alterations; (**c**) severe alteration due to the proximity to open flame. The fibres partially melted and are fused together. (Image: F. Coletti)

Fig. 4.2 Thermal degradation of wool fibres. The fibres are fused together, showing a compact, shiny and smooth surface. (Image: F. Coletti)

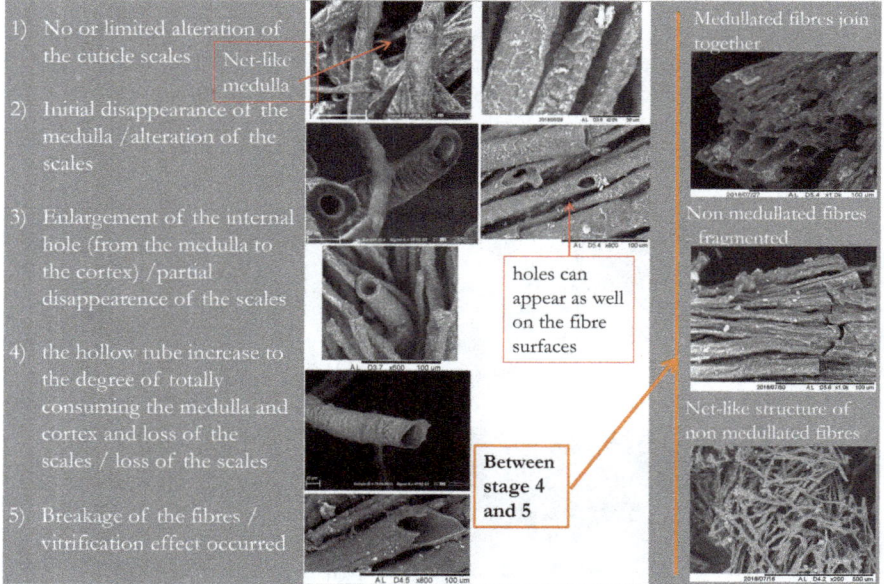

Fig. 4.3 Thermal degradation and the micro-tube effect of wool fibres from Pompeii. (Image: F. Coletti)

leading to a sort of vitrification effect. Between stages 4 and 5, the fibres occasionally showed an increase in their diameters (like swelling), and fusion between two or more fibres also occurred. This phenomenon was detected in both fibre types, those in the form of micro-tubes and the non-medullated ones, creating a net-like structure. The non-medullated fibres did not show any alteration of the internal fibre structure but fragmented occasionally. Relating to the last stage of carbonisation, stage 5, the macroscopic appearance of these fabrics was of irregular structure, like those with highly degraded bast fibres. In both cases, the fibres were fused together, showing a compact, shiny and smooth surface.

4.3.2 Reference Material

Microscopic and SEM examination showed a decrease in the diameters of all cellulosic fibres, especially cotton, which became even more intense as the temperature increased. Also, the inherent convolutions of the cotton fibres became more pronounced after carbonisation. For the flax fibres, an interesting observation was that they developed longitudinal lacerations with ragged edges, whereas the hemp fibres acquired a ridged or rather rippled appearance, and the Nettle fibres became wavy. A very important observation was that shrinkage occurred at both fibres and thread levels for all cellulosic fibres, affecting the weave count that increased after carbonisation. Equally important though was the fact that although certain patterns of degradation developed in the different fibres, they did not affect the morphology to a degree that one could not identify them (Fig. 4.4).

In general, the proteinaceous samples were far more susceptible to the effects of heat than the cellulosic ones and did not seem to be able to withstand temperatures above 250–300 °C (Margariti, 2020). As far as the wool fibres were concerned, they first fragmented, then swelled and, as the swelling progressed, they first lost their scales and finally burst (Fig. 4.5). However, the effect of micro-tubing did not seem to have occurred in any of the fibres examined after artificial carbonisation.

A possible explanation could be that the experiments reported here took place in a limited oxygen environment rather than a completely anoxic one. Experiments by Dong Su et al. (2018) (See also Istrate, 2011; Istrate et al., 2016) further support this hypothesis, as wool fibres were subjected to different temperatures in an anoxic environment by the introduction of Argon inside the furnace. The applied temperature range was from 200 to 450 °C, and the fibre samples were analysed step by step at the different degrees (Dong Su et al., 2018, 6352 fig. 6). When the samples were examined with an SEM, it was obvious that the micro-tubing effect had occurred at 200–300 °C. As temperature rose, the inner cortex of the fibres expanded, and the empty space of the hollow tubes was increased, while the cuticle became compact and smooth, losing its scales. At 450 °C degree the surface of the cuticle layer became completely smooth, and the fibres had started breaking. As part of the same experiments and for comparison, Merino non-medullated wool was heat-treated in an identical temperature range and in this case, there was no formation of hollow

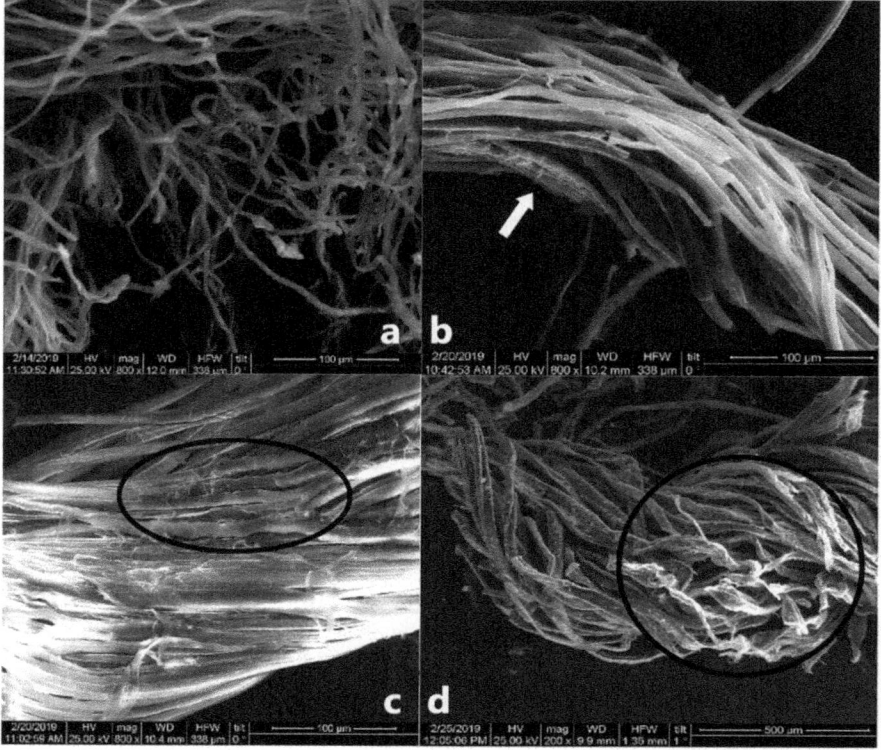

Fig. 4.4 Plant fibres: Scanning electron micrographs of (**a**) cotton fibres after carbonisation at 500 °C for 1 h, at which point the inherent convolutions of the fibres had intensified; (**b**) flax fibres after carbonisation at 500 °C for 1 h, where lacerations along the length of the fibres could be observed; (**c**) hemp fibres after carbonisation at 350 (**a**) and 500 °C (**b**) for 1 h, when they exhibited a rippled effect; and (**d**) nettle fibres after carbonisation at 500 °C for 1 h, where they acquired a wavy and ragged appearance. (Image: C. Margariti)

microtubes. It seems therefore that the micro-tube effect occurs only in medullated fibres. This thermal degradation process, strongly related to the complete oxygen exclusion and temperature rise, appears closer to the different carbonisation stages documented for the archaeological wool fibres from Pompeii (Fig. 4.6).

4.4 Conclusion

As both the Pompeian textiles and the artificially carbonised ones showed, cellulosic fibres are not particularly susceptible to the process of carbonisation, and the fibres' morphology can generally be preserved. Still, the fibre diameters of the cellulosic fibres appear to shrink gradually at different degrees as the temperature

4 The Effects of Carbonisation on the Morphology of Textile Fibres: Comparison… 51

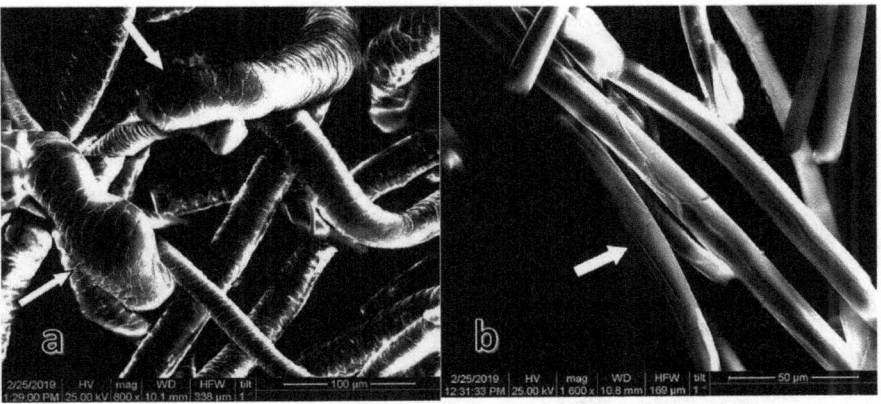

Fig. 4.5 Wool fibers: Scanning electron micrographs of (**a**) wool gabardine fibres after carbonisation at 250 °C for 6 mins, at which point they had fractured and started to melt without yet loosing the scale pattern; and (**b**) after one more minute, when swelling progressed the scales were lost and the fibres burst. (Image: C. Margariti)

increases. Examination of the Pompeian finds showed that bast fibres acquired very small diameters, even below 6 μm. The fibres on the artificially carbonised swatches exhibited marked degradation patterns, such as lacerations in flax, ridges in hemp, raggedness in nettle, and cracks in silk fibres. The proteinaceous swatches were generally destroyed at temperatures above 250–300 °C. Conversely, the wool fibres from Pompeii seemed to survive without alteration to an unrecognisable degree, even at higher temperatures. This distinct effect seems related to the complete exclusion or extremely limited presence of oxygen in context. For the experimental tests, the effects of carbonisation on wool fibres seemed less straightforward, and it became apparent that the amount of oxygen present, or the elimination of it, might lead to entirely different results.

The archaeological wool samples from Pompeii had undergone a process of thermal degradation that occurred during the experiments reported in the literature (Dong Su et al., 2018; Istrate, 2011, 40–45; Istrate et al., 2016, 593–595), resulting in a microtubing effect. This could mean that the wool fibres of Pompeii were originally modulated and/or that oxygen exclusion was most probably established in Pompeii and could be attributed to: (1) the high temperature and the hot gases of the pyroclastic flow, which included among others carbon dioxide that moved and excluded the oxygen in its surrounding atmosphere; (2) the occurrence of very specific micro-environmental conditions in the context where the textiles were located, like the exclusion of oxygen due to the complete coverage of the textiles by debris from the houses and roofs that collapsed because of the earthquake and the fallout of volcanic products during the eruption. Unfortunately, the majority of textiles from the Vesuvian area come from old excavations and their exact location and conditions have not been recorded.

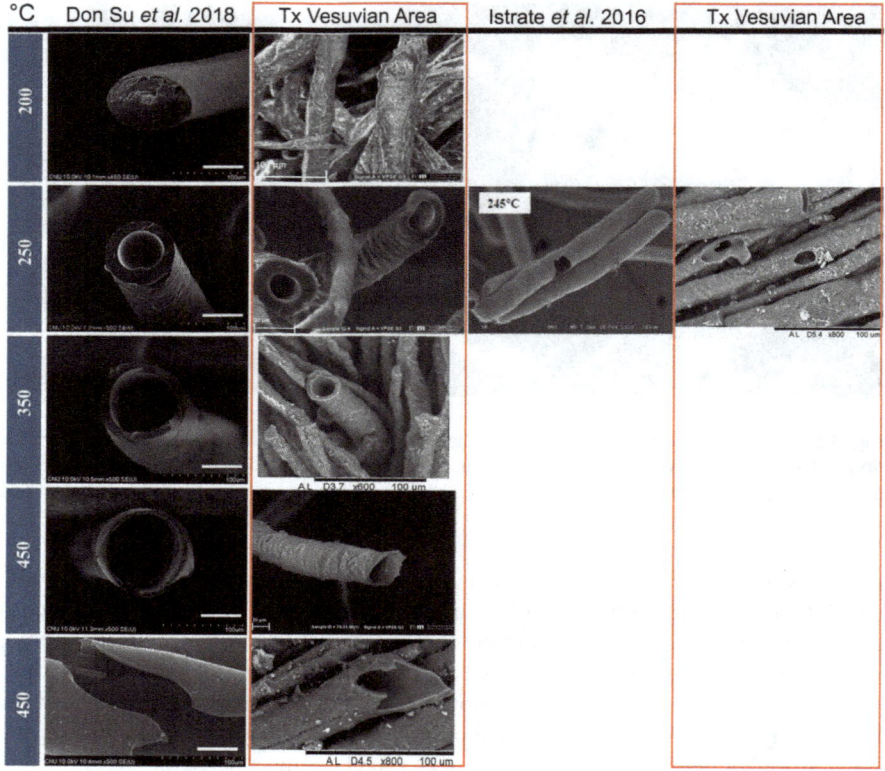

Fig. 4.6 Thermal degradation and micro-tube formation. The wool fibres from Pompeii show a similar process of thermal degradation occurred during the experiments conducted in literature. (Image modified after Dong Su et al., 2018, fig. 2, and Istrate et al., 2016, fig. 2)

The situation is very different with the textiles recently retrieved from Regio V by the Archaeological Park.[3] Comparison of the carbonised textiles discovered at the older excavations in Pompeii and the new findings from the recent investigations of room 10 in the House of Orion suggests that the melting of the fibres, as well as the fibres with different degrees of carbonisation within the same textile, are due to proximity or contact with an open flame and therefore oxygen (Fig. 4.7).

The surrounding context of the textiles was in fact, affected by a fire, which caused part of the roof to collapse right over the textile material. There, the flames most probably attenuated and were extinguished due to muffling because of the sudden decrease in oxygen. The organic material placed under the collapsed roof, such as textiles and two wooden beds, is fragmented but preserved its morphology. The

---

[3] Osanna and Zuchtriegel (eds) forthcoming. The excavation activities and the investigation conducted by The Archaeological Park of Pompeii in the Regio V will be published in the "Studi e Ricerche del Parco Archeologico di Pompei" series.

Fig. 4.7 Textiles from the House of Orion at Pompeii (V, 2, 15) with different degrees of carbonisation. (Image: F. Coletti)

textile fragments recovered under the collapsed roof have indeed preserved the original appearance of the textile weave and the morphology of the fibres.

All in all, the carbonised Pompeii textiles seemed to have been preserved in two different stages of carbonisation, each of them likely corresponding to different micro-environments: (1) the melted fibres that are likely the result of a combination of very high temperatures, with the occurrence of fire in the context, as possibly an amount of oxygen was present; (2) the fibres with the intact morphology, where oxygen and open fire were most probably excluded from their context. This clearly shows the difference in the condition of carbonised fibres directly correlates to the different micro-environments they were found in, making therefore these findings a valuable source of information not only for textile studies but also for understanding the archaeological context. The investigation related to the thermal degradation of the Pompeian textiles adds important data to the issue, currently under discussion in vesuvian archaeology (see Luongo et al., 2003; Ongaro et al., 2008; Mastrolorenzo et al., 2010), concerning the effect of the volcanic eruption on ancient artefacts caused by the natural disaster and the temperatures reached in the city of Pompeii during the vesuvian eruption in the 79 AD.

Acknowledgements The authors would like to thank the General Director of the Italian Museum Prof. M. Osanna, the Director of the Archaeological Park of Pompeii Dr. Gabriel Zuchtriegel and the archaeologists Dr. F. Zabotti and Dr. T. Virtuoso for providing useful discussions and suggestions related to the riding of the context. Moreover, we would like to thank Dr Elisavet Dotsika, Dr Giorgos Diamantopoulos, and Petros Karalis, Institute of Nanoscience and Nanotechnology, National Centre for Scientific Research "Demokritos".

Authors' Contributions Introduction: FC; Archaeological Material: FC; Reference Material: CM. All the authors equally contributed to the discussion and conclusion.

References

Andersson Strand, E., Frei, K. M., Gleba, M., Mannering, U., Nosch, M.-L., & Skals, I. (2010). Old textiles—New possibilities. *European Journal of Archaeology, 13*(2), 149–173.

Coletti, F. (2020). *I tessuti di Pompei: materiali, tecniche di lavorazione e contesti*. PhD thesis, Sapienza University of Rome and Ruprecht Karl University of Heidelberg.

Coletti, F. (forthcoming). *I reperti tessili di Pompei e d'area vesuviana*. Edizioni Quasar.

Dong Su, I., Min, H. K., Jung, H. S., & Park, W. H. (2018). Formation and characterization of hollow microtubes by thermal treatment of human hair. *ACS Sustainable Chemistry & Engineering, 6*(5), 6350–6357.

Galli, M., Coletti, F., Lemorini, C., & Mitschke, S. (2018). The "textile culture at Pompeii" project. In M. S. Busana, M. Gleba, & F. Meo (Eds.), *Purpureae Vestes VI. Textiles and dyes in the Mediterranean society and economy. International symposium*, 17–20 October 2016, Padova (pp. 275–293).

Galli, M., Coletti, F., & Casa, G. (2019). Cultura tessile a Pompei: impianti e materiali per la lavorazione della lana (lanariae). *Analysis Archaeologica, an International Journal of Western Mediterranean Archaeology, 5*, 275–284.

Gillard, R. D., Hardman, S. M., Thomas, R. G., & Watkinson, D. E. (1994). The mineralization of fibres in burial environments. *Studies in Conservation, 39*(3), 132–140.

Gleba, M., & Mannering, U. (2012). *Textiles and textile production in Europe. From prehistory to 400AD*. Oxbow Books.

Grömer, K. (2016). *The art of prehistoric textile making*. Natural History Museum.

Harris, S. (2015). Folded, layered textiles from a Bronze Age pit pyre excavated from Over Barrow 2, Cambridgeshire, England. In K. Grömer & F. Pritchard (Eds.), *Aspects of the design production and use of textiles and clothing from the Bronze Age to the early modern era, NESAT (North European Symposium of Archaeological Textiles) XII* (pp. 73–82). NESAT/Natural History Museum.

Huisman, H. D. J., Braadbaart, F., van Wijk, I. M., & van Os, B. J. H. (2012). Ashes to ashes, charcoal to dust: Micromorphological evidence for ash-induced disintegration of charcoal in Early Neolithic (LBK) soil features in Elsloo (the Netherlands). *Journal of Archaeological Science, 39*, 994–1004.

Istrate, D. (2011). *Heat induces denaturation of fibrous hard α-keratins and their reaction with various chemical reagents*. PhD thesis. Aachen.

Istrate, D., Er Rafik, M., Popescu, C., Demco, D. E., Tsarkova, L., & Wortmann, F. J. (2016). Keratin micro-tubes: The paradoxical thermal behavior of cortex and cuticle. *International Journal of Biological Marcromolecules, 89*, 592–598.

Jakes, K. A., Thompson, A. J., & Baldia, C. M. (2010). Revealing clues from textile particulate through microscopy, Infrared spectroscopy, and X-ray microanalysis. *Text, 8*(3), 322–340.

Kanstrup, M., Thomsen, I. K., Mikkelsen, P. H., & Christensen, B. T. (2012). Impact of charring on cereal grain characteristics: Linking prehistoric manuring practice to $\delta^{15}N$ signatures in archaeobotanical material. *Journal of Archaeological Science, 39*, 2533–2540.

Luongo, G., Perrotta, A., & Scarpati, C. (2003). Impact of the AD 79 explosive eruption on Pompeii, I. Relations amongst the depositional mechanisms of the pyroclastic products, the framework of the buildings and the associated destructive events. *Journal of Volcanology and Geothermal Research, 126*, 201–223.

Malmius, A. (2002). Cremation grave textiles: Examples from Vendel upper class in the Vendel and Viking periods. *Journal of Nordic Archaeological Science, 13*, 59–74.

Margariti, C. (2019). The application of FTIR microspectroscopy in a non-invasive and non-destructive way to the study and conservation of mineralised excavated textiles. *Heritage Science, 7*(63). https://doi.org/10.1186/s40494-019-0304-8

Margariti, C. (2020). The effects of artificial incomplete burning on the morphology and dimensions of cellulosic and proteinaceous textiles and fibres. *Studies in Conservation, 65*(7), 388–398. https://doi.org/10.1080/00393630.2019.1709307

Mastrolorenzo, G., Petrone, P., Pappalardo, L., & Guarino, F. M. (2010). Lethal thermal impact at periphery of pyroclastic surges: Evidences at Pompeii. *PLoS One, 5*(6), e11127. https://doi.org/10.1371/journal.pone.0011127

Mannering, U., & Skals, I. (2020). Textiles and fabrics: Conservation and preservation. In C. Smith (Ed.) *Encyclopedia of Global Archaeology.* https://doi.org/10.1007/978-3-030-30018-0_488

Médard, F. (2020). *L'artisanat du textile à Pompéi au Ier siècle après J.-C.: Vestiges textiles et outillages.* Centre Jean Bérard.

Ongaro, T. E., Neri, A., Menconi, G., de' Michieli Vitturi, M., Marianelli, P., Cavazzoni, C., Erbacci, G., & Baxter, P. J. (2008). Transient 3D numerical simulations of column collapse and pyroclastic density current scenarios at Vesuvius. *Journal of Volcanology and Geothermal Research, 178,* 378–396.

Osanna, M., & Zuchtriegel, G. (Eds.). (Forthcoming). *La Regio V, Studi e ricerche del Parco Archeologico di Pompei.*

Rottoli, M. (2005). Tessuti e intrecci della preistoria al medioevo: recupero, conservazione e anaisi. Le esperienze del laboratorio di archeologia dei Musei Civici di Como. In N. Zini (Ed.), *Intrecci vegetali e fibretessili da ambiente umido. Analisi Conservazione e Restauro* (Incontri di Restauro 4) (pp. 69–92). Provincia Autonoma di Trento.

Srinivasan, R., & Jakes, K. A. (1997). Optical and Scanning electron microscopic study of the effects of charring on Indian hemp (Apocynum cannabinum L) fibres. *Journal of Archaeological Science, 24*(6), 517–527.

Styring, A. K., Manning, H., Fraser, R. A., Wallace, M., Jones, G., Charles, M., Heaton, T. H. E., Bogaard, A., & Evershed, R. P. (2013). The effect of charring and burial on the biochemical composition of cereal grains: Investigating the integrity of archaeological plant material. *Journal of Archaeological Science, 40,* 4767–4779.

Chapter 5
Multi-analytical Approach for the Characterisation of Ancient Mineral Fibres: Tracing the Use of Asbestos in the Italic Peninsula

Francesca Coletti, Alessandro Ciccola, and Paolo Postorino

Abstract This paper presents the multi-analytical approach performed by microscopic analysis using Optical and Scanning Electron Microscope (SEM-EDX) and Raman spectroscopy. These techniques allow us to recognise asbestos fibres and precisely characterise their mineral nature. Using Raman micro-spectroscopy, which is often used to discriminate tiny mineral fibres, it was possible to precisely characterise the mineral composition of the asbestos fibres from ancient central-southern Italy by comparing their manufacture through the identification of the specific asbestos phase.

The results obtained highlight the extraction activity of the mineral fibres and the use of long hair-like fibres to manufacture textile objects in the ancient Italic Peninsula.

Keywords Asbestos fibres · Archaeological textiles · Raman spectroscopy · SEM-EDX

5.1 Introduction

The analysis of textile and fibre remains allows the investigation and the reconstruction of the relationship between humans and the use of land and natural resources, as well as their exploitation and processing in antiquity.

F. Coletti (✉)
Department of Science of Antiquities, Sapienza University of Rome, Rome, Italy
e-mail: francesca.coletti@uniroma1.it

A. Ciccola
Department of Environmental Biology, Sapienza University of Rome, Rome, Italy

P. Postorino
Department of Physics, Sapienza University of Rome, Rome, Italy

© The Author(s), under exclusive license to Springer Nature Switzerland AG 2024
F. Coletti et al. (eds.), *Multidisciplinary Approaches for the Investigation of Textiles and Fibres in the Archaeological Field*, Interdisciplinary Contributions to Archaeology, https://doi.org/10.1007/978-3-031-73812-8_5

Despite geographical discrepancies in the survival of textiles and organic materials, given the differences in climate and thermo-hygrometric conditions, the analysis of extant textiles and fibres gives us a fast-growing picture of the natural resources used in antiquity, thanks to the application of natural science methods in the field of archaeology. Organic fibres are commonly used in textile manufacture. Diverse cellulosic and proteinaceous fibres were used in antiquity varying based on the period, geographical area and cultural traditions. In addition to organic materials, asbestiform minerals were used to produce different everyday objects, including textile artefacts, although asbestos textiles are scanty in the archaeological record.

The use of asbestos fibres is well-attested by ancient written sources. It appears that Greeks and Romans were aware of the fibre's mineral nature, its properties, and the dangerous illness suffered by the workers. Ancient Greek and Latin sources include asbestos among the raw materials used to make yarns and fabrics for specific uses. The Greek nouns ἀμίαντος and ἄσβεστος, with the meaning respectively of incorruptible and inextinguishable, refer to the material's resistance to fire and its thermo-insulating properties, for which the material had assumed a close link with the sphere of magic and ritual. Dioscorides in the treatise *De materia medica* (first century AD) correctly attributes its mineral nature to asbestos, specifying how the fibrous matter was extracted from the rocks. Furthermore, the author recalls the peculiarities of asbestos fibres, which, without catching fire in the flames, came out candid and shiny without deteriorating. The functions of asbestos fabrics were linked to fire, the sources specify how these were used to wrap deceased body at the time of cremation, to obtain lamp wicks, and also intended for practical purposes to make fabrics for use in theatres and tablecloths for domestic use, which were cleaned with fire after use. Despite knowing the properties and uses of asbestos, Pliny the Elder in the Naturalis Historia (first century AD) seems to misunderstand its mineral nature, called it *linum vivum* coming from India (Plinio, Naturalis Historia XIX, 4) and Arcadia (Plinio, Naturalis Historia, XXXVII, 54). Regarding the raw material and its extraction, the authors generally refer to the eastern Mediterranean and Greece; Pausanias points to the Greek island of Cyprus while Strabo mentions the locality of Karistos in Euboea. The sources do not transmit information on areas of extraction and production of asbestos products in the Italian peninsula, however, we know that the karst and volcanic rocks from which the material is obtained were widespread in ancient times, as in the present day, in the northern Apennines and the Alps.

Despite the ancient written records, direct archaeological evidence of asbestos fibres and fabric is scarcely known. Its inorganic nature, however, allows it to survive in archaeological contexts. Thus, the lack of evidence may be attributed to the absence of records during archaeological excavations of these finds or, most probably, because many textiles in museum collections largely remain unpublished. At present state, we know that fragments of asbestos fibres and textiles mainly come from central and southern areas of the Italian peninsula.[1] Seventeen, eighteen-century travellers refer to one fragment of asbestos fabric found in 1633 in Pozzuoli (Campania Region) dated to the second century BC and preserved at the Barberini Gallery in Rome (Cameron et al., 2015, 167; Yates, 1853; Daremberg & Saglio, 1877; Urban, 1857; Gilroy, 1845; Keysler, 1757, 174). A remarkable fragment of asbestos cloth found in a marble sarcophagus in Rome, outside Porta Maggiore, was described in a letter of 1702, included in Montfaucon's Travels through Italy (Nibby, 1849; Yates, 1853, 359) and deposited in the Vatican Library (Cameron et al., 2015, 167 with literature). Further discoveries in the city of Rome are the fragments found in 1845 along Via Appia (Lanciani, 2000, 266) and in Via Triumphalis, in 1957 (Steinby, 2003, 158; Di Gennaro et al., 2008).[2] Stored together with part of the Vesuvian textile collection at the National Archaeological Museum of Naples, a fabric woven with asbestos fibres was excavated in the middle of the nineteen century in the Roman necropolis of Vasto (the ancient Histonium in Abruzzo Region, Italy) which was subject to Rome in the fourth century AD (Laufer, 1915, 309; Yates, 1853, 359–360). The Museums also held a remarkable quantity of asbestos fibres which were found in the ancient city of Pompeii. Since scientific investigations of all these finds are still missing, this paper aims to present the interdisciplinary analysis carried out on the two finds stored at the Museum of Naples found in the Necropolis of Vasto and Pompeii. In this study, the archaeological remains were analysed with in situ and laboratory analysis. In order to acquire exhaustive and reliable data, Raman spectroscopy was coupled with morphological and semi-quantitative data obtained with Optical Microscopy and SEM-EDX. After the preliminary morphological analyses, which allow to acquire data about the presence of mineral asbestos fibres, samples were subjected to EDX and Raman spectroscopy in order to: (1) confirm the initial hypotheses about the composition of the fibres and (2) to individuate the specific mineral constituent.

The spectroscopic methods present several advantages for the characterization of textile fibres. Most of them are not destructive so, after the analysis, the sample can be collected and subjected to further diagnostics, with the consequent implementation of data and results. Several spectroscopic methods do not require pretreatments of the samples, so they provide results rapidly to the conservators. Moreover, several instrumental setups are usually available, extending the possibilities of analysing archaeological textiles, which could be difficult to manipulate.

Less deepened applied to the characterisation of textile fibres than Fourier-Transformed InfraRed spectroscopy, Raman spectroscopy is based on the anelastic scattering of monochromatic radiation in the Visible light range (usually provided from a laser source) with the investigated sample material: the scattering of the radiation allows recovering its vibrational spectrum. The minor application of Raman spectroscopy to the investigation of ancient fibres is relatable to the higher

---

[1] The only known object from northern Italy is that reported by Brusin, 1936, 21–22. He refers to the presence of a net made of asbestos in the Archeological Museum in Aquileia, in Friuli Venezia Giulia Region, exhibited in the first part of the twentieth century.

[2] The object is currently stored in the Vatican Museum.

interference of other radiative processes, for instance, fluorescence, which could hinder the acquisition of the Raman spectrum: the typical vibrational peaks could result not observable because covered by the broad bands deriving from fluorescence emission. This issue is particularly frequent in the case of ancient textiles, which are prone to fluorescence because of ageing processes and contaminant species. However, in the case of asbestiform materials, due to its mineral matrix, Raman spectroscopy is frequently used for the identification of the specific mineral phase, as reported in the literature in the case of environmental analysis (Petriglieri et al., 2021; Rinaudo & Croce, 2019; Rinaudo et al., 2003, 2004, 2005; Kloprogge et al., 1999; Bard et al., 1997. From this point of view, it is important to highlight that Raman spectroscopy does not need any preparation of the samples, so it is highly attractive because it represents a non-invasive methodology and it does not involve any risk of change of the mineral phases present in a sample, especially in eventual minor amounts in the case of mixed materials.

In this perspective, with reference to the advantages of SEM-EDX and Raman spectroscopy for the identification of asbestos materials, the combination of the two techniques was exploited for the characterization of the two above-mentioned remains. This represents an interesting technology transfer of a multi-analytical methodology, usually applied for environmental and safety issues, in the archaeometric field, which could be applied for further research on ancient textiles. The successful results of these case studies show the performativity of the adopted approach and add new archaeological information on textile manufacturing from inorganic fibres in ancient times.

5.2 Material and Methods

5.2.1 *Archaeological Remains*

The analysed remains are currently stored in the National Archaeological Museum of Naples (Italy), and both were excavated in the nineteenth century. The lack of scientific excavations, unfortunately, leads to absent or poor information related to the context of recovery of both finds.

The findings are different in their appearance and state of processing.

Object 1, discovered in workshop V, I, 13 at Pompeii in 1875 (Fiorelli, 1875, 253), was conserved in the climate chamber of the Laboratory of Applied Research of the Archaeological Park of Pompeii at the time of this research. It is composed of bundles of long asbestiform fibres. It shows some fibre bundles slight s-twist and a relatively good length of about 16 cm (Fig. 5.1b, d).

Object 2 is a well-preserved textile fragment found in the Vaso Necropolis (Abruzzo Region, Italy) (Fig. 5.1a, c). The eighteen-century excavation reports contain unclear information about the attribution of the fabric to the burials in which it was found, precluding the exact dating of the find based on the funerary inscription.

5 Multi-analytical Approach for the Characterisation of Ancient Mineral Fibres... 61

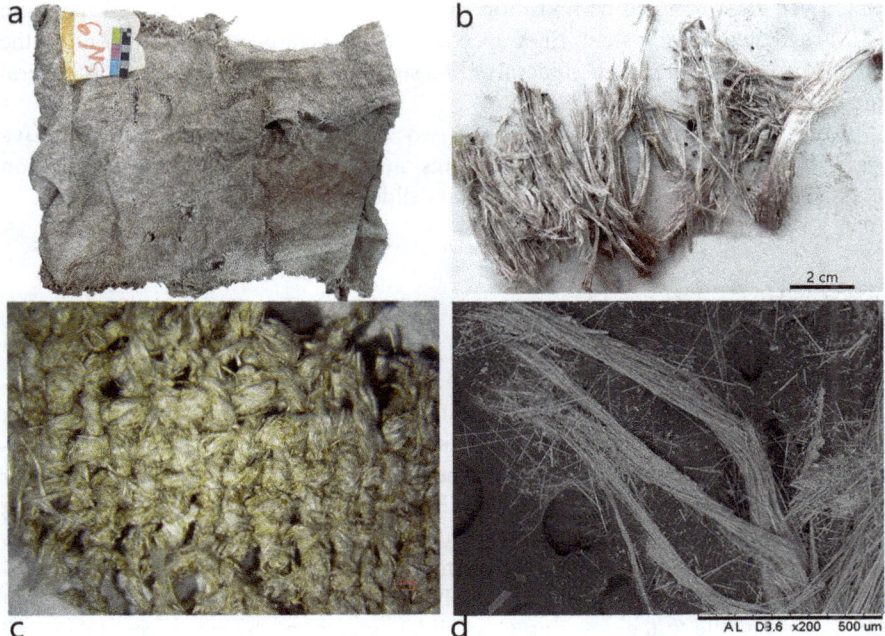

Fig. 5.1 Image of the finds: (**a**) Object 2; (**b**) Object 1; (**c**) magnification of the Object 2; (**d**) SEM micrograph of fibre bundles (Object 1). (Images: F. Coletti)

However, the excavation report refers to the asbestos shrouds covering the human remains of a child inside a square marble sarcophagus (Marchesani, 1838, 306). The fabric (37 × 225 cm) is woven in a simple balanced tabby with 2S-ply of 0.75–1.40 mm in diameter, realised with slightly s-twisted single yarns. The thread count is 7–8 threads per cm in both warp and weft. The fragment shows simple longitudinal selvedge, but no borders are preserved. At the four corners of the finds, ornamental S-ply silk threads of green colour (about 1 mm in diameter) are most probably later additions.

5.2.2 Microscopic Investigation and Energy Dispersive X-Ray Analysis

The investigation was carried out using optical microscopy and Scanning Electron Microscope (SEM). The documentation of the findings was performed with the portable microscope USB Veho VMS-004 with magnification up to 400X. The morphological analysis on the fibre samples was conducted using both the transmitted light microscopy Nikon Eclipse E600Pol, with 10x oculars using 10x, 20x, 40x plan achromatic objectives, and SEM Hitachi TM 3000 at 15 kV, without coating.

Moreover, the chemical composition of both samples was investigated using an SEM-mediated EDX system. EDX spectra were constantly collected to confirm the chemistry of the observed minerals. Measurements were performed on several points on both sample surfaces.

After the optical investigations, the two samples were mounted on adhesive stubs. To minimise the risk of loss of fibres during handling, the stubs were put on glass slides and covered with another glass slide.

5.2.3 Raman Spectroscopy

For the Raman analysis of samples, a Horiba Jobin-Yvon HR-Evolution micro-Raman setup, equipped with a 632.8 nm laser and a motorized XY Mapping Stage, was used. Experimental acquisition conditions were changed according to the characteristics of the samples, minimizing the risk of material damage under the laser probe. Raman analysis was performed directly on the samples under the covering glass slide, through proper focusing. Raman spectra were acquired in the ranges 40–1200 and 3215–3955 cm^{-1}, concerning the reference ranges reported in the literature for the identification of asbestos. In order to individuate eventual interfering bands attributable to the covering glass slides, spectra of the same were taken and compared with the spectra obtained focusing on the asbestos textiles. Spectra were calibrated through Neon emission, and they were processed through subtraction of a polynomial background; only in few cases, a smoothing processing was applied (Savitzky-Golay; number of points ≤15), with the aim of minimise noise effects. Origin was used as data analysis software. For the identification of the vibrational modes and the specific mineral phases, the collected Raman spectra were compared with reference spectra reported in the literature (Petriglieri et al., 2021; Rinaudo & Croce, 2019; Rinaudo et al., 2003, 2004, 2005; Kloprogge et al., 1999; Bard et al., 1997).

5.3 Results

5.3.1 Microscopy

The two samples show fibres with similar dimensions and morphology (Fig. 5.2). The analysis with optical transmitted light microscopy allows us to recognise in both samples mostly small fibre bundles ranging from 4 and 15 μm, and single fibres of 1.7–2 μm in diameter.[3] The measurements were confirmed by the

---

[3] The terms "Single fibres" refers to mineral particle elements with fibres-like appearance, whereas "fibre bundle" is used to indicate a group of parallel elements bound together.

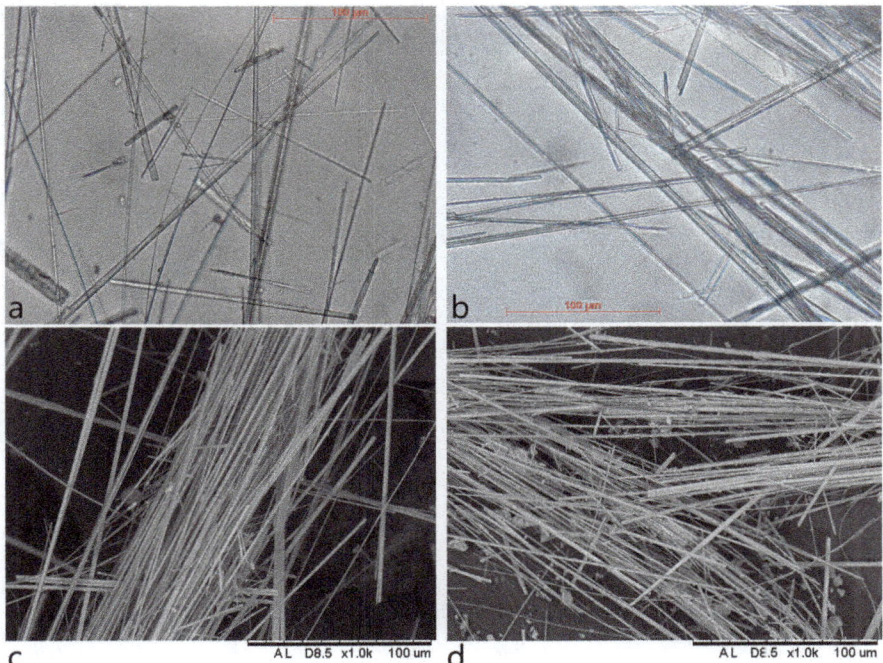

Fig. 5.2 Transmitted light microscopy and SEM micrographs of the fibres: (**a, c**) Object 2; (**b, d**) Object 1. (Images: F. Coletti)

investigation carried out with the SEM. The morphological analysis reveals fibres with elongated prismatic habit, smooth surface appearance and truncated or blade ends. The fibres are straits, and no ribbon-like appearance was documented. The fibre length is not a relevant parameter to consider in the case of archaeological artefacts.

The comparisons with reference materials in the literature highlight the differences between the characteristic morphology of the chrysotile asbestos fibres in terms of appearance and dimension (Rinaudo & Croce, 2019, Fig. 5.2 c, f).

5.3.2 Energy Dispersive: X-Ray Analysis

The elements detected throughout semi-quantitative analysis using EDX are collected in Tables 5.1 and 5.3.

The achieved EDX data were compared with the elemental characterisation of different type of asbestos minerals reported in the literature (Saiful Islam Khan et al., 2022; Li et al., 2019; Fisher & Morchat, 1993). In particular, the comparison with the relative elemental concentrations normalised to Si reported by Saiful Islam

Table 5.1 Average elemental percentages normalised to Si number of atoms for Object 1 and Object 2, compared to the theoretical ones calculated for different asbestos

	Obj1 Av	Obj2 Av	Act	Am	Crys	Croc	Trem	Ant
Mg/Si	56.6	37.3	0 < x < 62.5	0 < x < 87.5	150	/	62.5	0 < x < 87.5
Fe/Si	5.3	24.1	0 < x < 62.5	0 < x < 87.5	/	62.5	/	0 < x < 87.5
(Mg + Fe)/Si	62.0	61.4	62.5	87.5	150	62.5	62.5	87.5
Ca/Si	24.8	68.6	25.0	/	/	/	25.0	/

Table 5.2 Single and average elemental percentages normalised to Si number of atoms for Object 1, compared to the experimental ones for different asbestos reported in literature

	Obj1 Area1	Obj1 Area2	Obj1 Area3	Obj1 Area4	Obj1 Av	Act	Am	Crys	Croc	Trem	Ant
Mg/Si	64.8	52.9	52.2	63.7	56.6	63.1	19.4	146.4	13.0	62.3	86.5
Fe/Si	5.5	5.3	5.2	5.0	5.3	60.3	59.8	/	50.2	1.9	9.4
(Mg + Fe)/Si	70.3	58.2	57.4	68.7	62.0	123.4	79.2	146.4	63.2	64.2	95.9
Ca/Si	25.5	23.7	25.2	24.6	24.8	24.9	/	/	/	25.4	/

Table 5.3 Single and average elemental percentages normalised to Si number of atoms for Object 2, compared to the experimental ones for different asbestos reported in literature

	Obj2 Area1	Obj2 Area2	Obj2 Area3	Obj2 Av	Act	Am	Crys	Croc	Trem	Ant
Mg/Si	38.9	33.5	39.6	37.3	63.1	19.4	146.4	13.0	62.3	86.5
Fe/Si	15.5	27.4	29.4	24.1	60.3	59.8	/	50.2	1.9	9.4
(Mg + Fe)/Si	54.4	60.9	68.9	61.4	123.4	79.2	146.4	63.2	64.2	95.9
Ca/Si	56.2	79.1	70.6	68.6	24.9	/	/	/	25.4	/

Khan et al. (2022) was considered, with reference to the general remarkable content of Ca, Mg and Fe observed in the experimental data. The results of the different element percentages are reported regarding the theoretical formula of the different asbestos (Table 5.1) and to published experimental data (Tables 5.2 and 5.3). Particularly, besides the single Ca/Si, Mg/Si and Fe/Si ratios, also the cumulative (Mg + Fe)/Si ratio is reported, because of the variability in the atomic counts of these two elements in the theoretical formula of some minerals.

For Object 1, the average Ca/Si, Mg/Si and Fe/Si ratios are 24.8%, 56.6% and 5.3%, respectively, with a general reproducibility for the different analyzed areas. These data evidence higher similarity with those reported for tremolite. For Object 2, instead, the data presents a higher dispersion, but the high content of Calcium (Ca/Si: 68.6%) would allow restricting the possible mineral phases to either actinolite or tremolite, even if the content of the two other elements (Mg/Si: 37.3%; Fe/Si: 24.1%) are quite different from both the asbestos.

5 Multi-analytical Approach for the Characterisation of Ancient Mineral Fibres...

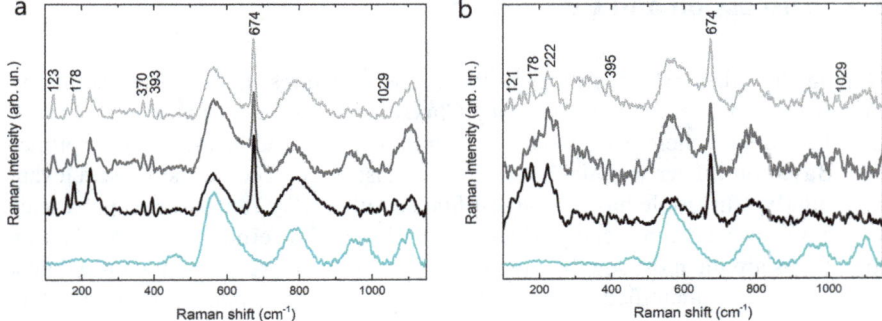

Fig. 5.3 Raman spectra for the analysed points in Object 1 (**a**) and in Object 2 (**b**), where some characteristic peaks of tremolite are evidenced; the spectrum of the glass slide (teal line) is provided to highlight the bands attributable to the covering substrate. (Images: A. Ciccola)

5.3.3 Raman Spectroscopy

The Raman spectra obtained for Object 1 clearly show peaks attributable to the characteristic peaks of an asbestos material (Fig. 5.3a). In particular, three defined peaks at 123, 162 and 179 cm^{-1} can be attributed to the vibrations of coordinated cations, while a signal at 224 cm^{-1}, along with a shoulder at 232 cm^{-1}, is indicative of the metal-oxygen modes. The bands at 370 and 394 cm^{-1}, which present a similar intensity, and a signal at 418 cm^{-1}, are indicative of the same vibrations, while the intense signal at 674 cm^{-1} is attributable to the Si-O-Si bridge symmetric stretching modes. Two weak bands at 932 and 1029 cm^{-1}, not visible in all the spectra, are attributable to the non bridging Si-O and bridging Si-O-Si antisymmetric stretching, respectively. At high wavenumbers, in the range 3500–3800 cm^{-1}, the characteristic signals of OH- stretching modes should be observable, but, in our case, only a very weak band at 3672 cm^{-1} could be considered barely visible in the spectrum in only one of the measured points. However, with reference to the cumulative set of peaks, it is possible to identify the mineral phase constituting the sample as tremolite (Petriglieri et al., 2021; Rinaudo et al., 2004; Rinaudo & Croce, 2019; Bard et al., 1997).

About the spectra obtained for Object 2 (Fig. 5.3b), it is fundamental to highlight that the signal/noise ratio decreases and the individuation of Raman peaks results more complex. However, it is possible to observe an intense signal at 674 cm^{-1}, while lower intensity peaks are at 121, 159, 179, 222, 370, 395 cm^{-1}. The signals at 418 and 932 cm^{-1}, which are observable in the spectra of the previous sample, are not distinguishable in the analogues for this sample, while a very weak peak at 1028 cm^{-1} is present only in one spectrum. However, taking into account the overall similarity, it is possible to hypothesize that, also in this case, the constituting mineral is tremolite.

5.4 Discussion and Conclusion

Among the thirty asbestos types with fibrous structures, Crocidolite, Actinolite, Tremolite, Amosite, Anthophyllite and Chrysotile were used thanks to their excellent thermal and chemical resistance, sound-absorbing and heat-insulating properties. Based on higher technical qualities, the last three become the most relevant. Particularly, Chrysotile has the longest fibres, with a silky-like surface appearance, which was also a commercially widely used species. Concerning textile production, long fibres are the most suitable for spinning activity. Interestingly the investigated fibres were both identified as tremolite, belonging to the amphibole-group, which are usually shorter fibre length. This assignment was based on the analytical data available from scientific research for environmental analytics, where Raman spectroscopy is addressed as a powerful technique for the discrimination of the mineral phases in asbestos. In particular, regarding the above-mentioned textile production practises, it was considered fundamental to identify the presence of Chrysotile in the samples. Both the EDX and Raman analyses were very useful for this aim. EDX highlighted that both archaeological finds present a remarkable content of Ca and Fe, elements which are not components of this mineral in its theoretical formula, while the experimental Mg/Si ratio for both of them is very far from the analogues reported in the literature. About Raman spectroscopy, according to the published data, a signature peak of this serpentine mineral should be present at 692 cm^{-1} and characterised by strong intensity (Petriglieri et al., 2021; Rinaudo et al., 2003, 2004, 2005; Rinaudo & Croce, 2019; Kloprogge et al., 1999; Bard et al., 1997). In all the investigated points of the two different samples, this peak -attributable to Si-O-Si bridge stretching modes- is not observable, while an analogue one can be identified around 672–675 cm^{-1} in both samples. This allowed excluding the hypothesis of Chrysotile as constituting material of the fibres in the two remains confirming the results obtained by the morphological analysis. Moreover, the symmetric Si-O-Si symmetric stretching peak at similar Raman shift values was observed only in the case of amphibolic silicates, specifically actinolite, anthophyllite and tremolite (Rinaudo & Croce, 2019). From the Raman point of view, these mineral phases can be further distinguished on the base of the antisymmetric stretching of Si-O-Si bonds. According to the literature, indeed, actinolite presents a peak at 1064 cm^{-1}, and anthophyllite at 1044 cm^{-1}, while tremolite is characterized by two peaks at 1031 and 1062 cm^{-1}. In the Raman spectra of both samples, no signal is observable around 1044 cm^{-1}, so the use of anthophyllite can be excluded. Peaks around 1060–1065 cm^{-1} are not distinguishable in any spectrum of both samples, while a peak at 1029–1030 cm^{-1} is observable in some spectra of both. Regarding the spectral background interference, the lower signal-to-noise ratio for Object 2 from Vasto and the slightly lower intensity of the 1062 cm^{-1} peak in comparison to that at 1031 cm^{-1} in Raman spectra of the tremolite references reported in literature, the acquired data suggest that, in both the samples, tremolite corresponds to the constituting fibres (Petriglieri et al., 2021; Rinaudo & Croce, 2019). Further confirmation derives from signals at low wavenumbers: according to the literature, in fact, the set of peaks at 160, 179, 224, 370 cm^{-1} -visible in the spectra of both the samples- are all present in the spectra of tremolite. In fairness, it is important to mention that the peaks at 418 and 932 cm^{-1}, which are considerably indicative of tremolite, appear only in object 1 from Pompeii, but also in this case the lower quality of the spectrum could hinder the individuation of these low-intensity signals. Finally, the absence of a clear visible spectral pattern in the 3215–3955 cm^{-1} range would confirm, indirectly, the presence of tremolite in the samples. According to the literature, indeed, this mineral does not present high-intensity peaks in this range (Rinaudo & Croce, 2019); few papers reported the weak band around 3672 cm^{-1} (Petriglieri et al., 2021; Bard et al., 1997), which, however, was detected only in the point of the Pompeii sample (object 1). EDX data confirm the tremolite hypotheses, even if a distinction among the two samples should be made from the point of view of data interpretation, which result more complex for the Object 2 in comparison to the Object 1. For this one the Si-normalised percentages for Ca, Mg and Fe result in agreement with those reported for tremolite in the literature; only the Fe content is slightly higher, but the Mg/Si ratio, close to the theoretical one, suggests that this difference could be attributed to the presence of contaminants. About Object 2, instead, the Ca/Si and Mg/Si ratio results are very different from the characteristic values reported in the literature, while the Fe/Si analogue is intermediate among the typical ones for asbestos and it does not correspond to any mineral phase. In this perspective, some deductions must be made. The high Ca content -which, however, must present a certain contribution from other species is indicative of two asbestos, actinolite and tremolite. Both of them present a similar content of Mg, but in the case of actinolite the Fe/Si ratio is high, while it is very low for tremolite. Taking into account these aspects and with reference to the Raman data, it is likely to hypothesise that the original fibre was constituted by tremolite, while some contamination or atom-substitution processes could have occurred during the deposition periods or the conservation history of the matrix.

Therefore, the research carried out demonstrates the processing of tremolite for extracting fibers and their in textile production, highlighting the high skills of ancient spinners and suggesting the versatile use of asbestiform fibres in such production.

Acknowledgements The authors are grateful to the Archaeological Park of Pompeii and the National Archaeological Museum of Naples (MANN), represented by the Director G. Zuchtriegel and the Director of the MANN, P. Giuglierini, as well as the General Director of the Italian Museums, Prof. M. Osanna for the kind permission to allow us to work on the textile remains. Our deepest thanks also go to Dr. L. Melillo, Prof. E. Pernicka.

Authors' Contributions Introduction: FC, AC; Textile and fibre analysis: FC; Energy Dispersive. X-ray Analysis: FC, AC;

Raman Spectroscopy: AC, PP. All the authors equally contributed to the discussion and conclusion.

References

Bard, D., Yarwood, J., & Tylee, B. (1997). Asbestos fibre identification by Raman microspectroscopy. *Journal of Raman Spectroscopy, 28,* 803–809. https://doi.org/10.1002/(SICI)1097-4555(199710)28:10<803::AID-JRS151>3.0.CO;2-7

Brusin, G. (1936). *Il Regio Museo Archeologico di Aquileia,* Roma, 21–22.

Cameron, J., Indrajaya, A., & Manguin, P. Y. (2015). Asbestos textiles from Batujaya (West Java, Indonesia): Further evidence for early long-distance interaction between the Roman Orient, Southern Asia and island Southeast Asia. *Bulletin de l'Ecole Francaise d'Extreme-Orient (Bulletin of the French School of Asian Studies), 101,* 159–176.

Daremberg, C., & Saglio, E. (1877). *Dictionnaire d'Anti- quités greques et romaines.*

Di Gennaro F., Ferro D., Marconi A., Masato L., & Rapinesi I. A. (2008). Trattamento e restauro dei materiali d'amianto di natura archeologica. In D. Ferro & A. L. Coluzza, *Kermes* 72, 64–66.

Fiorelli, G. (1875). *Giornale degli scavi di Pompei* (Vol. 3). Napoli.

Fisher, G. C., & Morchat, R. M. (1993). Asbestos characterization using scanning electron microscopy/Light element X-ray spectrometry technical memorandum 93/206, National Defence, Research and Development Branch, Canada.

Gilroy, C. G. (1845). *The history of silk, cotton, linen, wool and other fibrous substances.* Harper & Bros.

Keysler, J. G. (1757). *Travels through Germany, Bohemia, Hungary, Switzer- land, Italy and Lorrain* (Vol. II). Londra.

Kloprogge, J. T., Frost, R. L., & Rintoul, L. (1999). Single crystal Raman microscopic study of the asbestos mineral chrysotile. *Physical Chemistry Chemical Physics, 1,* 2559–2564. https://doi.org/10.1039/A809238I

Lanciani, R. (2000). *Storia degli scavi di Roma e notizie intorno le collezioni romane di antichità* (Vol. VI).

Laufer, B. (1915). Asbestos and Salamander. *T'oung Pao, 16*(1), 299–373.

Li, J., Li, H., Zheng, B., & Yu, Z. (2019). Comparison of analysis of asbestos fibres in drinking water using phase contrast microscopy and micro-FTIR spectrometry with scanning electron microscopy and energy-dispersive X-ray spectroscopy. *Environmental Science Water Research and Technology, 5,* 543–551.

Marchesani, L. (1838). *Storia di Vasto, città in Abruzzo Citeriore.* Napoli, Da' Torchi dell'Osservatore medico.

Nibby, A. (1849). *Analisi storica-topografica della carta de' dintorni di Roma* (Vol. III). Roma.

Petriglieri, J. R., Bersani, D., Laporte-Magoni, C., Tribaudino, M., Cavallo, A., Salvioli-Mariani, E., & Turci, F. (2021). Portable Raman spectrometer for in situ analysis of asbestos and fibrous minerals. *Applied Sciences (Switzerland), 11,* 287. https://doi.org/10.3390/app11010287

Rinaudo, C., & Croce, A. (2019). Micro-Raman spectroscopy, a powerful technique allowing sure identification and complete characterization of asbestiform minerals. *Applied Sciences, 9*(151), 3092. https://doi.org/10.3390/app9153092

Rinaudo, C., Gastaldi, D., & Belluso, E. (2003). Characterization of chrisotile, antigorite and lizardite by FT-Raman spectroscopy. *The Canadian Mineralogist, 41,* 883–890.

Rinaudo, C., Belluso, E., & Gastaldi, D. (2004). Assessment of the use of Raman spectroscopy for the determination of amphibole asbestos. *Mineralogical Magazine, 68,* 455–465. https://doi.org/10.1180/0026461046830197

Rinaudo, C., Gastaldi, D., Belluso, E., & Capella, S. (2005). Application of Raman Spectroscopy on asbestos fibre identification. *Neues Jahrbuch fur Mineralogie, Abhandlungen, 182,* 31–36. https://doi.org/10.1127/0077-7757/2005/0030.C

Saiful Islam Khan, M., Yoo, H., Wu, L., Lee, H., Kim, M., & Ro, C. (2022). Single-particle Mineralogy of Asbestos Mineral Particles by the Combined Use of Low-Z Particle EPMA and ATR-FTIR Imaging Techniques. *Asian Journal of Atmospheric Environment, 16*(4), 2022110.

Steinby, E. M. (2003). La necropoli della Via Triumphalis, in Memorie. *Atti della Pontificia Accademia Romana di Archeologia* III, XVII. Roma.
Urban, S. (1857). *The Gentleman's Magazine and historical review*. Londra.
Yates, J. (1853). *Textrinum Antiquorum. An account of the art of weaving among the ancients*. Londra.

Chapter 6
Revealing the Unknown: How Multi-technical Approach Can Be Crucial in Identification of Dyes and Protein in Archeological Remains

Ilaria Serafini, Alessandro Ciccola, Roberta Curini, Gabriele Favero, Gwénaëlle M. Kavich, Timothy P. Cleland, and Caroline Solazzo

Abstract The analysis of archaeological textiles is a challenging undertaking, because of the high information content that characterizes these precious remains. Their realization, from the point of view of the dyes and yarns used, can have multiple meanings, for example the wealth of the commissioner and reflect the cultural taste of the society. The raw materials also can reveal the commercial routes, this may not be evident from literary sources and become clear from the archaeometric study of these artifacts. However, the alteration processes to which these materials have been subjected to, such as thermal aging and carbonization, mineralization, etc., represent an extremely critical point for their study and conservation, because these chemical processes are not entirely known and could bring to a complete modification. For these reasons, the identification of their composition requires high sensitivity techniques, characterized also by great versatility.

Recently, multi-technical approaches, based on spectroscopic and spectrometric techniques, have been revealed as powerful strategies in providing information about chemical composition of archaeological relics; they have been employed for characterization of dyes and moreover proteomics and genomics. In this chapter a review of the state of the art of FTIR, Raman and mass spectrometry analyses

---

I. Serafini (✉)
Department of Environmental Biology, Sapienza University of Rome, Rome, Italy

Museum Conservation Institute, Smithsonian Institution, Suitland, MD, USA
e-mail: ilaria.serafini@uniroma1.it

A. Ciccola · G. Favero
Department of Environmental Biology, Sapienza University of Rome, Rome, Italy

R. Curini
Department of Chemistry, Sapienza University of Rome, Rome, Italy

G. M. Kavich · T. P. Cleland · C. Solazzo
Museum Conservation Institute, Smithsonian Institution, Suitland, MD, USA

applied to archaeological fabrics will be provided, also reporting several case studies to highlight the potential of these multi-technical analyses.

Keywords Dyes · FTIR · Raman · Proteomics · Multi-technical approach

6.1 Introduction

The analysis of archaeological textiles is a challenging undertaking. These remains hold the key to understanding ancient societies from the point of view of social, economic, and technological aspects, and thus reconstructing evolutionary paths that would otherwise only be conceivable but not demonstrable (Ciccola et al., 2020; Good, 2001; Gleba, 2011; Gleba & Mannering, 2012; Ortiz et al., 2016).

Their importance then only comes in understanding their composition and realization of technologies. It is important to highlight that these remains are often representative of objects of common use, so their preservation conditions over time are extremely related to their previous wear, the conservation environment and their eventual symbolic value, aspects which involve a difference in comparison to historical art objects, usually subjected to remarkable care for their recognized intrinsic value. Moreover, because of the processes they are subjected to, such as burial phenomena and mineralization, fire (due to funeral pyres, or catastrophic events such as volcanic eruptions, etc.) or bacterial attack, they are mostly or completely altered or fragmented.

With reference to the diagnostics, a series of aspects must be considered for characterization. First, the professionals involved in the study and conservation of the textile artifacts must be aware of the complexity in composition of the original material. A textile consists of at least of two chemical species: the fiber and the dye. These present totally different properties—the fiber is a polymeric material with variable affinity for water but not soluble in it, the (ancient) dye is a mixture of several chromophores with variable solubility in water according to their chemical nature, so they behave differently with reference to the environmental conditions and the biological and chemical agents. Moreover, some classes of dyes, for example anthraquinones, flavonoids and in some cases phenoxazones, require the presence of a third species, the mordant, which could be inorganic (metals) or organic (e.g. tannins), whose role is to bind the dye on the fiber and, consequently has an influence on the chemical properties of the two other species (e.g. the solubility of the dye). Secondly, the above-mentioned conservation conditions involve a degradation and alteration of the chemical composition of these components resulting in altered and degraded chemical compounds that have a physical chemical behavior that is partly or entirely different from the original components and in turn influence degradative phenomena. Consequently, greater complexity in sample processing and analysis is faced. These altered compounds must be identified to obtain direct information about the "state of health" of the item and, indirectly, details about the conservation environment; furthermore, they are fundamental to define a restoration intervention, if required or necessary. A final aspect to be evaluated in every eventual restoration treatment is if the textile might have been subjected to previous treatments in its history because this usually implies the presence of new or newer materials, which should be identified and could interfere with the analyses.

For all of the above reasons, analyzing precious textile remains means inevitably the development of specialized analytical methodologies, which require a sensitive multi-analytical approach involving several analytical techniques because of their complex chemical composition. From this point of view, a complete analytical protocol should move from observation of the object through microscopic techniques to identification of all the compounds by means of specific analytical tools. Since an exhaustive dissertation of all the possible techniques usable for the characterization of both the fibers and the dyes, from an analytical point of view, is beyond the scope of this chapter and many reviews have thoroughly discussed the subjects, the authors have focused their attention in providing a brief but comprehensive review of the state of art of spectroscopic and spectrometric analyses applied to archaeological fabrics, also reporting several case studies to highlight the potentiality of the multi-technical approach.

6.2 Dyes

6.2.1 Spectroscopic Techniques: Case Studies

The main advantage of several spectroscopic approaches for the identification of dyes is the possibility of analyzing the objects without any invasiveness: several analytical techniques are available as portable instruments, which allow their application directly on the object for the acquisition of characteristic spectra, whose features can be correlated to specific dyes. In particular, the combination with optical fibers usually represents the favored setup for the acquisition of spectra directly on-site: the fiber can transmit, through the total internal reflection the light from the source directly to the analyzed area on the object, where the interaction with the chemical components occurs (reflection, scattering, etc.). The light deriving from this interaction is then transmitted to the detector, with the consequent acquisition of spectral data (Bacci et al., 1992; Fabbri et al., 2001; Picollo et al., 2007; Montagner et al., 2011; Cosentino, 2015; Peruzzi et al., 2021).

From this point of view, one of the analytical spectroscopies which is widely applied for the identification of the dyes is the Fiber Optic Reflectance Spectroscopy (FORS), which can be combined with different light range sources, from ultraviolet to visible to near infrared light, to obtain different typology of information (Montagner et al., 2011; Aceto et al., 2014; Maynez-Rojas et al., 2017). In the case of dyes, the application of a visible light source is highly appropriate because all the investigated analytes are highly absorbing species in that range, and the acquired spectrum is directly relatable to the chromatic features of the object. The first information achievable from the visible light reflectance spectrum is the identification of the dye family: generally, the reflectance bands are attributable to a specific class of molecules in terms of frequencies and number of signals, which can be also interpreted with reference to the visible light absorption properties. This allows discriminating different families of dyes with the same color. For instance, the blue indigoid dyes (indigo and woad) are characterized in the reflectance spectrum by a maximum around 430–480 nm and an inflection point at around 710–720 nm, while by HOMO-LUMO and HOMO2-LUMO electronic transitions respectively at 660 and 350 nm in the pseudo-absorbance spectrum, while the logwood blue dyes present two reflectance bands around 430 and 455 nm with an inflection point shifted between 630 and 710 nm, according to different typologies of mordant (Gulmini et al., 2013). For some dyes, such as yellow ones, the discrimination among classes could be more difficult, but in some cases slight differences were observed in the pseudo-absorbance spectra (a maximum between 445 and 460 nm for proto-berberines; two maxima at around 445 and 470 nm for carotenoids; only one maximum at 420–440 nm for flavonoid dyes as weld; a different one between 400 and 420 nm for gamboge, silver grass and other dyes) (Tamburini & Dyer, 2019). In some cases, FORS spectra allow distinguishing dyes belonging to the same molecular class: for instance, in the case of anthraquinone red dyes it is possible to differentiate dyes from plant sources like madder (two band maxima at 510–515 and 540–545 nm) from those of animal origin (two band maxima at 520–525 and 550–565 nm) (Aceto et al., 2014; Gulmini et al. 2013). Interestingly, in some cases the FORS features could suggest details about the manufacturing of the item: for instance, according to Tamburini & Dyer, (2019) the sappanwood dye extracted in neutral conditions presents a broad maximum at 530–540 nm, while its analogue extracted in alkali conditions has a narrow band at 560 nm (Tamburini & Dyer, 2019), Fig. 6.1. Additional information could be obtained from the study of reflectance spectra and their first derivative, according to the typology of colorant. Peruzzi et al. (Peruzzi et al., 2021) report that lac dyes are distinguishable from cochineal ones by a maximum at around 670 nm in the derivative spectrum, which is not present in the cochineal analogue, while, from the studies of Fonseca et al. (2019), a differentiation between cochineal-tin and cochineal-aluminum complex would be possible basing on their pseudo-absorbance (maxima at 485, 520 and 555 nm for the tin mordant; at 493, 538 and 574 nm for aluminum one), even if it is important to highlight that these data refer to solid lake pigments.

Along with the reflectance properties, the fluorescence emission following the absorption of UV and Visible light represents a further physical process, which could be helpful for the identification of the dye. The fluorescence represents a main mechanism, through which the molecules absorbing the radiation recover the initial energy ground state from the excited one emitting radiation at higher wavelength. With reference to the complexity of vibronic states of a molecule, the emitted radiation is not monochromatic but it is a band in a range of energy. The obtained spectrum of radiation could be considered indicative, as the reflectance one to the class of dye. The main advantage of fluorescence spectroscopy is represented by the high sensitivity, and for this reason it represents one of the most successful and

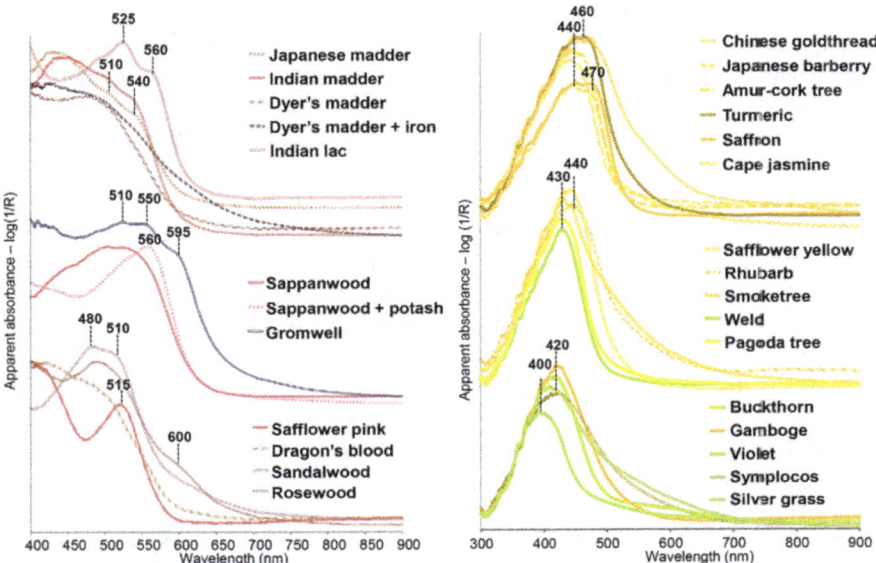

Fig. 6.1 FORS spectra (apparent absorption) of reference dye samples. (Reprinted with permission from Tamburini & Dyer (2019). Copyright 2019 Elsevier Ltd.)

traditional approaches used for the characterization of textile natural dyes. For instance, Wallert (1986) highlights the discriminant properties of the spectrofluorimetric approach, applying the method to solutions of quinone, lichen and redwood colorants. The analysis of extracts from historical samples was useful for the identification of dyes with comparison to data collected on an internal database, allowing at least the identification of the chromophore class. Since then, the technique has been used for different dyes and case studies: for instance, Clementi et al. (2006) applied the technique to the characterization of orchil dyes in solution and on different fiber substrates, confirming its suitability for diagnostics by successfully detecting the dyes on a Renaissance tapestry. The same research team extended the application to indigo, with successful identification of the blue colorant on several tapestries of the same period (Clementi et al., 2009). It is also worth mentioning that the fluorescence techniques could be coupled with different typologies of light sources. Abdel-Kareem et al. (2011) built a database of natural dyes for Laser Induced Fluorescence (exciting wavelength: 405 nm), while Aceto et al. (2015) used the fluorescence induced by a 350 nm LED source as part of a characterization study dedicated to the discrimination of folium and orchil dyes (it is fundamental to mention that the investigated mock-ups were dyed parchments, even if the used methodology is the same used for mordant dyeing of textiles).

One of the main drawbacks of fluorescence spectroscopy is represented by the fact that the spectrum is collected as emission radiation induced by excitation at a single wavelength, but this wavelength may not be suitable for the specific dye present on the sample (especially if preliminary information is not available). A strategy to overcome this issue is represented by multidimensional fluorescence spectroscopy, which has the advantage of revealing the mixture of dyes: the multidimensional spectrum, represented by the combination of excitation, emission and intensity axes in a "topographic map" plot, allows observing multiple fluorescence emission maxima, which are highly discriminant and informative. This three-dimensional approach is cited in the work of Wallert (1986), but it has been widely deepened in the following decades. In the work of Nakamura et al. (2009), excitation-emission matrix (EEM) fluorescence was combined with UV-Vis reflectance spectroscopy to investigate some eighth century textiles from Japan. This study showed the importance of correlating the wavelength of excitation λ_{ex} and emission λ_{em} in a 2D plot: for instance, this approach successfully distinguishes among different yellow dyes, while this represents one of the main issues of UV-Vis reflectance spectroscopy. Moreover, it was possible to differentiate the use of a same dye (*Kariyasu* yellow, extracted from eulalia, *Miscanthus tinctorius*) with different mordants (alum and lime) from the variation of the fluorescence matrices: if only one peak at $\lambda_{ex} = 441$ nm/$\lambda_{em} = 532$ nm is observable in the first case, two signals at $\lambda_{ex} = 371$ nm/$\lambda_{em} = 529$ nm and $\lambda_{ex} = 459$ nm/$\lambda_{em} = 534$ nm are observable in the second one. The work is also interesting because it highlighted the variation of spectral features from aging, which found a confirmation in the analysis of historical samples. For instance, the shift of the characteristic peak of *Kariyasu* yellow from $\lambda_{ex} = 371$ nm/$\lambda_{em} = 529$ nm to $\lambda ex = 371$ nm/$\lambda em = 519$ nm. To the clarity of the reader, the authors even mentioned when the EEM fluorescence approach did not produce useful results (e.g. the *ai* blue based on indigo), but the combination with UV-Vis reflectance could represent a totally non-invasive strategy for the complete characterization of dyes. This was the starting point for the work of Selberg et al. (2023), who collected the fluorescence EEMs of 31 dyed wool yarns, obtained from 18 natural dyes—among which some had quite peculiar results, in comparison to the dyes studied in the previous literature—alone and in mixture and used this database for the application on case studies (Fig. 6.2). The obtained patterns resulted in a range of information: some dyes were highly discriminable on the basis of their EEMs (e.g. lupine, bedstraws), others did not present fluorescence at all (e.g. indigotin-based ones, confirming Nakamura results). In other cases, the main potential of the technique was represented by the ability to distinguish dyes of different families and similar color: for instance, red dyes of Rubiaceae can be easily discriminated from wood dyes. Moreover, in the first family, it is possible to separate the bedstraw colorants because their two emission maxima at 600 nm, while madder and cochineal present maxima shifted to 625 nm. In the case of bedstraw dyes harvested in different periods, it was even possible to detect differences in relative intensity and shape of the fluorescence emission peaks, which were considered potentially indicative of different origins. An interesting result in this study is related to yellow dyes: if these dyes are generally considered difficult to discriminate with on-site techniques (for instance FORS), the EEMs spectra of northern firmoss and, especially, safflower are quite characteristic, so the technique can be used as a confirmation method if preliminary hypotheses on the presence of these dyes were

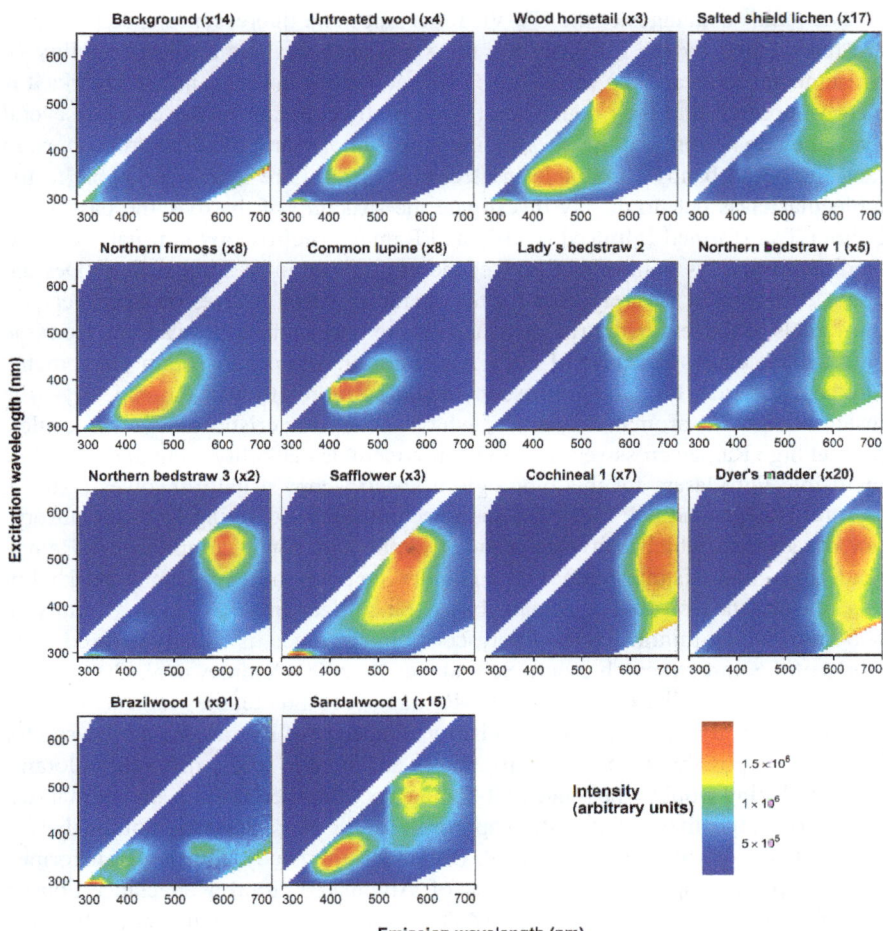

Fig. 6.2 Selection of characteristic EEM spectra of dyed wool reference samples, undyed wool and background material. For visualization purposes, the fluorescence intensities of some EEMs are multiplied by factors indicated in parentheses. Rayleigh and Raman scatter have been removed from all spectra (diagonal cuts). (Reprinted with permission from Selberg et al. (2023). Copyright 2023 Elsevier Ltd.)

formulated. Another aspect evaluated in the study is the effect of different mordants on the fluorescence: high fluorescence intensity, for example, can be correlated with higher binding of the mordant towards the dyes, even if, according to the study, the extension to a wider set of dyes is fundamental to deepen this aspect. The application of the EEM approach to a set of case studies (a tapestry from 1547 and a carpet from 1930) successfully identified dyes from the Rubiaceae family (results confirmed by liquid chromatography), even if a certain ambiguity with cochineal dyes was assessed.

The main advantages of the UV-Vis reflectance and fluorescence spectroscopies are represented by the affordability, the short analytical time, the portability of instrumental setup and the versatility. However, even if in the mentioned works it is clearly reported that they could be efficiently discriminant in the case of several dyes, they do not present the information potential of vibrational spectroscopies. In fact, the broad bands observable in electronic spectra are usually relatable to the molecular class but, to deeply investigate the structure of the dye, the passage to Fourier Transformed InfraRed (FTIR) and Raman spectroscopy is usually considered necessary. As pointed out by Degano et al. in an interesting review (Degano et al., 2009), FTIR is rarely used for the characterization of dyes on fiber, because the signals of the textile matrix are usually more intense than those arising from the colorant molecules, because of both concentration and cross-section phenomena. On the other side, Raman spectroscopy could be more efficient theoretically—the insaturations and aromatic moieties, which are characteristic of dye molecules, present high Raman cross-sections and consequent detectability—but the use of UV or Visible light lasers for this typology of spectroscopy usually involves a strong spectral background due to the fluorescence emission—deriving from the absorption of radiation, which is favored as radiative phenomenon in comparison to Raman scattering—and this interference could hinder the observation of Raman peaks. For this reason, the use of FT-Raman, based on a Near-InfraRed laser (usually at 1064 nm) which minimizes the fluorescence interference, is usually favored. Two works of the same research group (Schrader et al., 2000; Andreev et al., 2001) demonstrate the possibility of acquiring FT-Raman spectra on textiles indicative of the present natural dyes: besides the acquisition of spectra of the raw materials used for dyeing, it is possible to observe differences attributable to the different colorants used for dyeing wool in the related FT-Raman spectra, even if these are not marked.

In this perspective, an interesting approach for the characterization of the dyes in textiles was presented by Bruni et al. (2011). In this study, Fourier Transformed Raman spectroscopy, in combination of Attenuated Total Reflectance-Fourier Transformed InfraRed spectroscopy (ATR-FTIR; for more details about the technique, see paragraph "Spectroscopic characterisation of proteins" in this chapter) was applied to discriminate different dyes on wool, silk and cotton. With reference to preliminary data, the use of FTIR, both in ATR and transmission mode, was not particularly useful for the identification of dyes, because the FTIR spectra are generally dominated by signals characteristic of the fiber and only slight differences in the spectral pattern could be conducted to the presence of a dye, while, in the case of FT-Raman, the main issue was represented by the fluorescence interference, even if in most of the spectra signals attributable unambiguously to the dye were present. To overcome these issues, after acquiring ATR spectra of the dyed fibers, transmission FTIR spectra of pure dyes and FT-Raman of both the typologies of samples, the spectra were treated with range delimitation and calculation of the second derivative. Two libraries were built on InfraRed and FT-Raman data. The application of algorithms, based on the mean centering of sample and reference spectra and resulting correlation and derivative correlation coefficients, were applied, with the calculation of a relative quality index. For FTIR data, several cases using a library search for the identification of the dyes were made possible by working on the residual spectrum obtained by the subtraction of the fiber reference spectrum from the sample analogue: in this way, the interference of the textile substrate could be eliminated, favoring the recognition of the present dye from the second derivative spectrum. In the case of FT-Raman spectra, the application of the same algorithms resulted in determination of the dye with a high-quality index, especially in the case of the residual spectrum obtained by difference with the fiber reference one. The library search method for the combination of the two techniques was even applied to a set of ancient samples, constituted by Kaitag textiles and a Chinese Ningxia carpet: the method successfully identified the dyes among the first five hits suggested by the algorithms, and it was also able to identify different dyes in mixture (e.g. indigo and dyer's broom for a green sample).

Despite its advantages for the detection of dyes, the FT-Raman approach is usually not available in the form of portable instrumentation. Some portable instruments are available exploiting lasers at longer wavelengths (for instance, the BRAVO Raman) for Sequentially Shifted Excitation Raman Spectroscopy (Conti et al., 2016), which minimizes the fluorescence interference through diode lasers operating at different temperatures and, consequently, providing slightly shifted excitation wavelengths, but, to our knowledge, they have not been applied yet to the characterization of dyes on textiles—even if their application to organic pictorial pigments was quite successful (Pause et al., 2021). This methodology should be deepened, to exploit its potential on textiles of historical importance. Another interesting approach to eliminate fluorescence interference is represented by Subtracted Shifted Raman Spectroscopy (SSRS). From an experimental point of view, it is the difference of two Raman spectra acquired at two different grating positions. This involves a shift for the Raman bands, which is sufficiently small to leave the fluorescence background unvaried practically, by choice of the operator, because of the broadness of the luminescence band. The final difference-spectrum is characterized only by Raman derivative-like peaks, while the fluorescence background is almost nonexistent. Rosi et al. (2010) applied the SSRS approach to a series of dyes and lake pigments, to evaluate advantages and drawbacks of the methodology, and then to two textiles of Egyptian manufacturing (tenth to eleventh century). In both cases, the SSRS spectra showed the presence of madder from the typical anthraquinone peaks, while no interference of the Raman signal of the fibers were observed. According to the literature, however, this approach requires large instrumentation, and the reconstruction of the Raman spectrum from the acquired data could be difficult.

Extending the perspective on the potential of the technique, it is worth noting that Raman Scattering spectroscopy is commonly used for the identification of dyes in its Surface Enhanced variant. The Surface Enhancement Raman Scattering (SERS) phenomenon consists of a complex effect, usually interpreted as the combination of Raman spectral enhancement and fluorescence quenching (Pozzi & Leona, 2016). This phenomenon is generated by the surface interaction of the analyte with noble metal (Au or Ag, principally) nanostructures. For the interpretation of the process, a mechanism based on the combination of electromagnetic (Jeanmaire & Van Duyne,

1977) and charge-transfer ones (Albrecht & Creighton, 1977) is accepted, but it is fundamental to highlight that the enhancement to occur requires a close interaction between the nanostructure and the analyte molecules. In this way, the molecule is subjected to a strong amplification of the local electromagnetic field, which corresponds to an increase of the probability of Raman scattering and, consequently, to higher intensity Raman signals. For this reason, traditionally SERS measurements were performed dropping metal nanoparticle colloids on the sample, which, in the case of dyed textiles, could be constituted by fibers of the investigated material or by extracts of the dyes. The sensitivity of SERS is remarkably high, but these typologies of approach cannot be considered totally noninvasive, because they require the sampling of a textile fragment for the extraction or they involve the surface adhesion of the metal nanoparticles on the surface of the objects, with consequent addition of non-original material and chromatic variations. In this context, an interesting complementary strategy uses gel substrates for extraction and consequent SERS analysis. This approach is based on the ability of gel, soaked or loaded with proper solutions, to extract dyes from the surface of the object they are put in contact with. In this way, theoretically, only the dyes are sampled on a molecular scale, while no actual removal of macroscopic material is promoted. The dyes, entrapped in the gel matrix in very low concentrations, can be revealed by SERS after their contact with the nanoparticles. To facilitate this interaction, two different approaches are reported in the literature. The first method involves the loading of a noble metal colloid during the preparation of the hydrogel, which is intrinsically SERS-active: in this way, the dye molecules start their interaction with the SERS nanostructures directly during the extraction, and this interaction is increased by shrinkage of the gel by evaporation of the solvent after the extraction. Following the approach tested by Leona et al. (2011) and based on the use of a methacrylate-based copolymer gel for the extraction and detection of natural and synthetic dyes, Lofrumento et al. (2013) tested the agar gel, loaded with silver nanoparticles (Ag NPS) and an extracting solution of ethylenediaminetetraacetic acid (EDTA) for extracting anthraquinones from textile items. In this series of works (Lofrumento et al., 2013; Platania et al., 2014, 2015), the dependence to the excitation wavelength of SERS signals was investigated for several anthraquinone dyes. Lasers at 514.5 and 785 nm were compared (Lofrumento et al., 2013), and it was possible to observe that the first laser granted higher intensities for peaks at higher wavenumbers, while the second for those at lower wavenumbers, probably for the occurrence of Resonance Raman in the first case and for specific interaction between agar and Ag NPS involving a red shift to the localized surface plasmon resonance in the second. The extraction performances were evaluated according to different typology of fibers (wool, silk and printed cotton) (Platania et al., 2014) and different extraction times were identified with dependence to the typology of textile: for instance, 50 min were found to be necessary for the wool because of the limited adhesion of agar gel on the fiber and the higher strength of dye-fiber interaction, while, for the silk, high quality SERS spectra were acquired on gel cubes after an extraction of 15 min. The methodology even allowed the identification of an alizarin-containing dye on a historical Peruvian textile and its general efficiency was also confirmed by analyses performed by chromatographic techniques on the mock-up and samples. The same approach was also devoted to the identification of indigoids (Platania et al., 2015), even if in this case the Ag-agar gel was not loaded with the extraction solution, but a drop of NaOH/$Na_2S_2O_4$ solution—able to reduce the indigoids to their soluble leuco-form—was added on the top of it and then in contact with the object. After testing on reference samples dyed with indigo or Tyrian purple, the procedure was applied on different typologies of textile artworks (a precolombian textile, a fifteenth century cotton tablecloth, a sixteenth century tapestry): in all the cases, the SERS spectra allowed identitification of an indigo-based dye, when standard Raman spectra did not provide recognisable features for the dye.

The second approach, reported in the literature, for identification by SERS directly on the extraction gel was presented by Germinario et al. (2020). In this case, along with the agar gel, the Nanorestore Gel—a commercial gel used for restoration cleaning—was tested for the extraction in combination with a mild solution based on ammonia and EDTA. These gels did not contain Ag nanoparticles inside the matrix, but a colloid was dropped on the surface of the gel substrates after the extraction on dyed yarns. In this case, the aggregation of the nanoparticles was not granted by the shrinkage of the gel for evaporation of the solvents, but chemically induced by addition of a salt. The two gels were tested with different laser wavelengths on madder and cochineal and it was possible to identify and discriminate the typical features of the two dyes (Fig. 6.3). This approach, deepened by Bosi et al. (2023) in the case of pigment lakes in hydrophilic pictorial films, presents the advantages of being more feasible to achieve in the laboratory, because no gel-loading of the colloid is necessary and commercial ready-to-use gels can be utilized. On the other hand, it is important to highlight that, in this second approach, the contact between the analytes and the nanoparticles occurs on the surface of the gel substrate, so it cannot benefit from the shrinkage of the gel matrix. However, with reference to both approaches, it is undeniable that the use of gel-systems for the localized extraction of dyes from textiles presents a great potential to fill a void in

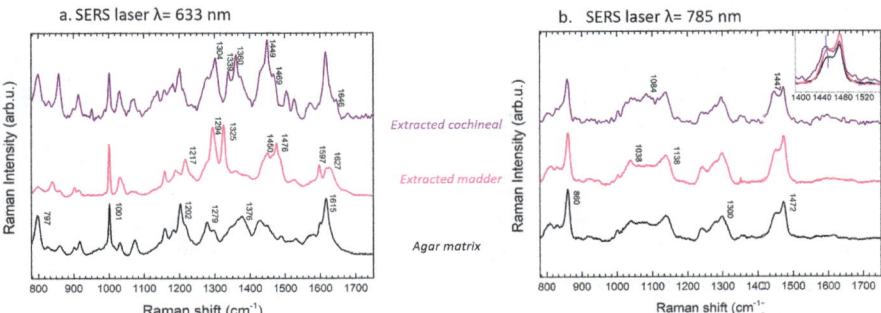

Fig. 6.3 Comparison of SERS spectra for the agar gel blank (bottom), the extracted madder on agar (middle) and the extracted cochineal analogue (top) using the laser at $\lambda = 633$ nm (**a**) and at $\lambda = 785$ nm (**b**). (Reprinted with permission from Germinario et al. (2020). Copyright 2020 Elsevier Ltd.)

archaeometry for the micro-invasive characterization of organic compounds, building a bridge between a totally noninvasive approach and laboratory analytics. Moreover, through a secondary re-extraction phase, these methodologies could be easily combined with other techniques working with samples in solution, like the chromatographic and spectrometric technique, which are discussed in the following section.

6.2.2 Spectrometric Techniques: Case Studies

The first papers on the extraction and analysis of dyes through a spectrometric approach from historical textiles date back to the mid-1970s–1980s. These first attempts for looking at the dye compositions on historical textiles, started from extraction from fibers and then the application of different techniques, such as paper chromatography, UV-Vis and FTIR spectroscopy, to identify the dye (Shahid et al., 2019; Wouters, 1985; Wouters & Verhecken, 1989; Wouters & Rosario-Chirinos, 1992; Tiedemann & Yang, 1995; Taylor, 1983; Gillard et al., 1994). These papers represented the beginning of this new field, which saw from the very beginning a very close connection between art historians, analytical chemists and experts in separation techniques, and archaeologists.

Its driving force undoubtedly came from technological advances in the field of analytical instruments. The association between extraction protocols with separative techniques, such as HPLC, introduced by Wouters and Verhecken, was applied to study an archaeological Coptic textile (Wouters, 1985; Orska-Gawrys et al., 2003) and demonstrated in this case to be able to identify the main compounds in the dye mixture to give a first insight in the matrices employed in ancient times.

The association between separative techniques and UV-Vis but mostly mass spectrometry has represented a powerful accelerator in the field of studying dyes in archaeological textiles (Shahid et al., 2019). Liquid chromatography in fact makes it possible to resolve complex mixtures and open the possibility of identifying the components of dye mixtures. In particular, HPLC/UHPLC-MS analyses (especially with MS/MS fragmentation patterns) and in combination with high-resolution MS (HRMS) may allow detailed analysis of dye components which are isomers or very close in ion mass (Lech & Fornal, 2020).

From an analytical point of view, there are several factors that contribute to the good results of LC-MS analyses, such as the column employed for the separation, the mobile phase, etc. but certainly the most crucial aspect is the extraction method (Lombardi et al., 2016; Serafini et al., 2017; Valianou et al., 2009; Karapanagiotis et al., 2021). The reason lies mainly in the fact natural dyes, unlike synthetic dyes, are not composed by one or a few dye molecules, but a complex mix of chromophores, mostly based on anthraquinones (cochineal, madder, kermes), flavonoids (weld and many other plants), indigoids (indigo, purple, etc.), phenoxazones (orchil), etc. (Serafini et al., 2023). As in the case of madder, it is possible to count at least 45–60 anthraquinone species contributing to the color and, as in the case of cochineal, many are structural isomers. The characterization of the whole molecular pattern, or most of it, is fundamental to yield information about the geographical provenances of the dye plants or insect employed. Moreover, researchers demonstrated that these data can be used with the scope of differentiating even within a single plant species (Degano et al., 2009; Wouters, 1985; Wouters & Verhecken, 1989; Ford et al., 2017, 2018; Mantzouris & Karapanagiotis, 2015; Stathopoulou et al., 2013; Shahid et al., 2019), trying to define criteria for their distinction through a chemometric approach (Serrano et al., 2015; Koren, 2023): to have a clear vision of the sources employed allows for defining the commercial routes, historical provenances as mentioned before. Therefore, any possible alteration should be avoided, strongly impacting the identification of the primary source or any possible information related (Koren, 2023).

The first proposed methods for dye extraction was presented by Wouters, and it mainly consisted of a solution of H_2O:MeOH:HCl 37% (1:1:2) at 100 °C for 10 min (Wouters, 1985; Shahid et al., 2019). This method was also applied together with the first application of HPLC-UV-Vis for the purpose of having quantitative dyes analyses. It was applied to study archaeological textiles, particularly four samples, two brown threads, one red and one purple Coptic textiles, coming from different artworks. Starting from an extraction of 3N HCl for 30 min, the extraction yielded madder based dyes in all the samples, even if with different shades, with the addition of carminic acid in one of the brown threads (Wouters & Rosario-Chirinos, 1992).

In the work of Orska-Gawrys, to study archeological silk Coptic textiles, the same method was investigated with a double approach, a first extraction with a solution of 3M HCl-Ethanol (1:1) for 15 min at 100 °C and the fiber residue treated with warm pyridine to detect indigoids compounds (Orska-Gawrys et al., 2003). In this case, the authors recognized the decomposition of glycosidic parts, but they reported to be still able to hypothesize the presence of madder, weld, lac-dye, indigo and cochineal, together with some tannins, probably employed to increase the weight of the silk (Orska-Gawrys et al., 2003). However, further evaluation on the source of these matrices is obviously not possible, due to the lack and the probable modification of the minor components.

A similar double approach has been applied for the study of other archaeological remains: in the work of Liu, several textiles, excavated from the graveyard at Yingpan, Xinjiang, on the ancient Silk Road, were analyzed. In this case, a multi-technical approach was applied to investigate both fiber and dyes. For the dyes, 9 silk and wool samples were analyzed (Fig. 6.4).

To identify the matrices in the red/brown or yellow yarns and a solution of H_2O/MeOH/37%HCl (1/1/2, v/v/v), at 105 °C for 10 min was employed (Wouters, 1985; Liu et al., 2011). For green or blue shades, the solution employed has been 37% HCl/DMSO (1/20, v/v) at 80 °C for 5 min (Puchalska et al., 2004) and analyzed through HPLC-PDA analyses. The analyses identified alizarin, as the main component, and purpurin in the sample YP15-1, confirming the use of a madder dye plants, widely present in China. Furthermore, observing the ratio between the two components, the authors hypothesize the also the use of *Rubia tinctorum* L., a local dyestuff. Alizarin and purpurin were also identified in four other red/brown samples.

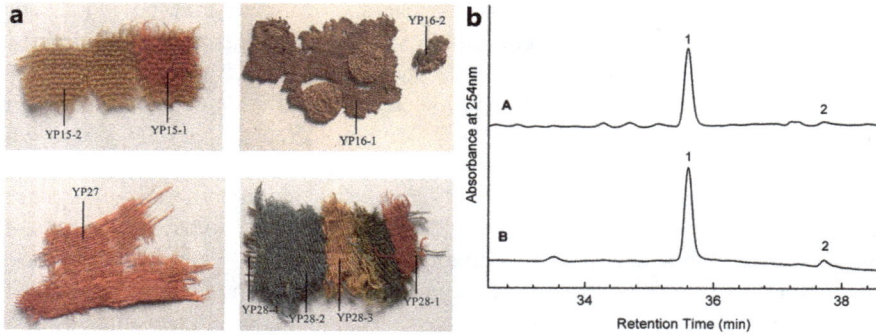

Fig. 6.4 (a) Photographs of the textile fragments from Yingpan burial sites used for dyestuffs analysis. (b) HPLC chromatograms of Rubia tinctorum L. of Xinjiang (A) and red sample YP15-1 (B). Peaks 1 and 2 correspond to Alizarin and Purpurin, respectively. (Reprinted with permission from Liu et al. (2011). Copyright 2011 Elsevier Ltd.)

For blue dyes, indigo and indigotin were identified while the most interesting result came from the yellow dyes. Luteolin and luteolin-like flavonoid were identified, and the authors reports that weld, safflower and dyer's broom were not documented in the ancient Chinese sources but were widely used for dyestuff manufacture in Western Asia and Europe in ancient times, so their use is to be referred to the ancient trades on the silk route (Liu et al., 2011; Zhang et al., 2008).

Another collection investigated with the same extraction method comes from Egypt, 27 ancient Egyptian fabrics of the Fill-Trevisiol collection (Karapanagiotis et al., 2019), with different shades, from red to deep violet–blue wool weft threads, Z-twist. The procedure employed is again with H_2O:MeOH:37% HCl (1:1:2, v/v/v) at 100 °C for 10 min (Wouters, 1985); the residue subjected to a double extraction with DMSO and heated at around 80 °C for 5 min. Of particular interest is the identification of cochineal dyes, which the authors refer to the use of *Porphyrophora hamelii* Brandt, Armenian cochineal. Together with cochineal, kermes dyes were be detected, easily recognizable for the absence of carminic acid. In this case, the authors support previous findings that the use of kermes or cochineal in only certain kinds of textiles in the collection, must be referred to the Islamic period of Egyptian textiles, while they are not used before the Arab conquest (Karapanagiotis et al., 2019; Pfister, 1936).

Together with the red insect and madder dyes, indigo dyes were identified, referable to the use of a mollusk source. The HPLC results of the molluscan dye detected in a Roman fabric were hypothesized to be from *Hexaplex trunculus* L. (Koren, 2008; Koren & Verhecken-Lammens, 2013; Karapanagiotis et al., 2019). The molluscan dye was also detected in a Byzantine sample in combination with madder (Karapanagiotis et al., 2019).

Despite the pioneering character of the Wouters method and application to LC analyses, this extraction method, although achieving very high yields, led to a variety of degradative phenomena such as decarboxylation, excessive hydrolysis (such as partial hydrolysis of pseudopurpurin and munjistin (Shahid et al., 2019; Wouters, 1985), and for the fiber itself, and especially glycosidic bond disruption in the chromophoric components, which are naturally present in the source employed and are fixed on the yarns during the dyeing process (Derksen et al., 2002; Lombardi et al., 2016; Serafini et al., 2017; Hofenk de Graaff, 2004; Delamare & Monasse, 2005; Mouri & Laursen, 2012; Shahid et al., 2019; Blackburn, 2017; Serrano et al., 2015). For example, for the cochineal dyes, other papers confirmed that the HCl method is not a suitable protocol to distinguish the cochineal source, because of several O-glucosides that must be considered to have a correct identification (Shahid et al., 2019; Lech et al., 2015; Lech & Jarosz, 2016; Serrano et al., 2015; Serafini et al., 2017). For this reason, different methods have been developed with the aim of having a more complete vision of the dye composition (Valianou et al., 2009; Sanyova, 2008; Sanyova & Reisse, 2006). It is worthy of mention that in the previous work of Karapanagiotis (2019), it is reported that the acid hydrolysis method does not have any noticeable effect on the relative composition of the molluscan dye.

Looking at alternative methods for HCl, Tiedemann and Yang (Tiedemann & Yang, 1995) propose the use of the organic solvent, DMF, in association with 0.1% EDTA (Serrano et al., 2011). Another common method proposes the use of DMSO, often in association with other extraction protocols.

An interesting paper reporting DMF extraction is those proposed by Sabatini on Paracas textiles (Sabatini et al., 2020). In this paper, a combined analytical approach is presented, to evaluate the state of conservation of Paracas textiles, made of dyed cotton yarns and camelid yarns, these latter generally used for the embroidery, conserved in Peruvian and Swedish Museums. The importance of this work lies in the paucity of information we have for such artifacts compared with the European-Western textiles, aiming at determining the dye sources employed in pre-Columbian textiles (Sabatini et al., 2020; Tamburini et al., 2019a). All the samples analyzed were subjected to an extraction process with 0.1% sodium EDTA in water and DMF, 99.8% (1:1, v/v), at 60 °C for 1 h in an ultrasonic bath, and then filtered before the analysis in HPLC-DAD and HPLC-ESI-Q-ToF (Sabatini et al., 2020). The chromatographic runs of red threads reported the presence of several anthraquinone compounds and based on literature information, seemed to refer to *Relbunium* vegetal species. In particular, the authors compared with reference materials dyed with different species of *Relbunium*, such as *R. hypocarpium*, *R. ciliatum*, *Relbunium*-unknown species. The similarities suggested *R. hypocarpium*, even if some differences can be detected, which can be referred to a differing dyeing processes or degradation processes (Cardon, 2007; Sabatini et al., 2020). The small differences in composition could be due to the use of a mixture of distinct *Relbunium* species, different dyeing processes, or degradation of the textiles. The importance of reference materials is highlighted also by the investigation on blue dyes, which revealed the presence of indigoids. They could come from two different plants, *Indigofera suffruticosa* and *Cybistax antisyphilitica* (Sabatini et al., 2020), which have not been investigated yet. Furthermore, the balance of the different compounds of indigoids could also be related to the extraction procedure from the plants and dyeing recipes (Sanz et al., 2012). In fact, the author ascribed the higher amount of indirubin in the samples as a possible effect of a south American vat dye technology that could be reasonably different from European ones. Yellow dyes in association with indigotin in the green or brown yarns were identified as flavonoid-based dyes but the reference materials didn't provide information regarding a possible source employed; because of the similarity with *Reseda luteola* L., authors hypothesized the use wild *Salix humboldtiana*, which has a similar chemical profile, even if further investigation are suggested (Sabatini et al., 2020).

An example of a double-extraction approach, based on the use of DMSO, comes from Dyer's work (Dyer et al., 2018). This work presents once again the possibility of a multi-technique approach to reduce, through a series of multispectral and non-invasive techniques, the number of samples for subsequent micro-destructive investigations. The study is focused on Late Antique textiles from Egypt, from the British Museum collection. As the authors reported, generally the origin and date of such textiles were largely determined by style and iconography. However, the application of analytical approach offers a deep inside into the materials composition, clarifying their sources, etc., and it is opening new scenario on the textile production, dyeing practices, trade routes and the economy (Dyer et al., 2018; Karapanagiotis et al., 2019).

The chosen objects of investigation were rubbish dumps of the city of Antinoupolis and three are from the Monastery of Apa Thomas at Wadi Sarga, both in Middle Egypt; the authors reported that reason behind the investigation is to answer differences in dye source, trade and/or practice associated two different contexts (an urban versus monastic one) and to fully understand their original shades (Dyer et al., 2018). In this case, 0.1 mg (2–3 mm) of sample were extracted in 200 μL DMSO and heated at 80 °C for 10 min. The residue was subjected to a second extraction, with 200 μL of methanol/acetone/water/0.5 M oxalic acid 30:30:40:1 (v/v/v/v), at 80 °C for 15 min. The DMSO extract was combined with the oxalic acid extract and the solution was centrifuged for 10 min, before the HPLC-MS analyses (through a HPLC-DAD-ESI-Q-ToF system) (Dyer et al., 2018). The dye analyses reported the presence of madder dyes, also for samples which appeared with different shades, suggesting possible differences in the dye bath conditions, such as the pH, but excluding a difference in the mordant process. The source employed is probably *Rubia tinctorum* L., but the authors underline how the chemical distinction between different species should be thoroughly considered and carefully evaluated, due to several factors that can affect the final dye composition (Dyer et al., 2018). Furthermore, the environmental condition of preservation should be considered, which can alter the final molecular pattern obtained by the extraction, which is a further element that can affect the chemical composition of the dye mixture (Fig. 6.5). The green color were obtained by indigo and yellow in a double dyeing process, and it is important to underline how in some case, the FORS and Multispectral Imaging measurement detected the presence of indigo with some peaks related to the flavonoids colorant (probably *Reseda luteola* L.) and in some cases, they were not detected by the HPLC-MS analyses, probably because of a strong degradation process which brought these yellow dyes under the limit of detection. This confirms the importance of a comprehensive and integrated study to assess the composition and constituent materials of the objects of investigation.

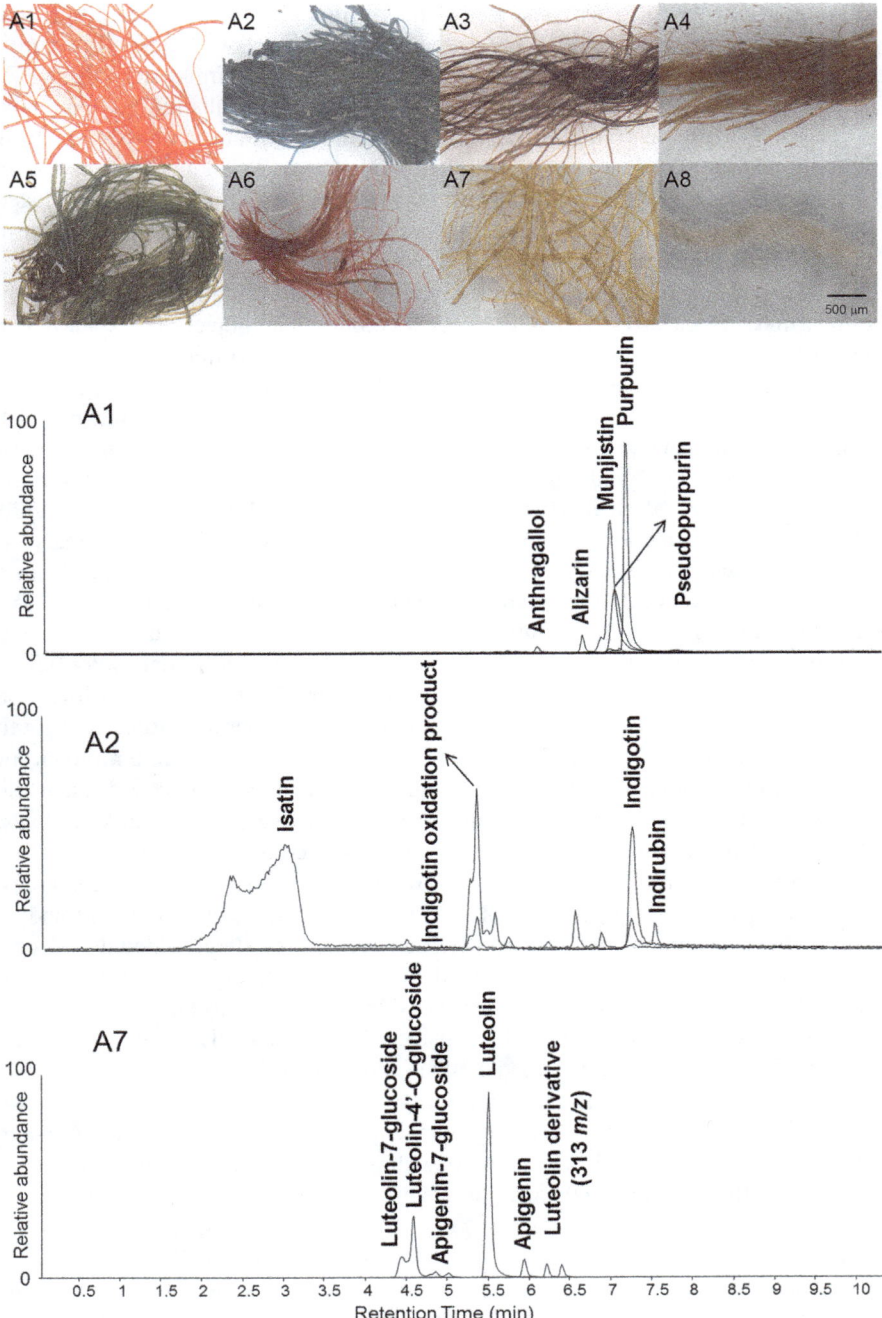

Fig. 6.5 Micrographs of selected samples at 80x magnification and Extract Ion Chromatograms (EICs) obtained by HPLC-ESI-Q-ToF analysis of samples A1, A2 and A7, showing the dye compounds identified. (Reproduced by Dyer et al. (2018). Copyright: © 2018 Dyer et al)

Another example of successful multi-analytical approach, which employed the DMSO extraction procedure, is represented by dye analyses of Chinese silk embroidery from Dunhuang (Tang dynasty), excavated from the temple site of Qian Fo Dong, near Dunhuang, one of the most famous archaeological sites in China, now at the British Museum (Tamburini et al., 2019b). The importance of the dye analysis for such textiles can be ascribed to limited evidence on Asian colorant matters in literature: in fact, as reported by the authors, even if at least 40 plants are listed among the most common raw materials for dyeing blue, red, yellow and brown in ancient China, investigations on ancient textiles often report the detection of unknown dyes, thus prompting research to fill this gap (Tamburini et al., 2019b; Tamburini & Dyer, 2019; Zhang et al., 2007, 2008). The object of this study is a textile displaying a standing Buddha Shakyamuni, on the Vulture Peak, with bodhisattvas and his disciples on both sides, dated around 618–907 AD. The object is composed of extensive embroidery made with numerous silk floss, stitched on a silk ground and hemp backing. It was discovered in 1908 and subjected to a first restoration campaign in 1912 and a new one in 2017 (Tamburini et al., 2019b). From the point of view of analytical investigations, after the visual examination and SEM EDX (Scanning Electron Microscopy with Energy Dispersive X-Ray analysis) analyses, 25 samples of about 3 mm (from 50 to 150 µg) were taken to obtain a complete overview on the dyes and mordant salts employed. The extraction was performed through a DMSO solution, at 80 °C for 10 min. Also in this case, a second extraction was performed with a solution of methanol/acetone/water/0.5 M oxalic acid 30:30:40:1 (v/v/v/v), heated at 80 °C for 15 min. After centrifugation and evaporation, the two solutions were combined and further centrifugated prior to injection in the HPLC system. The analyses confirmed the use of alum mordant for red and purple color, respectively anthraquinone and naphtoquinone dyes, while iron mordant was associated with tannins. The other dyes, for the pink, yellows, blue and green, were used as direct or vat dyes. Brown color was obtained by tannin-based dyes, probably from *Quercus acutissima*, one of the most common sources. In this case, degradation products of silk, such as 4-hydroxybenzoic acid and 2-hydroxybenzoic acid, were also identified and could be easily considered as degradation production of the tannin dyes, but their presence in every samples make them referable to degradation process of the fiber (Degano et al., 2011); in that case, the latter hypothesis is more likely to be considered, because of the poor preservation state of the silk embroidery threads. Blue colors, also the base for green yarns, showed different shades and two different profiles were obtained: a first one with indigotin as the main compound, together with isatin, indirubin, isoindigotin (an isomer of indigotin) while the second one showed the same compounds but with indirubin as the same one, indicative of two different dye sources. In this case, however, as reported by the author, even if different plants have effectively been used traditionally, from *Indigofera tinctoria* to *Isatis tinctoria* but also *Polygonum tinctorium* and *Strobilanthes cusia* (syn. *Baphicacanthus cusia*), the latter two in the Chinese tradition (Cardon, 2007), a discrimination should always be done with a critical thought, because the components of their extracts essentially the same and the environmental, conservation conditions, together with dye bath etc., can strongly influence the final dye pattern fixed on the yarn, making the identification of the primary source extremely difficult (Tamburini et al., 2019b). The yellow dyes showed two different profiles also in this case: one is to be referred to flavonoid dyes, due to the present of luteolin, apigenin and their glycosides, extremely common in different plant extracts. The second profile reported the presence of berberine and its degradation product. Nonetheless, no other alkaloids were found, even if they are reported by the literature, probably suggesting another plant employed to obtain this dye, not the traditional Chinese ones such as *Phellodendron amurense* or *P. chinense*. Also in this case, several factors can influence the final dye composition, such as the part of the plant used to obtain the dye bath, the dye bath condition (in terms of pH, temperature, etc.) and the degradation process, which bring the authors to only hypothesize the dye provenance. Pink color was composed by carthamin and two degradation products of carthamin, related to the use of safflower (*Carthamus tinctorius*), a very light sensitive dye. Together with that, some flavonoids were detected, which could be related to the use of other plants but also to a dyeing process used in antiquity: safflower dye bath required the adjustment of the pH and natural substances were used to obtain this condition in ancient times (e.g. dark plum juice), which could explain the presence of other compounds. Different red dyes sources were also employed; some yarns showed the presence of madder dye compounds, while other again flavonoid compounds. Other red yarns showed some unknown compounds, which still require further investigation on Chinese ancient dyeing culture (Tamburini et al., 2019b).

Moving forward in soft extraction methods, some papers have presented new protocols based on milder acid conditions, such as formic acid (FA:MeOH, 5:95, v/v) at 40 °C for 30 min and H_2EDTA: acetonitrile: MeOH (2:10:88, v/v/v) at 60 °C for 30 min by Zhang and Laursen, to avoid glucosyl moieties disruption (Zhang & Laursen, 2005). The formic acid method was successfully employed by Zhang in the investigation of archaeological remains from mortuary and settlement sites, including mummified bodies, from Xinjiang Province, China, dated from about 1400 BC to the late first millennium BC. The textiles for dye analyses were extracted through the formic acid procedure and analyses through LC-DAD-MS analyses. The blues were indigoids, the yellow dyes were several flavonoid-based dyes with their glycosyl components. They hypothesized the use of *Reseda luteola* L., which should be confirmed by palaeoethobotanical study on southwest Xinjiang area, to understand if this plant was grown in that area. Also, glycosyl dyes from madder were identified, such as lucidin primeveroside, ruberythric acid, etc. (Zhang et al., 2008).

Together with these methods, acetic acid (Hofenk de Graaff, 2004) or trifluoroacetic acid (TFA), citric acid and oxalic acid (Valianou et al., 2009; Mantzouris et al., 2014) were proposed and compared by Valianou, in the following way: citric acid (5 M) or oxalic acid (1 M) or TFA (2 M) in 1:1 with a solution of MeOH:H_2O solution (1:1 v/v) at 100 °C for 15 min for citric or oxalic acid, while 10 min for TFA. The extract was then evaporated, reconstituted with DMSO, and only the upper solution was injected for HPLC analysis. The formic acid procedure has been slightly modified by the author, which uses a solution 1:1 of 5 M formic acid solution and MeOH:H$_2$O (1:1 v/v), at 100 °C for 5 min; then, a solution of EDTA 0.5 mM is added to the mixture and heated for another 5 min (Valianou et al., 2009). Even if the TFA could significantly reduce the efficiency of ionization if a mass spectrometer is employed because of the strong ion-pairs between TFA and dye molecules (Kostiainen & Kauppila, 2009), this method has been successfully employed in different papers, such as on silk textiles (Valianou et al., 2009; Shahid et al., 2019) for madder dyes and from Serrano et al. (2011) to develop a statistical method (through the principal component analyses) to distinguish among cochineal insects. In that case, several methods were compared, three on acid condition, formic acid-methanol, oxalic acid and TFA, plus an organic-solvent based extraction (acetone/methanol/H$_2$O), and TFA and oxalic acid seemed to provide the best results, in terms of yield of extraction and TFA for chromatographic resolution (Shahid et al., 2019; Serrano et al., 2011).

A combination of DMSO and oxalic acid extraction was used to identify the dyes in the production of barkcloth from Pacific islands (Tamburini et al., 2019a). Barkclothes, known also as tapa, are typical non-woven material made from beaten inner bark and often considered as a bast fiber (Flowers et al., 2019). Because of this origin, both dyes and earth pigments have been used together to obtain the color, traditionally; furthermore, the dyes are frequently used as a surface coating without use of a mordant, so not strongly bound to the fibers (Flowers et al., 2019). The textiles, coming from the British Museum, were subjected to a multi-analytical approach through noninvasive analyses, which led to the identification of several and a two-step extraction for the following HPLC-Q-ToF analyses. The two-step extraction procedure consisted of 200 μL of DMSO per 2–3 mm of samples, heated at 80 °C for 10 min. The residue was mixed with 200 μL of MeOH/acetone/H$_2$O/0.5 M oxalic acid 30:30:40:1 (v/v/v/v) and heated at 80 °C for 15 min to retain mild extraction conditions. The solution was evaporated and reconstituted using MeOH/H$_2$O 1:1 (v/v) and then the DMSO extract was combined with the oxalic acid extract, for the HPLC-MS analyses, following the previous literature (Han et al., 2017; Tamburini et al., 2019c). This work has provided an important overview on a type of resources of dye plants employed in contexts far from the European one, thus identifying the use of fiber referable to *Broussonetia papyrifera* (paper mulberry), *Artocarpus altilis* (breadfruit tree), *Ficus spp.* (fig/banyan) including *Ficus prolixa*, *Pipturus albidus* (māmaki) and *Hibiscus tiliaceus* (hau, beach hibiscus) thanks to SEM analyses, while the dyes employed seemed to be referred to the use of *Morinda citrifolia* (or noni), *Curcuma longa*, indigo and tannins, this latter probably from local plants, such as the bark of the kukui or candlenut tree (*Aleurites moluccana*) or the toa tree (*Casuarina equisetifolia*) (Tamburini et al., 2019a; Colantonio et al., 2022). The use of *Morinda* is recurrent in literature and even in Hawaii more than 10 plant species were identified as historic red dye sources. Most of the samples analyzed in different research so far shows that the red came from *Morinda citrifolia*, in association in some cases with an iron oxide pigment; Flowers suggested that this choice lies mainly in the stability of the dyes (Flowers et al., 2019). Moreover, for indigo samples in Tamburini's work, an important difference with common indigo mixture is reported: authors were able to detect isatin, indigotin and an oxidation product of indigotin, but not indirubin, commonly found in most indigo-containing samples, suggesting a completely different pattern for certain berries of some plants, as the *Leea indica* in Papua New Guinea and the *Dianella* spp. in the Hawaiian Islands, used to obtain the blue color (Tamburini et al., 2019a).

In another paper, from Zhang et al. (2017), a multi-technical approach is applied aiming at identifying the fiber and dyes together from archaeological textiles, from the Chinese Qing Dynasty Royal Palace (sixteenth to nineteenth century). For dye identification, four kinds of solvents or solvent mixtures were investigated to extract the yellow dye from the silk fiber, MeOH, MeOH/formic acid (FA) (95:5, v/v), MeOH/10 mM EDTA aqueous solution (9:1, v/v) and MeOH/FA/10 mM EDTA aqueous solution (85:5:10, v/v/v), all of them at 60 °C for 50 min. In this case, the separation was performed on a UHPLC coupled with a Q-ToF mass spectrometer, to also have the MS/MS information. The method with MeOH, FA and 10 mM EDTA gave the best results, highlighting that higher concentration of EDTA could interfere with the extraction effectiveness (Zhang et al., 2017). Similarly, for Liu et al. (2011) the results were compared with the UHPLC-MS profile of the water extract from some plants, traditionally employed to obtain yellow shades, in particular the *Sophora japonica* L.'s (huaimi) buds and flowers, the cortex of *Phellodendron amurense* Rupr., *Gardenia* and turmeric, evaluating differences in fingerprints of their extracts. The authors were able to hypothesize that the textiles were not dyed with only one kind of plants, but with the cortex of *Phellodendron amurense* Rupr., due to the presence of barberine, and the flowers and buds of *Sophora japonica* L. This fact represents the first demonstration of these two plants used together to dye bright yellow textiles in Chinese culture (Zhang et al., 2017). It is also worth noting that the absence of some compounds, expected to be in the textile's extract, such as the quercetin, should always suggest further evaluation, as it could be indicative of environmental conditions (light, water, temperature, soil, etc.) that have led to the alteration and degradation of some of the chromophores; the quercetin, for example is, as the authors reported, is unstable (Zhang et al., 2017).

A further method based on softer acid condition is the extraction through HF in organic solvent, firstly proposed by Sanyova (2008) for lake-pigments and more recently employed by Leona and other authors for SERS analyses.

Unlike using acids is the approach in a basic environment, starting from the proposal of the use of pyridine/water/1.0 M oxalic acid in water (95:95:10) at 100 °C for 15 min, even if the use of pyridine should be avoided for health issues (Mouri & Laursen, 2012).

Good extraction yields and results in the extraction of the glycosylated component come also from the ammonia method, proposed by some of the authors themselves, which first showed better extraction efficiency than the DMF method (Lombardi et al., 2016) and revealed how, by modifying the extraction process, some compounds considered as markers of Polish cochineal, were present in the American cochineal as well (Serafini et al., 2017).

A completely different approach based on the use of aqueous solution of 0.4% d-(+)-glucose to extract 2 mg wool sample at 90 °C for 15 mins (in a ratio of 1:1

mass ratio of glucose to wool sample), which avoids the use of acid conditions and extracts glycosyl moieties thanks to hydrogen bonding interactions. The authors also analyzed three different sources of madder, Iranian, Turkish and English madder, hypothesizing for each of them a different compositional profile and comparing these profiles with the extract of the same dyed wool samples (Ford et al., 2017).

Various extraction methods have been proposed and the different case studies reported show the critical use of different methods, with the ultimate goal of maximizing the information content of individual analyses. It is undoubted that noninvasive approaches can strongly affect the successful use of micro-invasive dye characterization: when a hypothesis of which class of dyes is present on the textiles, it is easier to develop a tailored extraction protocol to maximize the yield, looking always at preserving all the components of the dye mixture.

Another point that should be considered is also the amount of sample available. The objective is to evaluate extraction methods that are as mild as possible to respect the internal molecular pattern and allow characterization from a minimum quantity of material (Campos Ayala et al., 2021), which generally varies from 1 mg to few μg. However, thanks to increasingly sophisticated and sensitive techniques, it is opening the possibility of pushing toward the identification of the entire molecular pattern of the dye mixture by being able to strongly reduce the amount of material sampled. In this context, several techniques which move in that direction; some of them do not involve canonical extraction but allow direct dye analysis in the MS system without prior sample preparation or through imaging spectrometric approach (Shahid et al., 2019; Newsome & Martin, 2023). Others, instead, involve an *in situ* micro-extraction process, such as the gel system, effectively extracting the dye but without resorting to actual sampling of the textile material.

Going into details, matrix desorption/ionization time of flight mass spectrometry (MALDI-ToF-MS) or laser desorption mass spectrometry (LDI-MS) are methods that have been successfully applied to the study of pigments and dyes in archaeological objects and in archeological textiles; for example, LDI-MS has been used to evaluate the possibility of obtaining a mass spectral fingerprint of shellfish purple and consequently applied to some archeological ceramics (Ribechini et al., 2013) or to evaluate colorants in Roman make-ups by Van Elslande et al. (2008). Its first application to textiles is provided by Wyplosz, on an ancient Peruvian red dyed fiber, to identify madder dyes main components (Wyplosz, 2003). In this case, together with alizarin and other known compounds, there are some peaks that seem assignable to aluminum complex of the dyes, confirming the possibility of applying of this technique directly to dyed fiber, even if the same authors report that interpretation of the spectra is very complex for the sample.

Kramell offered another example of MALDI-TOF mass spectrometric analysis on wool and silk textiles from the archeological site of Niya, in the Tarim basi, Xinjian, China dated second century BC- fifth century AD) or from Icham culture, Peru, date 1100–1400 AD (Kramell et al., 2014). In this paper, the authors investigate a further application of this technique: because the MALDI-TOF is applied in different fields, such as forensics, as MS Imaging to investigate traces of substances and their spatial distribution on fibers, Kramell develops a method to obtain similar information for natural dyes on archeological textiles. In particular, the authors evaluate different sample preparation and assessed the optimal conditions (such as the proximity to the probe, the necessity of some differences in the z-axis that should be corrected with a calibrant before and after the acquisition), also highlighting some limits. For example, direct laser on sensitive fiber, like silk, can cause damage and could prevent this technique's use on this type of material. For this reason, to obtain spatial information on textiles, the fiber was immersed in paraffin, to produce thin sections to avoid irregular signal intensity, mass shifts or sample damage. The method was then successfully applied to the previously mentioned textiles and the MS spectra and distribution of indigo dyes was obtained (Kramell et al., 2019) (Fig. 6.6).

A different application of direct analysis through MS spectrometry is reported in the work of Campos Ayala (Campos Ayala et al., 2021), where an interesting comparison among LC-MS and direct analysis in real time time-of-flight mass spectrometry (DART-MS) and paper spray MS were presented. The work is focused on the study different textiles from Paracas Necropolis and from the Michael C. Carlos Museum, from which textiles from Nazca, Wari and Lambayeque civilization were considered (dated from 100 CE to 1450 CE). It is interesting to note how the authors highlight some preliminary differences and limits of DART-MS analyses refer to LC, such as the difficulty to distinguish structural isomers, such as indigotin and indirubin, or alizarin and xanthopurpurin, most of the anthraquinone structures in cochineal, because of the absence of a chromatographic separation. In detail, authors report how yellow colorants are difficult to differentiate with DART-MS alone because of the source cause complex spectra for mixtures (Campos Ayala et al., 2021; Day et al., 2013). Unlike DART and paper spray, LC analyses require sampling and extraction that are extremely critical step in the dye's identification. So, in this case, the results from the two techniques, ambient ionization (through DART-MS and paper spray) and LC-MS were compared to further evaluate the promise of

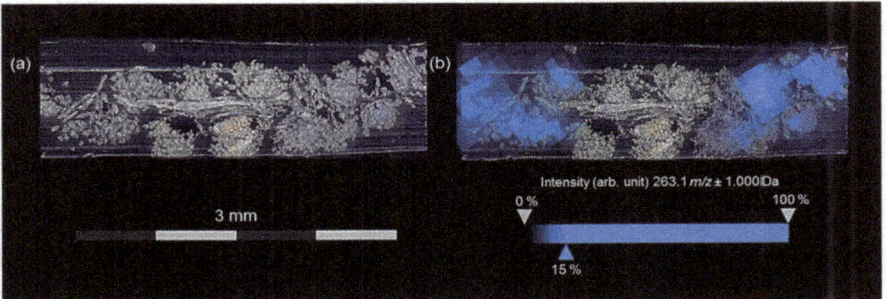

Fig. 6.6 MALDI-TOF-MS imaging results for Technovit7100-embedded fabric sections of a historic fabric fragment (sample ID: 95MNIM5-43B). (**a**) Optical image of a Technovit7100-embedded fabric section. (**b**) Visualization of indigo (m/z 262. 1 [M]•+ and m/z 263.1 [M + H]+) and measured in reflector positive mode with Universal MALDI matrix (half-transparent overlay of an optical image and MALDI-TOF-MS imaging data). (Reproduced by Kramell et al. (2019). Copyright 2019 Nature, Scientific reports)

these instruments. For the analyses of blue yarns, indigo is obviously the main source, and different species are ascribed as potential matrices for it, such as *I. suffructosa* and *I. truxillensis*, *Cybistax antisyphilitica*, or other such species native to South America (Campos Ayala et al., 2021). The results confirm the difficulties of DART in differentiating isomers, so basically observing one peak for indigo and indirubin; furthermore, due to an extreme sensitivity of this technique to indigoids, their peak often dominates the spectra; for paper spray, due to solubility issues of indigoids, the signal is very variable in paper spray mass spectra, making this technique not perfectly suitable for this class of dye. Obviously, LC-DAD analyses perfectly fit with the purpose of identifying the two different isomers, even if the authors observed that the ratio of indigotin / indirubin, suggested to be indicative of the dyeing process or other conditions in the preparation, are variable depending on which wavelength has been used for integration. Furthermore, samples extracted in DMSO changed color, from blue to reddish-purple, after the extraction, which wasn't followed immediately by LC-DAD analyses. This difference in color can be considered diagnostic of a molecular shift from indigotin to indirubin in solution, as demonstrated by the analyses that showed only the indirubin peak. The re-extracted sample, with methanol/HCl, instead revealed the presence of both isomers, with a higher concentration of indigotin (Campos Ayala et al., 2021). For red plant sources, LC-DAD identified the purpurin as the main component, together with other aglycone compounds; DART-MS is not able to distinguish between the isomers, such as alizarin and xanthopurpurin but also in UV-Vis detection mode it is hard to distinguish them, because of their similar spatial structure (they differ only for the position of one hydroxyl group). However, when DART-MS is employed under collision- induced dissociation conditions, reference samples of alizarin and xanthopurpurin yielded different mass spectra, as reported by Armitage and Szostek (Armitage et al., 2015; Szostek et al., 2003). Nonetheless, the complexity of the dyed yarn spectra obtained in this condition still doesn't allow a unique differentiation between these compounds. The anthraquinones from cochineal, such as carminic acid, dcofka—the O-glucopyranoside of flavokermesic acid, etc. aren't effectively identified through DART-MS; the author suggested the reason could be that these cannot be desorbed from the fibers solely by heat. Paper spray instead worked with the extracted solution for HPLC. For the yellow dyes, several peaks related to degradation products were found and the identification wasn't possible; in some cases, both DART-MS and LC analyses were able to detect signals referable to a specific source, the *Bidens andicola*, also thanks to reference materials. For other color, the authors confirmed that the success of DART-MS analyses depend on the mordants employed, such as Fe, Sn and Cu, and how the mordant and dye bind to cellulose and proteinaceous fibers, at least for some dyes, i.e. logwood (Campos Ayala et al., 2021).

Direct analyses on the fiber through MS analyses were presented also by Kramell, through a micro-extraction in situ, assessed with a flowprobe-electrospray ionization-high-resolution mass spectrometry (flowprobe- ESI-HRMS) (Kramell et al., 2017). This real-time in situ microextraction method was used to analyze different textiles, from south American and Chinese culture, proving to have a minimal invasiveness, without modifying the color of the spot analyzed. In this system, a couple of coaxial capillaries (probe outer diameter 1/4630 mm) are positioned close to the surface of the object and a continuous solvent flow forms a liquid microjunction between the probe and the sample surface and the extracted analytes are delivered to the ESI mass spectrometers. The study is performed on wool, silk and cotton yarns dyed with indigo-type and anthraquinone dyes; the system revealed the use of a cochineal dye and of a dye gained from plants of the Rubiaceae family for the investigated red hues and the use of the indigo for blue colorations. The confirmation of dye sources was notrelated to the materials or the state of conservation. However, the compounds identified were not sufficient to discriminate the specific source employed and the authord suggest coupling the system with a LC system, to differentiate the minor components (Kramell et al., 2017).

A similar approach has been suggested, even if with a different technique, by Germinario et al. (2020): with a micro-gel system, in that case Agar gel and Nanorestore were investigated, soaked in an ammonia-sodium EDTA extracting solution, it is possible to extract dyes fixed on the fiber, without any "sampling" of the yarns or moving the artifact to a "convenient" location for the probe. The micro gel system, after the micro extraction from the fiber, is usable as the substrate for both SERS analysis and subsequent re-extraction and analysis by HPLC-HRMS. While the SERS identification of the dyes was successfully carried out, the re-extraction allowed the detection of alizarin from madder dye fiber, but the limit relied on the clean-up protocol of the ammonia methodology. The liquid-liquid extraction, for the extraction from 1 mg of fiber, proved to be completely ineffective in much lower concentration of dyes, such as those extracted by gel system. For this reason, a new protocol to overcome this limit has been recently developed and it has been applied to Tuthankamon tomb's relics fibers and paint layers (Serafini et al., 2023 to be resubmitted to Analytica Chimica Acta; Peruzzi et al., 2023).

6.3 Proteins

6.3.1 Spectroscopic Characterisation of Protein

Different spectroscopic methods present a high potential for the identification of proteinaceous species, like those constituting the main animal fibers. Among these methods, the vibrational spectroscopies are of great importance, and in particular, FTIR spectroscopy. The power of the technique for the identification and the study of proteins and other biological compounds is well-known and showed by several reviews in the literature (Barth, 2007; Movasaghi et al., 2008). However, it is fundamental to highlight that this power also has an impact on the characterization of ancient textile fibers, among which wool and silk must be mentioned. These fibers, both of animal origin, are constituted of proteins, specifically keratin in the case of the wool and fibroin in the case of the silk. These proteins are not the only original constituent of materials directly obtained from the animal sources, but what is obtained after their anthropic processing. The keys to address the discrimination between different proteins are multiple, from the observable differences in the spectra—which, however, should be combined with morphological analyses of sample—to application of chemometrics, to elaboration of specific statistical models from FTIR spectra. However, with reference to the high versatility of FTIR approach according to the different typologies of textile samples, it represents one of the most powerful analytical techniques for their characterization. It is commonly known that several instrumental setups are available for FTIR spectroscopy, and this versatility can be exploited for the characterization of proteinaceous textiles. One of the most common methodologies is represented by the Attenuated Total Reflection (ATR) mode, which is widely used in cultural heritage for the analysis of different typologies of materials. The principles of the techniques are remarkably described in a series of reviews and papers, so in this section only a brief description will be provided (Glassford et al., 2013). In ATR, an IR beam is directed towards a crystal material, which is in contact with the sample to analyze. This crystal material requires a high refractive index: if the IR beam is directed at above a certain "critical angle", total internal reflection is obtained, with generation of the so-called "evanescent wave" totally reflecting inside the crystal and, consequently, fully interacting with the sample on the surface, where this evanescent wave is partially absorbed, in frequency and in intensity. The exiting wave, after the absorption (and consequently called "attenuated"), is directed to the detector, with the conversion into a FTIR spectrum. It is important to highlight that the evanescent wave decays exponentially to the distance from the surface of the crystal, so this technique provides information about the surface composition of the sample in contact with that; a penetration depth is defined, according to the angle of the incident beam and to the typology of crystal and samples, in the range of 0.5–2 μm, while the actual sampling depth is around 3 times this penetration depth. The technique is remarkably sensitive, so it can be applied to very small samples, in the order of 1 mm^2. The practicality of this FTIR approach has determined a great utility for the characterization of ancient fibers. For instance, Kramell et al. (2014) used ATR for identifying if some textiles of the late Bronze Age were constituted by vegetal (cellulosic) or animal (proteinaceous) fibers: the ATR spectra, showing two bands at 1600–1690 cm^{-1} and 1490–1560 cm^{-1}, attributable to amide I and amide II vibrations respectively, were considered unambiguous for the presence of proteins, so the animal nature of the fibers was assessed. Combining this information with the morphological one deriving from the use of optical and scanning electron microscopies, it was also possible to identify the fiber as wool. In a study of 2010 (Cao et al., 2010), an ancient Chinese fabric (25–420 AD) was analyzed with ATR, and in this case the presence of amide I and amide II bands, along with the N-H stretching at around 3300 cm^{-1}, allowed identifying the presence of wool as the constituting material. About the discrimination of wool typologies, an interesting study of McGregor et al. (2018) proved the efficiency of ATR-FTIR in distinguishing keratin-based fibers on the basis of the content of specific amino acids. In this study, cashmere, hair, wool, bison, qiviut and vicuña were subjected to ATR analyses (Fig. 6.7). After identification of specific

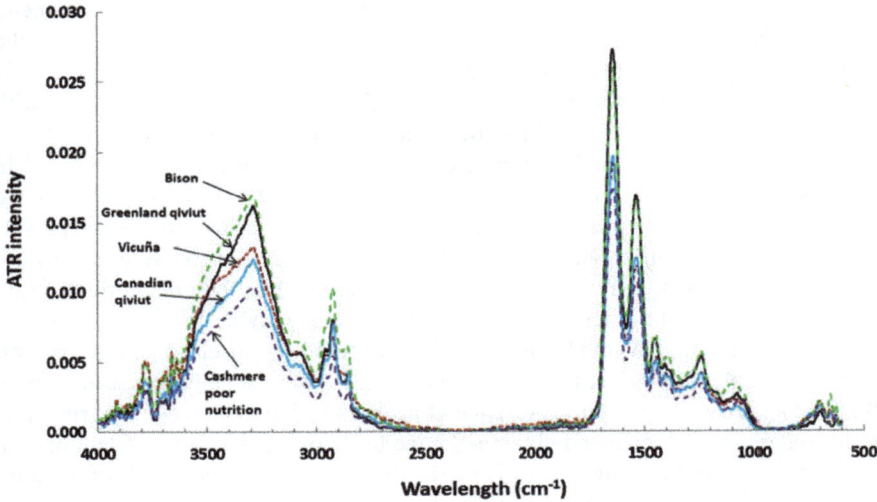

Fig. 6.7 The FTIR ATR spectra intensity for samples of vicuña, qiviut, bison and cashmere originating from the poorest nutritional treatment in the feeding experiment. Symbols to be read at wavelength 3300 cm^{-1}: bison, top dashed green line; vicuña, dotted red line; poor nutrition cashmere, lowest dashed purple line; Greenland qiviut, highest solid black line; Canadian tundra qiviut, lowest solid blue line. (Reprinted with permission from McGregor et al. (2018). Copyright 2018 Taylor & Francis)

wavenumber regions from the spectra and the calculation of the area under the bands in these regions, some parameters based on these values were calculated and correlated with the amino acids content in the different fibers. Moreover, the use of a statistical model based on random coefficient REstricted Maximum Likelihood (REML) mixed model was developed. This model provides a series of parameters, corresponding to the different spectral regions in ATR data, which differentiates samples of different typologies, showing interactions among the typology of fiber, its color and its origin in the different spectral regions. For instance, while the cashmere of Chinese origin had the highest intensity values for parameters in all the spectral regions, Chinese wool has lower values for some of them. Even if the calculated parameters could present some ambiguity in the discrimination of some fibers, the method presents a good potential for diagnostics, and a perspective could be represented by its use for the discrimination of fibers in ancient samples. However, the technique is even applied for the characterization of materials in textile samples characterized by high complexity. An interesting example is represented by the study of metal threads present in some Medieval embroideries and velvets, where organic yarn was wrapped with metal strips (Balta et al., 2017). In this case, ATR was used to investigate the composition of the different typologies of compounds present in three areas: the surface of the metal thread, the organic core and the junction area between the core and the organic yarn. The application of the ATR was successful not only for the identification of silk in the organic core, but also for the recognition of organic compounds present on the surface of metal threads, like beeswax and acacia gum, confirming the historical recipes about the manufacturing of items of that typology.

Interestingly, in this study, the ATR even allowed identifying sericin, along with fibroin, on the yarn in the core of the metal thread. The fingerprint bands at 1070 and 1400 cm^{-1} of sericin, which is a protective protein covering the fibroin fibers in native silk and which is removed by the degumming process, were used to evaluate if the original fiber was processed in the investigated objects and, in this way, it was possible to have identify historical manufacturing reported in treatises and to assess the use of raw silk in some embroideries. This method, based on the normalization of the intensity of the reference peaks with other attributable to fibroin, was proposed by Zhang and Wyeth Zhang and Wyeth (2010) and used to assess that two archaeological silk fragments from the Han dynasty were actually constituted only by fibroin, as confirmed by the presence of peaks at 975 and 1000 cm^{-1}, attributable to fibroin glycine-glycine and glycine-alanine backbone and clearly evident only in the case of reduced coating of sericin on the fibroin core. The use of ATR for studying the production technique of silk yarns was extended by de Palaminy et al. (2022). This work focused on the combination of ATR and chemometrics for the identification of the use of wild silks (obtained by non- or semi-domesticated species, like those from the Saturniidae family) in comparison to that obtained from the domestic *Bombyx mori*. The comparison of ATR spectra of wild silk spectra with those of the domestic one revealed that a peak at 965 cm^{-1} can be considered specific of the first one, and it is assigned to their higher content of polyalanine, while the spectrum of *Bombyx mori* silk presents a shoulder at 1260 cm^{-1} (fibroin β-sheet). Moreover, to discriminate unambiguously the species of silkworm, the obtained spectra were processed and characterized through chemometrics. This method, based on the second derivative spectrum of the portion between 1176 and 1239 cm^{-1} (amide III band), involved the Hierarchical Clustering and the Principal Components Analyses (HCA and PCA): the PCA score plot allowed discriminating the species *Borocera madagascariensis* from others, while the dendrogram separated efficiently these species from those of Saturniidae family, identifying potential subclasses (for instance, the species of *Epiphora bauhiniae*), Fig. 6.8. The study requires further validation, as identified by the authors, but it shows a great potential and encourages the exploitation of combining FTIR spectra with chemometrics to further deepen the set of achievable information in diagnostics. Interestingly, the matching of ATR with chemometrics represents a useful methodology also for the general discrimination of fibers: in this case, the use of microspectroscopy allowed mapping the composition of textile fragments. In the case of two-component materials, a general poor reproducibility of the spectra was observed, due primarily to the differences of contact between the ATR crystal and the fibers. For this reason, the preliminary observation of the material with a microscope and the acquisition of at least 25 spectra per sample were suggested (Peets et al., 2017). Nonetheless, this represents a good strategy for evaluating the homogeneity in composition of textiles and it could be useful to identify and differentiate the typology of fibers present in the same item. The combination with PCA increases the reliability of the analysis,

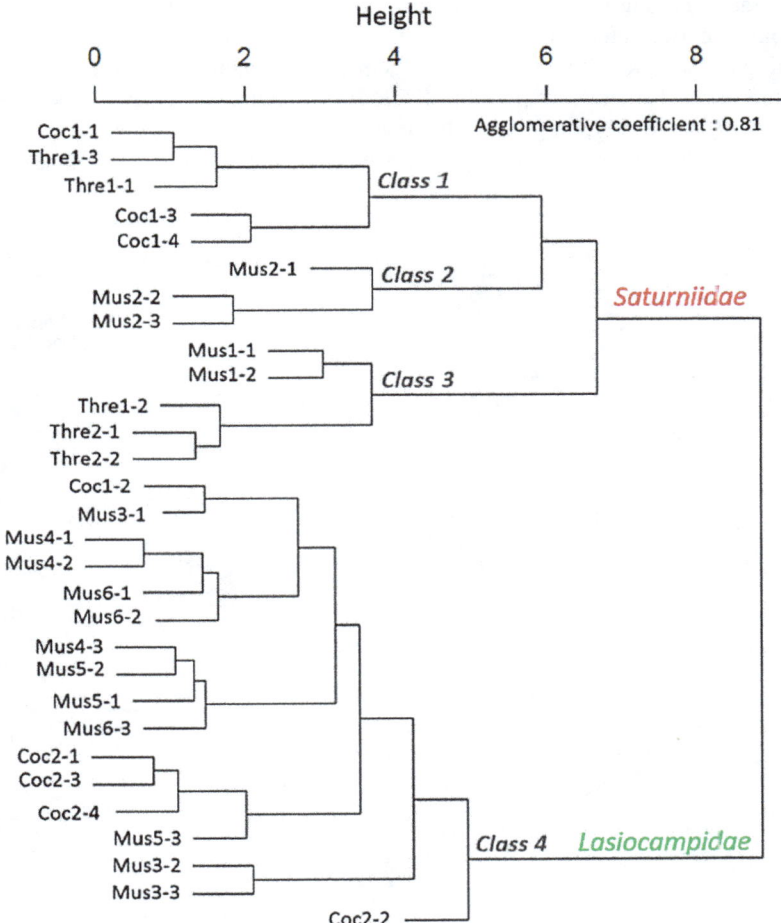

Fig. 6.8 Dendrogram obtained from the HCA of the second derivatives of the amide III band of wild silk samples (10 samples, 30 spectra) partitioned into 4 classes and 2 main groups corresponding to two different families of Lepidoptera: Lasiocampidae (class 4) and Saturniidae (classes 1, 2, 3). (Reprinted with permission from de Palaminy et al. (2022). Copyright 2022 Elsevier Ltd.)

but it is necessary to acquire a high number of reference spectra of mixed fiber textiles with different contents of the individual ones. Textiles can be made of different fibers, with different contents of the same ones (e.g.: for a textile made of two different fibers: 10–90%, 50–50%, 90–10%).

An interesting approach, which was compared to ATR for the characterization of the fibers, is represented by reflectance FTIR. In this case, the acquired spectrum results from the portion of light, which is reflected by the sample—so neither absorbed or transmitted—to the detector. This approach presents an undeniable advantage in comparison to ATR, because it is not necessary to apply pressure for the contact between the sample and the probe crystal, so this eliminates the risks of breaking the sample or the object under the piston and avoids the sampling phase—this approach characterizes portable FTIR instrumentation. In the work of Peets et al. (2019), sixteen typologies of fiber materials were investigated with reflectance FTIR and ATR, and the obtained spectra were compared (Fig. 6.9). If a general

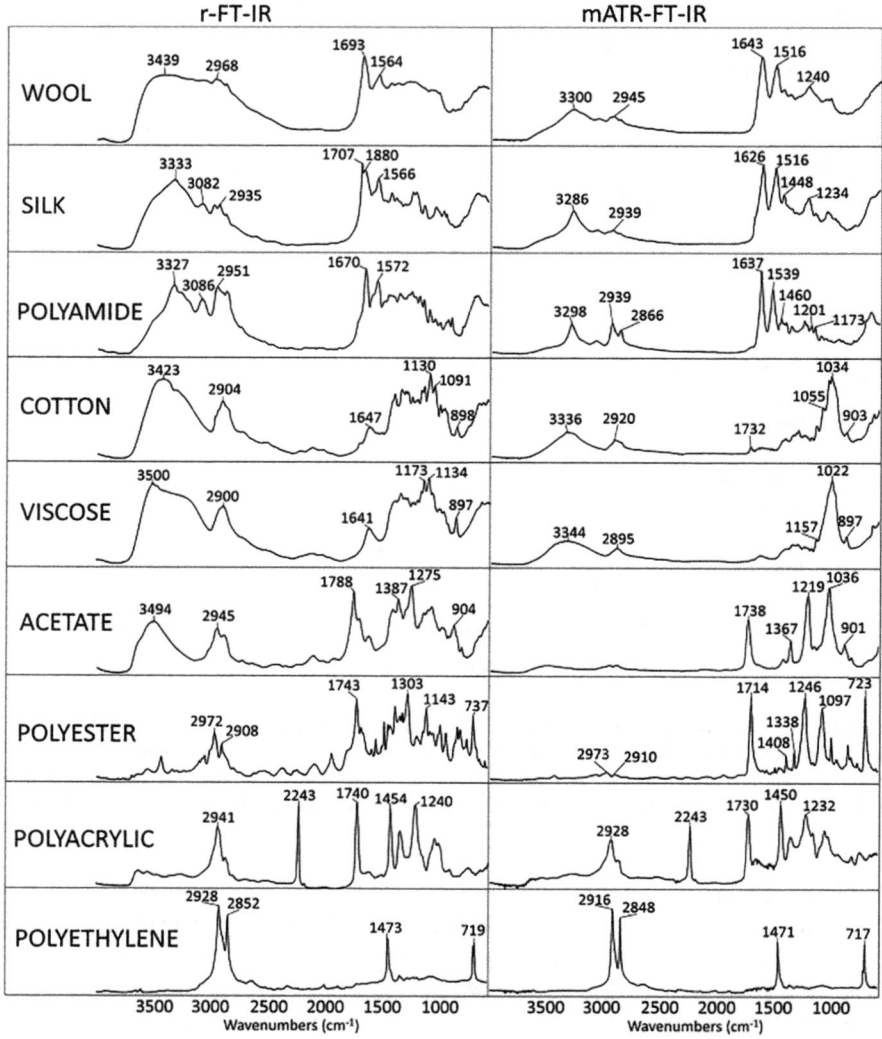

Fig. 6.9 r-FT-IR and mATR-FT-IR spectra of most common textile fibers. (Reprinted from Peets et al. (2019). The article is distributed under the terms of the Creative Commons Attribution 4.0 International License)

similarity between the spectra obtained from the two modes was observed, some differences could be detected. The main differences consist in a marked broadening of the obtained absorbance bands, along with wavenumber shifts and variation of the relative intensities of the peaks: these phenomena are attributable to the surface morphology of the fibers, which involves the combination of specular and diffuse reflectance of the radiation, with consequent deformation of spectral features. However, from the comparison with ATR spectra, it was possible to identify some interesting data from the diagnostic point of view. For instance, the spectra obtained in reflection mode for silk, wool and synthetic polyamide are remarkably different, while in ATR only slight shifts and broadening for amide I and N-H/OH stretching modes were observable. A peak at 1710 cm^{-1} was indicative of silk and distinguishes this fiber from wool fibers and the eventual compresence of polyamide fibers used in restorations. The combination of reflectance FTIR with chemometrics—both Discriminant Analysis (DA) based on Principal Component Analysis (PCA) and random forest-based machine learning algorithm—emphasized the potential of the technique. In particular, PCA showed the differences among different fibers in a space based on the first three components, which covers 88.0% of the variance, with a slight increase in comparison to the application of the same approach to ATR (87.8% of the variance).

This methodology was highly proficient in distinguishing not only proteinaceous and polyamide fibers, but also cellulose-based ones, which show higher similarities among each other. The methodology was also applied to a series of case studies, which showed that the reflectance approach presents a great potential, especially in discriminating amide-based textiles (like wool and silk), but also limitations in the case of samples of very small size or with surface contaminants. With reference to the actual advancements in the use of reflectance FTIR and to the availability of new portable FTIR spectrometers, this approach deserves further investigation and new applications to archaeological and historical textiles. Another possible approach for the identification of proteinaceous fibers is represented by Fourier-Transformed Raman Spectroscopy. This technique was used for the characterization of wool and silk, and it owns a discriminant potential. As highlighted in Section *Spectroscopic techniques: case studies* of this chapter, in comparison to standard Raman spectroscopy, FT-Raman allows acquiring spectra with a lower fluorescence background, so the vibrational pattern can be identified in a clearer way. The spectra obtained with FT-Raman and reported in the literature for wool and silk (Carter et al., 1994; Edwards & Farwell, 1995; Hogg et al., 1994) present a general high quality. Moreover, the two fibers are distinguishable from the different set of peaks, and this represents an undoubted advantage when there is ambiguity in the identification of the specific fiber. However, another strength—which makes the technique very powerful—is the possibility to identify information related to the origins and/or the processing of silk. In a study of Edwards and Farewell (Edwards & Farwell, 1995), several silk samples were analyzed with FT-Raman, from cultivated cocoons to wild silk, including raw fibers and weaved silk of different origins. The weaker bands in the 500–1800 cm^{-1} range were the most important ones to identify the main differences among the samples. For instance, the presence of a band at 1605 cm^{-1}, attributable to aromatic ring vibrations, is indicative of silk not subjected to degumming, as well as the aromatic bending at 854 cm^{-1}, while the absence of signals around 1515–1550 cm^{-1}, relatable to carotenoids, could show some chemical treatment applied to the fiber. At higher wavenumbers, the presence of a band at 2856 cm^{-1} is assigned only to cultivated silk, while the absence of the aromatic stretch at 3035 cm^{-1} is indicative of degumming, confirming previous data. From a methodological point of view, the spectra of a single silk fiber were also acquired. Some significant dissimilarities were noticed, involving shift in wavenumbers (e.g. shift of a band at 3279 cm^{-1} in the bulk sample to 3268 cm^{-1} in the single fiber) and intensity change (e.g. total disappearance of the signal at 2739 cm^{-1} in the single fiber spectrum). These variations must be considered, especially in the case of analyses on textile objects of historical or archaeological importance, where the sampling amount should be limited: if the analysis of a single fiber could represent a micro-invasive strategy, the comparison with reference samples obtained with the same setup should be mandatory to provide clear and accurate assignments. In this perspective, it would be interesting to test the FT-Raman on a series of case studies, whose number is limited in the literature and, usually, restricted to goals different from the discrimination of the specific typology of silk or wool. In this way, actual data on the performativity of this approach would be reported and a trustable evaluation of the advantages and drawbacks of the technique for diagnostics on historical matrices would be provided.

6.3.2 Spectrometric Characterization of Protein

Even if the first recovery of ancient protein was assessed through Edman degradation sequencing in 1990, it is in 2000 that for the first-time soft ionization MALDI-TOF is applied to detect protein osteocalcin from modern and ancient bones (Warinner et al., 2022; Ostrom et al., 2000). From here on out, thanks to the advance in mass spectrometry, especially with the introduction of the Orbitrap technology, mass spectrometry has become the leading technique for the identification of proteins in archaeological materials.

As stated in the introduction, an exhaustive and comprehensive review of all case studies in which mass spectrometry methods have been applied to the study of archaeological textile materials is beyond the scope of this chapter, and so the authors refer for further details and insights to extremely comprehensive reviews on the subject (Solazzo, 2019; Warinner et al., 2022). However, from the perspective of analytical methods for the study of textile materials, this section aims to provide an overview to stimulate the interest on this aspect and to underline the potential and possibilities of the current analytical techniques.

Proteins are biomolecules, which, starting from linear amino acidic chains, encoded by DNA and transcribed from RNA, built up in three-dimensional structures that preserve a part of this genetic signal of the organism; this fact makes them suitable to the purpose of taxonomic identifications and phylogenic reconstruction

(Warinner et al., 2022; Lee et al., 2022). Their chemical structure guarantees them a very longevity, over millions of years, more than the DNA: some specific proteins, such as the secreted hair keratins or silk fibroins, can last over centuries (Warinner et al., 2022). Keratins, coming from animal hair, are the most common proteins composing textiles (Solazzo, 2019). Fibers that come from mammalian hairs are composed of three structural parts: cuticle cells, which compose the outermost layer, and overlap following specific scale patterns (useful for microscopy identification); the cortex, made of macrofibrils and for some species a medulla as the central part. Macrofibrils are composed of longitudinally intermediate filaments (IFs) of trichocyte keratin, together with keratin-associated proteins (KAPs), that build the matrix surrounding the intermediate filaments (Solazzo, 2019).

Keratins are proteins generally composed of 400–500 amino acidic residues, divided into two types: acid type, Is, (from K31 to K40) and neutral-basic type, IIs, (from K81 to K87). A right-handed alpha-helix constitutes the central rod domain (segments 1A, 1B, 2A and 2B) that is interrupted by some amorphous segments called linkers (L1, L12 and L2) and ends by a long amorphous head and tail (N-terminus and C-terminus) (Solazzo, 2019; Plowman, 2018). Keratin associated proteins (KAPs) are a larger group of proteins, divided into High-sulfur (HSPs), ultra-high-sulfur (UHSPs) and High glycine-tyrosine (HGTPs) proteins (Solazzo, 2019), which are bound to the keratins through disulfide bridges in their head and tail regions. The interactions between KAPS and keratins influence the mechanical properties of the fibers; these interactions occur through phenomena of inter- and intra-molecular cross-linking of the amino acid cysteine residues, through the formation of disulfide bridges (Solazzo, 2019; Deb-Choudhury et al., 2015; Plowman, 2018).

Silk is instead a highly oriented and crystalline proteinaceous fiber consisting mainly of fibroin and sericin proteins. It is composed of two filaments of fibroin: one is a heavy chain, so-called H-fibroin, and the second considered as the light chain, L-fibroin, where sericin acts as glue. The molecular weights of the two chains are 350,000 Da and 25,000 Da, respectively. The two chains are linked by a single disulfide bridge, because of cysteine in the two chains (Tanaka et al., 1999; Inoue et al., 2000; Garside & Wyeth, 2007; Sionkowska & Planecka, 2011; Vilaplana et al., 2015). A third component indicated by Inoue, the glycoprotein P25, is present in lower proportion than the two others, exactly 6:6:1 molar ratio, but it is associated with the H- and L-fibroins by noncovalent forces (Vilaplana et al., 2015). The heavy fibroin chain consists of a primary structure of 20 amino acids; the most important are glycine (Gly) 45.9%, alanine (Ala) 30.3%, serine (Ser) 12.1% and tyrosine (Tyr) 5.3%. Inside the chain, there is an alternating of crystalline and amorphous regions. The principal component of the crystalline regions is a dipeptide motif, composed by Gly and a second amino acidic residue, which can be Ala, Ser or Tyr, with a relative abundance of 65%, 23% and 9%, respectively. These dipeptide units are arranged in two hexapeptides, counting for the 70% of this domain, that are: Gly-Ala-Gly-Ala-Gly-Ser, the most abundant, and Gly-Ala-Gly-Ala-Gly-Tyr (Vilaplana et al., 2015). The dipeptides are further distributed in 12 "crystalline" domains, folded in β-sheets packs, with varying length between 39 and 612 amino acid residues, separated by identical copies of boundary "amorphous" sequences (Vilaplana et al., 2015). The β-sheet packs are strongly aligned with the axis of fibers when the filaments are extruded, and are embedded in those amorphous regions, rich in residues with bulky and polar side chains (Garside & Wyeth, 2007). The amorphous regions break the dimer alternations and terminate the crystalline regions. In these regions, however, distorted β-sheets are present (Asakura et al., 2002). Nonetheless, if its chemical and physical properties affect its excellent mechanical performances, some research papers show that the same protein composition and the presence of amorphous regions makes it easily attacked by water, light, heat and microorganisms (Huang et al., 2013; Zhang & Yuan, 2010; Szostak-Kotowa, 2004). Moreover, silk fibroin contains some light-sensitive amino acids, such as phenylalanine, tryptophan and tyrosine (Boersma et al., 2007).

The initial identification of the textile fibers takes place through optical microscopy and is mainly based on identifying diagnostic characters of fibers, such as the shapes of the cuticula, the diameter of the fibers, the presence of the medulla, etc. However, this technique is highly dependent on the presence of a good database to distinguish between the inter- and intra- species differences and on the state of conservation of the textiles. Together with FTIR, as described in previous sections of this chapter, mass spectrometry is proving to be the technique of choice for the identification of fibers and for the identification of species.

The preparation of the samples is obviously different in the case of silk or wool. In the case of silk, this can be denatured in a solution of calcium chloride, ethanol, and water, generally at 95 °C and then digested with chymotrypsin, in solution or in gel. Wool, on the other hand, can be effectively extracted in a urea solution with a pH higher than 8 with the presence of reducing agents, (such as TCEP-HCl, etc.) to break the disulfide bonds, the reformation of which is prevented with a subsequent alkylation process, for example with iodoacetamide. In the case of soil contamination, urea has reduced effectiveness, so, recently, a new extraction at 95 °C with TCEP HCl and CAA gave the best results (Solazzo & Niepold, 2023). The extraction can be followed by a desalting procedure, such as paramagnetic beads (Solazzo & Niepold, 2023; Cleland, 2018) and then the trypsin digestion in solution. Subsequently, after a short purification, mass spectrometry analysis is carried out.

As mentioned, mass spectrometry analysis of archaeological textiles is certainly an extremely powerful tool, but a correct interpretation of the data requires some key aspects: although proteins endure much longer than even DNA, the identification of species is achieved through key markers, better if multiple markers, generally identified with altered profiles due to modifications that can occur (such as oxidation, deamidation, carbamidomethylation, etc.). Some of them can be referred to the aging process, some can be induced by the preparation of the samples (Solazzo, 2019).

Of particular interest in demonstrating the potential of the spectrometric approach in proteomic investigation is the work of Azémard, in which some archaeological textiles from two different sites in China have been characterized to their genus and species, in most cases (Azémard et al., 2019). Some fibers from eastern Xinjiang region, mainly dated at Iron and Bronze Ages, were studied. As mentioned earlier, this region is in the eastern part of Central Asia and represent a key point for commercial routes in ancient Asia, as part of Silk Roads; from this comes the importance that the study of such textile artifacts has for understanding the customs and aspects and cross-cultural contacts of ancient civilizations (Azémard et al., 2019). However, in approaching any proteomic study of fibers, as the author points out, one must consider that some difficulties arise. In the case of wool, keratins are characterized by high sequence similarity between keratins in closely related species (Plowman, 2007): for example, sheep and goat can be distinguished looking at diagnostic maker, a fragment of acid keratin K33, which differs by only one amino acid between the two species (Azémard et al., 2019; Solazzo et al., 2013, 2014a). In this sense, the authors underline the importance of further studies, to define new marker peptides, which are essential for improving the identification of archaeological fibers. Furthermore, the situation obviously becomes more complicated when the textile comes from an excavation such as the archaeological ones and has therefore been subjected to degradation and alteration processes, such as thermal processes (from pyre burials, volcano eruptions, etc.), burial, etc. which induced a series of modifications in the protein sequences. In the work of Azémard, the extraction was performed through 25 mM Tris-HCl, 2.4 M thiourea, 5 M urea (pH 8.5), and dithiothreitol (DTT, 100 mM) and then reduction and alkylation through DTT and iodoacetamide, respectively, before the trypsin digestion. Once the solution obtained is purified through C8 cartridge, it is analyzed by LC-MS. In the analyses of the data obtained by the mass analyses, the carbamidomethylation of cysteine was considered as a fixed modification and deamidation of glutamine and asparagine as well as oxidation of methionine and lysine carbamylation as variable modifications. Here in Table 6.1 is reported the table in which peptide markers has been identified.

As reported by the authors, the peptide coming from keratin type I K33B can be considered a good marker for the specificity in sheep (YSCQLSQVQSLIVNVESQLAEIR), goat (YSCQLNQVQSLIVNVESQLAEIR), human (primate, YSSQLSQVQRLITNVESQLAEIR), camel (YGSQLSQVQGLITNVEHQLAEIR) and undetermined caprine (YSCQLNQVQSLISNVESQLAEIR) (Solazzo et al., 2013; Clerens et al., 2010; Azémard et al., 2019). Along with that, the authors identify some other peptides specific to non-Bovidae and Bovidae, such as goat, sheep, cattle, camel. They identify a new non-cattle marker from keratin K31, GDLERQNQEYQVLLDVR, present in various mammals but not in cattle species, while some specific regions in type II keratins are instead specific to cattle, in the N-terminal and central region of the proteins, in particular AGYCSR, GLNMDNIVAEIK, and GLNMDNIVAEIKAQYDDIASR from keratin K83 and ALPAFSCVSACGPRPGR from keratin K86. Also, KAP can offer some specific markers, such as SSCCQPCCLPIR for cattle, SLCGSGYGYGSR for non-cattle Bovidae, and TSTLSRPCQTTYSGSLGFGSR for camel (Azémard et al., 2019) (Table 6.1). Other specific peptides of interests can be found also in the work of Solazzo et al. (2013).

In this work of peptide inference, the authors highlight how database incompleteness and intra-specific sequence variability may alter the study of protein specificity. At the end, on a total of 109 objects, the authors were able to identify 64 as

Table 6.1 List of peptide markers used to distinguish among species

Attribution	Sequence	Best match keratin	Number of observations	Mean scare ± sd	Reference
Type I keratin markers					
Sheep	YSCQLSQVQSLIVNVESQLAEIR	K33b	62	92.0 ± 14.6	Clerens et al. (2010) and Solazzo et al. (2013)
Goat	YSCQLNQVQSLIVNVESQLAEIR	K31, K33a	13	99.7 ± 13.8	Clerens et al. (2010) and Solazzo et al. (2013)
Non-caprine (cattle, deer)	YSCQLAQVQGLIGNVESQLAEIR	K31, K33a	9	127.7 ± 12.8	Clerens et al. (2010) and Solazzo et al. (2013)
Caprine (sheep, goat)	YSCQLNQVQSLISNVESQLAEIR	K31	45	78.1 ± 24.1	Clerens et al. (2010) and Solazzo et al. (2013)
Cattle deer	ILERSQQQEPLLCPNYQSYFR	K31	4	28.5 ± 4.2	This study
Non-cattle (various mammals)	GDLERONQEYQVLLDVR	K31	81	33.2 ± 110	This study
Non-cattle (various mammals)	ARLESEINTYR	K31, K33	90	39.3 ± 13.5	Clerens et al. (2010) and Solazzo et al. (2013)
Non-cattle (various mammals)	LESEINTYR	K31, K33	97	70.9 ± 10.6	Clerens et al. (2010) and Solazzo et al. (2013)
Goat	CGPCSSYVR	K31	15	41.2 ± 11.9	This study
Non-goat (cattle, sheep, deer)	CGPCNSYVR	K31	33	31.8 ± 15.5	Clerens et al. (2010) and Solazzo et al. (2013)

Camel	YGSQLSQVQCLITNVEHQLAEIR	K33	1	81	Solazzo et al. (2013)
Camel	CGPCNTFMR	K33a	1	32	This study
Camelid	QTEELNKQVVSSSEQLQSNQAEIIELRR	K33a	1	37	This study
Primate	YSSQLSQVQSLITNVESQLAEIR	K33a	2	99.5 ± 3.5	This study
Primate	YSSQLSQVQR	K31	2	75.0 ± 11.3	This study
Primate	LITNVESQLAEIR	K31	2	95.5 ± 9.2	This study
Primate	DNAELENLIR	K31, K33a	2	60.0 ± 2.8	This study
Type II keratin markers					
Non-cattle (various mammals)	DLNMDCIVAEIKAQYDDIASR	K83	22	13.7 ± 10.0	Clerens et al. (2010)
Caprine (sheep, goat)	GGVACGGLTYSSTAGR	K85	64	60.6 ± 17.5	Clerens et al. (2010) and Solazzo et al. (2013)
Non-caprine (cattle, deer)	GGVTCGGLTYSTTAGR	K85	9	78.0 ± 30.9	Solazzo et al. (2013)
Goat	(K)SDLEANAEALIQETDFLR(R)	K81	10	23.8 ± 12.5	This study
Cattle and primate	(K)SDLEANVEALIQEIDFLR	K81	4	18.8 ± 6.2	Solazzo et al. (2013)
Cattle	AGYCSR	K83	2	16.0 ± 14.1	This study
Cattle	GLNMDNIVAEIKAQYDDIASR	K83	3	45.3 ± 23.6	This study
Cattle	GLNMDNIVAEIK	K83	4	86.3 ± 6.2	Solazzo et al. (2013)
Cattle	ALPAFSCVSACGPRPGR	K86	5	32.2 ± 12.7	Solazzo et al. (2013)
Goat, horse, deer	AFSCVSACGPRPSR	K81	17	15.7 ± 6.8	This study
Sheep	QIASGPVATGGSITVLAPDSCQPR	K85	26	15.6 ± 14.2	Clerens et al. (2010) and Solazzo et al. (2013)

(continued)

Table 6.1 (continued)

Attribution	Sequence	Best match keratin	Number of observations	Mean scare ± sd	Reference
Non-sheep	QIASGPVATGGSITVLAPDSCVPCQPR	K85	6	22.2 ± 16.0	Solazzo et al. (2013)
Camelid	DLNLDCIVAEIKEQYDDIAR	K81	1	54	This study
Primate	GGVVCGDLCASTTAPVVSTR	K86	1	54	This study
Human	VSSVPSNSNVVVGTTNACAPSAR	K86	1	39	This study
KAPs markers					
Caprine (sheep, goat) and cattle	(R)FWPFALY	–	72	15.1 ± 1.8	Clerens et al. (2010)
Cattle	SSCCQPCCLPIR	–	1	26	This study
Non-cattle (caprine, deer, antelope)	SLCGSGYGYGSR	–	3	59.3 ± 11.2	Clerens et al. (2010) and Solazzo et al. (2013)
Camel	TSTLSRPCQTTYSGSLGFCSR	–	1	39	This study

Reprinted with permission from Azémard et al. (2019). Copyright 2019 Elsevier Ltd sheep, 17 as goat, 14 as undetermined caprine, and 9 as cattle, with a protein percentage coverage from 14% and 62% for the archeological samples; this identification helped the historians and the archaeologists to deduce that between the two sites there were similarities in fabrication and use of textiles. In particular, the authors were able to address the use of these fibers to a particular use: camel and human fibers seemed to be used occasionally, while the Bronze Age sheep were preferred to produce wool textiles, the goats employed mostly for furs and pelts, the cattle for shoes, while the shoelaces are made from sheep or undetermined caprine fibers.

An important parameter that should be considered in evaluating the proteomic profile of ancient fiber is the deamidation ratio, a value extensively studied and discussed for the information it can provide from the study of an archaeological artifact, as in the case of the study of two groups of artifacts from UK and Iceland proposed by Solazzo et al. (2014b). Deamidation has been a marker of degradation and a possible indication of aging in archeological and in general artistic protein-based materials; it is based on the degradation of two specific amino acids, asparagine (N) and glutamine (Q) that are converted in aspartic (D) and glutamic (E) acids or pyroglutamic acid (5-oxoproline), through a non-enzymatic reaction. In the previous paper of Azémard, the value of deamidation for archaeological fibers was the double of modern samples, around 46.8% for the archaeological textiles, 24.3% and 25.6% for goat and sheep modern samples. In Solazzo et al.'s paper, authors start its evaluation looking at deamidation rates on N and Q in 8 specific peptides in two groups of buried textiles: one coming from York (UK) sites, some dated ninth to thirteenth centuries (9 samples) and some tenth to eleventh centuries, and the other group from Iceland, dated thirteenth to sixteenth centuries, composed of 8 samples. This study, based also on a model study on dyed and undyed wool samples, elucidates some preferential mechanisms or conditions of deamidation in archaeological tissues and highlights some aspects that may favor or disfavor these degradative mechanisms in the relics and thus cannot be disregarded in the evaluation of this parameter. Starting from the model study, which is focused on 8 peptides, part of the central rod domain of alpha keratins, chosen as makers of deamidation, in conditions of accelerated aging dyed samples showed a higher deamidation value than undyed wool. Together with this, the buried textiles demonstrated that the burial conditions play a fundamental role in preservation of textiles and thus the degradation process. In fact, the Iceland samples appeared to be older in comparison to the UK's ones, but this is probably due to the thermal conditions of the Iceland sites, which were in a former farm close to hot spring conduits which allowed water and steam to circulate in the building and probably induced a higher soil temperature and accelerate deamidation; this fact should be carefully considered when deamidation is used to calculate the age of the artifacts. It is also interesting to note that in the Iceland sites, both were acid bogs but one with sphagnum moss, which has a protective effect against biodegradation, was better preserved with greater remains of dye, compared to the site where biodeterioration was favored. This confirms that deamidation is strictly connected to the temperature, which cause its acceleration, and it appears to be favored by low pH. However, authors suggest that in constant temperature condition, deamidation seems to steadily increase over time and it could be considered a good marker to establish the "age" of the relic or its conservation conditions, if these conditions are considered. In fact, deepening the matter, the authors further observe that, based on the primary structure, on the contrary of what was found for collagen-based materials (van Doorn et al., 2012; Orlando et al., 2013; Solazzo et al., 2014b), deamidation is faster on glutamine that asparagine on wool; moreover, deamidation of Q appears to be faster when it is directly preceded or followed by aspartic acid residues. In general, deamidation is accelerated with the presence of a charged residue, such as the basic residue histidine. Furthermore, the alpha-helical configuration plays a role too in the deamidation rate: the high-order structure poses some conformational constraints, so deamidation will start preferentially on linker peptides than in alpha coiled coil. However, this configuration brings different residues together in close proximity, for example in the region of a turn of the helix: i.e. the peptide LESEINTYR and its equivalent LEAEINTYR and LECEINTYR, the N in the first one is in proximity with the S, due to the helical configuration, and thus induced acceleration of deamidation in this peptide as possible catalytic effect of the hydroxyl group of the serine's side chain (Solazzo et al., 2014b).

All these aspects should therefore highlight how, once again, the study of archaeological finds cannot fall under preestablished rules but represents an almost standalone case study each time, where every component must be considered in detail and in relation to the whole.

Worthy of mention is the case of textiles strictly connected to metal artifacts that can lead to greater preservation of the artifact as in the case of species identification by peptide mass fingerprinting (PMF) in fiber products preserved in association with copper-alloy artefacts (Solazzo et al., 2014c). In that case, a series of objects (pelt and textile fragments) was found in association with copper-alloy objects with different degrees of mineralization. Mineralization is a process that results in the substitution of the sample's organic matrix with an inorganic one, forming positive and negative casts of the textile. It can be a partial or complete mineralization (pseudomorph textiles), even if this case seems to be rare. In some cases, mineralization can preserve the original dye (i.e. from a mineralized sample from Pompeii; Ciccola et al., 2020), the shape of the fibers (Solazzo et al., 2014c) and stop the biodeterioration of the materials. In the study by Solazzo, the samples studied came from a Viking-Age (tenth century) grave in Britain and from a burial in Mongolia, in which the textiles were wrapped around a copper alloy disk and a small hemisphere (third century BC to second century AD). In this case, the textiles presented different rates of mineralization. The proteomic analyses of mineralized samples showed a low signal to noise ratio, indicative of a high level of degradation, but the authors identified the presence of peaks related to the Caprinae family, up to *Ovis* genus in almost all samples, including pseudomorph type. This therefore indicates the possibility of tracing organic material for proteomic investigations in these materials as well. Deamidation seems to be much lower than in non-mineralized fibers, inhibited by the copper corrosion products (Solazzo et al., 2014c). Moving to silk identification cases, it is interesting to mention the work from Li, where the authors performed the analyses of soil textile imprints from a Chinese tomb to assess the previous presence of silk (Li et al., 2021). The study started from some considerations on literature on funeral tradition of noble people in China, where the use of silk was reported even if there was a lack of evidence from a scientific standpoint. Therefore, when some textiles imprint, the shape of textiles found on pottery, soil, or bronze, were found in a tomb from Dahekou cemetery, and no evidence of silk fiber were found, the authors moved to the analyses of the soil imprint to evaluate the presence of proteins related to silk or its degradation products. In that case, 5 peptides referable to heavy chain of *Bombyx mori* were detected (Li et al., 2021) (Table 6.2), thus offering initial evidence of the possible presence of silk in that context.

In the work of Lee, the authors offer a comprehensive study on different analytical protocols to analyze silk fibers and apply this workflow to 5 silk samples coming from Palmyra, an ancient oasis in the area that is today Homs province in Syria, NE to Damascus (Lee et al., 2022). Born around the third millennium BC, it was a key point in commercial routes from the Roman Empire because of its connection with Central Asia, the Far East and the Romans on the Silk Road. It is in the twentieth century that an archaeological campaign discovered several tower tombs and more than 2000 textiles have been found, in only 9 different tombs, which should be dated from first BCE -second CE centuries (Lee et al., 2022). The study of such findings provided the perfect opportunity to further study silk fibers, which show some analytical difficulties: for example, silk is much less prone to solubilization than wool, due to crystalline regions, hydrogen bonds, high hydrophobicity, etc. This is further exacerbated moving from domestic silk, *Bombyx mori*, to wild silk non-*Bombyx mori* species derived from wild or semicultivated silkworms, which do not solubilize in the same conditions of the domestic one (Lee et al., 2022). This could related to different species having different protein structures and consequently mechanical properties: the wild silk does not have heavy and light chains, together with the P25, but the silk from *Antheraea* and *Samia* only have the heavy chain coupled with disulfide bonds and a totally different polyalanine sequence, of at least 4 alanine residues such as $(X)A_{12}(X)$, where X residues can be glycine, serine or arginine (Lee et al., 2022).

Starting from the databases present for some silk species in the family Bombycidae and Saturniidae, different protocols were compared to maximize the solubilization of different silk species and thus define possible markers. In detail, the most effective protocol was identified as a 7 M solution of $Ca(NO_3)_2$ at high temperature (around 136 °C), with a double digestion of chymotrypsin first and trypsin after (Lee et al., 2022). The analysis by nano LC-MS allowed the detection of a unique peptides of Antharaea in all Palmyra samples, and the alignment with the database and the unique peptides identified suggests the attribution of these fragments to the species *A. mylitta*. This species is from India and historians suggested that Chinese silk was imported from India, but this finding could give a name to the exact traded species and confirmed the archaeologists hypothesize of a commercial silk route that involved Palmyra.

This last case described, as far as the study of Palmyra's silks is concerned, is an excellent example of how the study of textile fibers can be a key, once again, to

Table 6.2 Summary of the de novo homology matching performed on the results from the proteomic analysis of the Palmyra samples

Sample	Highest Scoring peptide	Accession	$-101gP$	Cov (%)	#Peptides (unique)	Unique peptides (position, $-101gP$)
A S8 warp	$SA_{12}GSGAGGRGD$ ($-10lgP$ = 47.33) *Antheraea specific*	Q8ISB3|ANTMY	163.41	30	31(12)	$SGA_{12}SGAGGR$ (243–263, 46–77) $SSA_{11}SAAR$ (484–500, 44.12)
		E1CGA3|ANTYA	160.30	7	35(7)	
		O76786|ANTPE	151.28	7	31(3)	
		A0A0K0KR73|ANTASA	121.62	8	18(7)	
B S8 weft	$GGYGSGSSA_{11}SAAR$ ($-10lgP$ = 53.66) *A. mylitta specific*	Q8ISB3|ANTMY	238.35	48	48 (29)	$GGYGSGSSA_{11}SAAR$ (478–500, 70.75)
						$SA_{14}GSGAGGRGDGGY$ (206–232, 41.95)
						$GA_{12}SGAGGR$ (244–263, 40.40)
						$GGGGFYETHDSYSSY$ (134–148, 37.28)
						$GSDSA_{13}GSGAGGVGGGYGR$ (346–375, 31.11)
						$SA_{15}SGAGGR$ (176–197, 27.45)
						$NIHHDEYVDSHGQLVER$ (20–36, 21.13)
		E1CGA3|ANTYA	197.23	11	44(14)	
		O76786|ANTPE	195.64	10	36(6)	
		A0A0K0KR73|ANTASA	156.27	8	16(8)	
C S48	$GAGSA_{10}GAGASR$ ($-10lgP$ = 49.64) *A. pernyi specific*)	O76786|ANTPE	131.54	8	12(5)	
		1CGA3|ANTYA	123.78	8	14(6)	$SA_{15}SGAGGR$(176–197, 39.04)
		Q8ISB3|ANTMY	115.17	22	12(7)	$SGA_{12}SGAGGRGD$ (243–265, 37.66)
						$SGSSA_{11}SAAR$ (482–500, 36.05)

D S49 T1	GYGSGSSA$_{10}$SAAR (−10lgP = 55.54) A. pernyi specific	Q8ISB3|ANTMY	179.20	36	17(13)	GSGSSA$_{11}$SAAR(481–500, 64.48)
						QASHGAGGAAGAAAGAAASSSVR (111–133, 44.75)
						SGA$_{12}$SGAGGR (243–263, 25.96)
						GQATVVMDGAMAAMVLTR (297–314, 20.53)
		E1CGA3|ANTYA	172.99	5	16(4)	
		O76786|ANTPE	170.24	6	18(5)	
E S49 T2	SA$_{11}$SAAR (−10lgP = 32.85) A. mylitta specific	E1CGA3|ANTYA	116.35	7	25(8)	
		A0A0K0KR73|ANTASA	105.68	5	19(2)	
		Q8ISB3|ANTMY	103.05	24	15(3)	SA$_{11}$SAAR (485–500, 32.35)
						GSDPGA$_{13}$ (452–469, 24.41)

Reproduced by Lee et al. (2022). Copyright Scientific reports 2022
Accession codes are in the format of UniProtKB. The −10lgP score indicates the statistical significance of the peptide-spectrum match. Peptides were filtered by −10lgP values ≥20, and the values ≥70 is usually considered significant for proteins

reconstructing parts of the histories of ancient civilizations that sometimes cannot be defined through bibliographic sources alone. In this context, the importance of such research is undoubted; however, as can be seen for both dyes and textile fibers, the analytical challenges are different. From the state of preservation of the textile, to the raw materials used (which can be the most varied), to the lack of databases and in most cases the need of samples. Considering this, the lack of a joint approach to the study of these materials is peculiar, a protocol that aims at studying dyes and fibers in a single extraction. For this reason, the authors of this chapter are pursuing a European community-funded project, PARCA, which involves the development of an innovative method for the extraction of dyes and proteins from wool artifacts using a single workflow. The results of this project will be submitted soon.

Acknowledgments

This project has received funding from the European Union's Horizon 2020 research and innovation program under the Marie Skłodowska-Curie grant agreement No 101029204.

This project was also supported by the Smithsonian Museum Conservation Institute Federal and Trust funds (GMK, TPC, CS).

References

Abdel-Kareem, O., Eltokhy, A., & Harith, M. A. (2011). Identification of natural dyes on archaeological textile objects using laser induced fluorescent technique, The 8th international conference on laser applications – ICLA. *AIP Conference Proceedings, 1380*(1), 70–76. https://doi.org/10.1063/1.3631813

Aceto, M., Agostino, A., Fenoglio, G., Idone, A., Gulmini, M., Picollo, M., Ricciardi, P., & Delaney, J. K. (2014). Characterisation of colourants on illuminated manuscripts by portable fibre optic UV-visible-NIR reflectance spectrophotometry. *Analytical Methods, 6*, 1488–1500.

Aceto, M., Arrais, A., Marsano, F., Agostino, A., Fenoglio, G., Idone, A., & Gulmini, M. (2015). A diagnostic study on folium and orchil dyes with non-invasive and micro-destructive methods, Spectrochimica Acta – Part A. *Molecular and Biomolecular Spectroscopy, 142*, 159–168.

Albrecht, M. G., & Creighton, J. A. (1977). Anomalously intense Raman spectra of pyridine at a silver electrode. *Journal of American Chemical Society, 99*, 5215–5217.

Andreev, G. N., Schrader, B., Schulz, H., Fuchs, R., Popov, S., & Handjieva, N. (2001). Non-destructive NIR-FT-Raman analyses in practice. Part 1. Analyses of plants and historic textiles. *Analytical and Bioanalytical Chemistry, 371*, 1009–1017.

Armitage, R. A., Jakes, K., & Day, C. (2015). Direct analysis in real time-mass spectroscopy for identification of red dye colourants in Paracas Necropolis Textiles. *STAR: Science & Technology of Archaeological Research, 1*(2), 60–69.

Asakura, T., Yao, J. M., Yamane, T., Umemura, K., & Ulrich, A. S. (2002). Heterogeneous structure of silk fibers from Bombyx mori resolved by 13C solid state NMR spectroscopy. *Journal of the American Chemical Society, 124*, 8794–8795.

Azémard, C., Zazzo, A., Marie, A., Lepetz, S., Debaine-Francfort, C., Idriss, A., & Zirah, S. (2019). Animal fibre use in the Keriya valley (Xinjiang, China) during the Bronze and Iron Ages: A proteomic approach. *Journal of Archaeological Science, 110*, 104996.

Bacci, M., Baronti, S., Casini, A., Lotti, F., Picollo, M., & Casazza, O. (1992). Non-destructive spectroscopic investigations on paintings using optical fibers. *MRS Proceedings, 267*, 265–283. https://doi.org/10.1557/proc-267-265

Balta, Z. I., Demetrescu, I., Cretu, I., & Lupu, M. (2017). ATR/FTIR investigation into the nature of the metal threads from Romanian medieval textiles. *UPB Scientific Bulletin, Series B: Chemistry and Materials Science, 79*, 25–36.

Barth, A. (2007). Infrared spectroscopy of proteins. *Biochimica et Biophysica Acta – Bioenergetics, 1767*, 1073–1101. https://doi.org/10.1016/j.bbabio.2007.06.004

Blackburn, R. S. (2017). Natural dyes in madder (Rubia spp.) and their extraction and analysis in historical textiles. *Coloration Technology, 133*, 449–462.

Boersma, F., Brokerhof, A. W., Van der Berg, S., & Tegelaers, J. (2007). *Unravelling textiles: A handbook for the preservation of textile collections*. Archetype Publications Ltd.

Bosi, A., Ciccola, A., Serafini, I., Peruzzi, G., Nigro, V., Postorino, P., Curini, R., & Favero, G. (2023). Gel microextraction from hydrophilic paint layers: A comparison between Agargel and Nanorestore Gel® HWR for spectroscopic identification of madder. *Microchemical Journal, 187*, 108447.

Bruni, S., De Luca, E., Guglielmi, V., & Pozzi, F. (2011). Identification of natural dyes on laboratory-dyed wool and ancient wool, silk, and cotton fibers using attenuated total reflection (ATR) fourier transform infrared (FT-IR) spectroscopy and fourier transform Raman spectroscopy. *Applied Spectroscopy, 65*, 1017–1023.

Campos Ayala, J., Mahan, S., Wilson, B., Antúnez de Mayolo, K., Jakes, K., Stein, R., & Armitage, R. A. (2021). Characterizing the dyes of pre-Columbian Andean textiles: Comparison of ambient ionization mass spectrometry and HPLC-DAD. *Heritage, 4*, 1639–1659.

Cao, Q., Zhu, S., Zhao, H., & Tu, H. (2010). Application of Fourier transform attenuated total reflection infrared spectroscopy to identifying archaeological fibres. *Research Journal of Textile and Apparel, 14*, 38–41.

Cardon, D. (2007). *Natural dyes: Sources, tradition, technology and science*. Archetype.

Carter, E. A., Fredericks, P. M., Church, J. S., & Denning, R. J. (1994). FT-Raman spectroscopy of wool-I. Preliminary studies. *Spectrochimica Acta Part A Molecular and Biomolecular Spectroscopy, 50*, 1927–1936.

Ciccola, A., Serafini, I., Ripanti, F., Vincenti, F., Coletti, F., Bianco, A., Fasolato, C., Montesano, C., Galli, M., Curini, R., & Postorino, P. (2020). Dyes from the ashes: Discovering and characterizing natural dyes from mineralized textiles. *Molecules, 25*, 1417.

Cleland, T. P. (2018). Human bone paleoproteomics utilizing the single-pot, solid-phase- enhanced sample preparation method to maximize detected proteins and reduce humics. *Journal of Proteome Research, 17*, 3976–3983.

Clementi, C., Miliani, C., Romani, A., & Favaro, G. (2006). In situ fluorimetry: A powerful non-invasive diagnostic technique for natural dyes used in artefacts. Part I. Spectral characterization of orcein in solution, on silk and wool laboratory-standards and a fragment of Renaissance tapestry. *Spectrochimica Acta – Part A: Molecular and Biomolecular Spectroscopy, 64*, 906–912.

Clementi, C., Miliani, C., Romani, A., Santamaria, U., Morresi, F., Mlynarska, K., & Favaro, G. (2009). In-situ fluorimetry: A powerful non-invasive diagnostic technique for natural dyes used in artefacts. Part II. Identification of orcein and indigo in Renaissance tapestries. *Spectrochimica Acta – Part A: Molecular and Biomolecular Spectroscopy, 71*, 2057–2062.

Clerens, S., Cornellison, C. D., Deb-Choudhury, S., Thomas, A., Plowman, J. E., & Dyer, J. M. (2010). Developing the wool proteome. *Journal of Proteomics, 73*, 1722–1731.

Colantonio, C., Lanteri, L., Ciccola, A., Serafini, I., Postorino, P., Censorii, E., Rotari, D., & Pelosi, C. (2022). Imaging diagnostics coupled with non-invasive and micro-invasive analyses for the restoration of ethnographic artifacts from French Polynesia. *Heritage, 5*, 215–232.

Conti, C., Botteon, A., Bertasa, M., Colombo, C., Realini, M., & Sali, D. (2016). Portable sequentially shifted excitation Raman spectroscopy as an innovative tool for: In situ chemical interrogation of painted surfaces. *Analyst, 141*, 4599–4607.

Cosentino, A. (2015). FORS spectral database of historical pigments in different binders. *e-Conservation Journal, 2*, 54–65.

Day, C. J., DeRoo, C. S., & Armitage, R. A. (2013). Developing direct analysis in real time time-of-flight mass spectrometric methods for identification of organic dyes in historic wool textiles. In R. A. Armitage & J. H. Burton (Eds.), *Archaeological chemistry VIII* (ACS symposium series) (Vol. 1147, pp. 69–85).

de Palaminy, L., Daher, C., & Moulherat, C. (2022). Development of a non-destructive methodology using ATR-FTIR and chemometrics to discriminate wild silk species in heritage collections. *Spectrochimica Acta – Part A Molecular and Biomolecular Spectroscopy, 270*, 120788.

Deb-Choudhury, S., Plowman, J. E., Rao, K., Lee, E., van Koten, C., Clerens, S., Dyer, J. M., & Harland, D. P. (2015). Mapping the accessibility of the disulfide crosslink network in the wool fiber cortex. *Proteins: Structure, Function, and Bioinformatics, 83*, 224–234. https://doi.org/10.1002/prot.24727

Degano, I., Ribechini, E., Modugno, F., & Colombini, M. P. (2009). Analytical methods for the characterization of organic dyes in artworks and in historical textiles. *Applied Spectroscopy Reviews, 44*(5), 363–410.

Degano, I., Biesaga, M., Colombini, M. P., & Trojanowicz, M. (2011). Historical and archaeological textiles: an insight on degradation products of wool and silk yarns. *Journal of Chromatography A, 1218*(34), 5837–5847.

Delamare, F., & Monasse, B. (2005). Le rôle de l'alun comme mordant en teinture. Une approche par la simulation numérique – Cas de la teinture de la cellulose à l'alizarine. In P. Borgard, J. P. Brun, & M. Picon (Eds.), *L'alun de la Méditerranée* (pp. 277–290). Publications du Centre Jean Bérard.

Derksen, G. C. H., Niederländer, H. A. G., & Van Beek, T. A. (2002). Analysis of anthraquinones in Rubia tinctorum L. by liquid chromatography coupled with diode-array UV and mass spectrometric detection. *Journal of Chromatography A, 278*, 119–127.

Dyer, J., Tamburini, D., O'Connell, E. R., & Harrison, A. (2018). A multispectral imaging approach integrated into the study of Late Antique textiles from Egypt. *PLoS One, 13*(10), e0204699.

Edwards, H. G. M., & Farwell, D. W. (1995). Raman Spectroscopic Studies of Silk. *Journal of Raman Spectroscopy, 26*, 901–909.

Fabbri, M., Picollo, M., Porcinai, S., & Bacci, M. (2001). Mid-infrared fiber-optics reflectance spectroscopy: A noninvasive technique for remote analysis of painted layers. Part I: Technical setup. *Applied Spectroscopy, 55*, 420–427.

Flowers, T. H., Smith, M. J., & Brunton, J. (2019). Colouring of Pacific barkcloths: identification of the brown, red and yellow colourants used in the decoration of historic Pacific barkcloths. *Heritage Science, 7*, 2.

Fonseca, B., Schmidt Patterson, C., Ganio, M., MacLennan, D., & Trentelman, K. (2019). Seeing red: towards an improved protocol for the identification of madder- and cochineal-based pigments by fiber optics reflectance spectroscopy (FORS). *Heritage Science, 7*, 1–15.

Ford, L., Henderson, R. L., Rayner, C. M., & Blackburn, R. S. (2017). Mild extraction methods using aqueous glucose solution for the analysis of natural dyes in textile artefacts dyed with Dyer's madder (Rubia tinctorum L.). *Journal of Chromatography A, 1487*(3), 36–46.

Ford, L., Rayner, M. C., & Blackburn, R. S. (2018). Degradation of lucidin: New insights into the fate of this natural pigment present in Dyer's madder (Rubia tinctorum L.) during the extraction of textile artefacts. *Dyes and Pigments, 154*, 290–295.

Garside, P., & Wyeth, P. (2007). Crystallinity and degradation of silk: correlations between analytical signatures and physical condition on ageing. *Applied Physics A, 89*, 871–876.

Germinario, G., Ciccola, A., Serafini, I., Ruggiero, L., Sbroscia, M., Vincenti, F., Fasolato, C., Curini, R., Ioele, M., Postorino, P., & Sodo, A. (2020). Gel substrates and ammonia-EDTA extraction solution: A new non-destructive combined approach for the identification of anthraquinone dyes from wool textiles. *Microchemical Journal, 155*, 104780.

Gillard, R. D., Hardman, S. M., Thomas, R. G., & Watkinson, D. E. (1994). The detection of dyes by FTIR microscopy. *Studies in Conservation, 39*, 187–192.

Glassford, S. E., Byrne, B., & Kazarian, S. G. (2013). Recent applications of ATR FTIR spectroscopy and imaging to proteins. *Biochimica et Biophysica Acta – Proteins and Proteomics, 1834*, 2849–2858.

Gleba, M. (2011). Textiles studies: Sources and methods. *Kubaba 2 – Journal of Ancient Southwest Asia and Eastern Mediterranean Studies, 2*, 2–26.

Gleba, M., & Mannering, U. (2012). *Textiles and textile production in europe: From prehistory to AD 400*. Oxbow Books.

Good, I. (2001). Archaeological textiles: A review of current research. *Annual Review of Anthropology, 30*, 209–226.

Gulmini, M., Idone, A., Diana, E., Gastaldi, D., Vaudan, D., & Aceto, M. (2013). Identification of dyestuffs in historical textiles: Strong and weak points of a non-invasive approach. *Dyes and Pigments, 98*, 136–145.

Han, J., Wanrooij, J., van Bommel, M., & Quye, A. (2017). Characterisation of chemical components for identifying historical Chinese textile dyes by ultra high performance liquid chromatography – Photodiode array – Electrospray ionisation mass spectrometer. *Journal of Chromatography A, 1479*, 87–96.

Hofenk de Graaff, J. (2004). *The colourful past. Origin, chemistry and identification of natural dyestuffs*. Archetype Publications.

Hogg, L. J., Edwards, H. G. M., Farwell, D. W., & Peters, A. T. (1994). FT Raman spectroscopic studies of wool. *Journal of the Society of Dyers and Colourists, 110*, 196–199.

Huang, D., Peng, Z., Hu, Z., Zhang, S., He, J., Cao, L., Zhou, Y., & Zhao, F. (2013). A new consolidation system for aged silk fabrics: Effect of reactive epoxide-ethylene glycol diglycidyl ether. *Reactive & Functional Polymers, 73*, 168–174.

Inoue, S., Tanaka, K., Arisaka, F., Kimura, S., Ohtomo, K., & Mizuno, S. (2000). Silk fibroin of Bombyx mori is secreted, assembling a high molecular mass elementary unit consisting of H-chain, L-chain, and P25, with a 6:6:1 molar ratio. *Journal of Biological Chemistry, 275*(51), 40517–40528.

Jeanmaire, D. L., & Van Duyne, R. P. (1977). Surface Raman spectroelectrochemistry: Part I. Heterocyclic, aromatic, and aliphatic amines adsorbed on the anodized silver electrode. *Journal of Electroanalytical Chemistry, 84*, 1–20.

Karapanagiotis, I., Verhecken-Lammens, C., & Kamaterou, P. (2019). Identification of dyes in Egyptian textiles of the first millennium AD from the collection Fill-Trevisiol. *Archaeological and Anthropological Sciences, 11*, 2699–2710.

Karapanagiotis, I., Abdel-Kareem, O., Kamaterou, P., & Mantzouris, D. (2021). Identification of dyes in Coptic textiles from the Museum of Faculty of Archaeology, Cairo University. *Heritage, 4*, 3147–3156.

Koren, Z. C. (2008). Archaeochemical analysis of Royal Purple on a Darius I stone jar. *Microchimica Acta, 162*, 381–392.

Koren, Z. C. (2023). Chromatographic characterization of archaeological Molluskan Colorants via the Di-Mono Index and ternary diagram. *Heritage, 6*, 2186–2201.

Koren, Z. C., & Verhecken-Lammens, C. (2013). Microscopic and chromato- graphic analyses of molluskan purple yarns in a late Roman Period Textile. *e-Preservation Science, 10*, 27–34.

Kostiainen, R., & Kauppila, T. J. (2009). Effect of eluent on the ionization process in liquid chromatography–mass spectrometry. *Journal of Chromatography A, 1216*, 685–699.

Kramell, A., Li, X., Csuk, R., Wagner, M., Goslar, T., Tarasov, P. E., Kreusel, N., Kluge, R., & Wunderlich, C. H. (2014). Dyes of late Bronze Age textile clothes and accessories from the

Yanghai archaeological site, Turfan, China: Determination of the fibers, color analysis and dating. *Quaternary International, 348*, 214–223.

Kramell, A. E., Brachmann, A. O., Kluge, R., Piel, J., & Csuk, R. (2017). Fast direct detection of natural dyes in historic and prehistoric textiles by flowprobe TM-ESI-HRMS. *RSC Advances, 7*, 12990.

Kramell, A. E., García-Altares, M., Pötsch, M., Kluge, R., Rother, A., Hause, G., Hertweck, C., & Csuk, R. (2019). Mapping natural dyes in archeological textiles by imaging mass spectrometry. *Scientific Reports, 9*, 2331.

Lech, K., & Fornal, E. (2020). A mass spectrometry-based approach for characterization of red, blue, and purple natural dyes. *Molecules, 25*, 322.

Lech, K., & Jarosz, M. (2016). Identification of Polish cochineal (Porphyrophora polonica L.) in historical textiles by High-Performance Liquid Chromatography coupled with spectrophotometric and tandem Mass Spectrometric detection. *Analytical and Bioanalytical Chemistry, 408*, 3349–3358.

Lech, K., Witkos, K., Wilenska, B., & Jarosz, M. (2015). Identification of unknown color- ants in pre-Columbian textiles dyed with American cochineal (Dactylopius coccus Costa) using High-Performance Liquid Chromatography and tandem Mass Spectrometry. *Analytical and Bioanalytical Chemistry, 407*, 855–867.

Lee, B., Pires, E., Pollard, A. M., & McCullagh, J. S. O. (2022). Species identification of silks by protein mass spectrometry reveals evidence of wild silk use in antiquity. *Scientific Reports, 12*, 4579.

Leona, M., Decuzzi, P., Kubic, T. A., Gates, G., & Lombardi, J. R. (2011). Nondestructive identification of natural and synthetic organic colorants in works of art by surface enhanced Raman scattering. *Analytical Chemistry, 83*, 3990–3993.

Li, L., Zhu, L., & Xie, Y. (2021). Proteomics analysis of the soil textile imprints from tomb M6043 of the Dahekou Cemetery site in Yicheng County, Shanxi Province, China. *Archaeological and Anthropological Sciences, 13*(7). https://doi.org/10.1007/s12520-020-01258-0

Liu, J., Guo, D., Zhou, Y., Wu, Z., Li, W., Zhao, F., & Zheng, X. (2011). Identification of ancient textiles from Yingpan, Xinjiang, by multiple analytical techniques. *Journal of Archaeological Science, 38*, 1763–1770.

Lofrumento, C., Ricci, M., Platania, E., Becucci, M., & Castellucci, E. (2013). SERS detection of red organic dyes in Ag-agar gel. *Journal of Raman Spectroscopy, 44*, 47–54.

Lombardi, L., Serafini, I., Guiso, M., Sciubba, F., & Bianco, A. (2016). A new approach to the mild extraction of madder dyes from lake and textile. *Microchemical Journal, 126*, 373–380.

Mantzouris, D., & Karapanagiotis, I. (2015). Armenian cochineal (Porphyrophora hamelii) and purpurin-rich madder in ancient polychromy. *Coloration Technology, 131*(5), 370–3731.

Mantzouris, D., Karapanagiotis, I., & Panayiotou, C. (2014). Comparison of extraction methods for the analysis of Indigofera tinctoria and Carthamus tinctorius in textiles by high performance liquid chromatography. *Microchemical Journal, 115*, 78–86. https://doi.org/10.1016/j.microc.2014.02.010

Maynez-Rojas, M. A., Casanova-González, E., & Ruvalcaba-Sil, J. L. (2017). Identification of natural red and purple dyes on textiles by Fiber-optics Reflectance Spectroscopy. *Spectrochimica Acta – Part A: Molecular and Biomolecular Spectroscopy, 178*, 239–250.

McGregor, B. A., Liu, X., & Wang, X. G. (2018). Comparisons of the Fourier Transform Infrared Spectra of cashmere, guard hair, wool and other animal fibres. *The Journal of the Textile Institute, 109*, 813–822.

Montagner, C., Bacci, M., Bracci, S., Freeman, R., & Picollo, M. (2011). Library of UV-Vis-NIR reflectance spectra of modern organic dyes from historic pattern-card coloured papers. *Spectrochimica Acta – Part A: Molecular and Biomolecular Spectroscopy, 79*, 1669–1680.

Mouri, C., & Laursen, R. (2012). Identification of anthraquinone markers for distinguishing rubia species in madder dyed textiles by HPLC. *Microchimica Acta, 179*, 105–113.

Movasaghi, Z., Rehman, S., & Rehman, I. U. (2008). Fourier transform infrared (FTIR) spectroscopy of biological tissues. *Applied Spectroscopy Reviews, 43*, 134–179.

Nakamura, R., Tanaka, Y., Ogata, A., & Naruse, M. (2009). Dye analysis of Shosoin textiles using excitation-emission matrix fluorescence and ultraviolet-visible reflectance spectroscopic techniques. *Analytical Chemistry, 81*, 5691–5698.

Newsome, G. A., & Martin, K. M. (2023). Non-proximate sampling and photoionization for damage-free mass spectrometric analysis of intact Native American Baskets. *Analytical Chemistry, 95*(28). https://doi.org/10.1021/acs.analchem.3c01468

Orlando, L., Ginolhac, A., Zhang, G., Froese, D., Albrechtsen, A., Stiller, M., Schubert, M., Cappellini, E., Petersen, B., Moltke, I., Johnson, P. L. F., Fumagalli, M., Vilstrup, J. T., Raghavan, M., Korneliussen, T., Malaspinas, A. S., Vogt, J., Szklarczyk, D., Kelstrup, C. D., Vinther, J., Dolocan, A., Stenderup, J., Velazquez, A. M. V., Cahill, J., Rasmussen, M., Wang, X., Min, J., Zazula, G. D., Seguin-Orlando, A., Mortensen, C., Magnussen, K., Thompson, J. F., Weinstock, J., Gregersen, K., Røed, K. H., Eisenmann, V., Rubin, C. J., Miller, D. C., Antczak, D. F., Bertelsen, M. F., Brunak, S., Al-Rasheid, K. A. S., Ryder, O., Andersson, L., Mundy, J., Krogh, A., Gilbert, M. T. P., Kjær, K., Sicheritz-Ponten, T., Jensen, L. J., Olsen, J. V., Hofreiter, M., Nielsen, R., Shapiro, B., Wang, J., & Willerslev, E. (2013). Recalibrating Equus evolution using the genome sequence of an early Middle Pleistocene horse. *Nature, 499*(7456), 74–78.

Orska-Gawrys, J., Surowiec, I., Kehl, J., Rejniak, H., Urbaniak-Walczak, K., & Trojanowicz, M. (2003). Identification of natural dyes in archeological Coptic textiles by liquid chromatography with diode array detection. *Journal of Chromatography A, 989*, 239–248.

Ortiz, J., Alfaro, C., Turell, L., & Martinez, J. (eds.) (2016). *Textiles, basketry and dyes in the ancient Mediterranean world. In Purpureae Vestes V. Textiles et Dyes in the Ancient Mediterranean World. Proceedings of the Vth international symposium on textiles and dyes in the Ancient Mediterranean World* (Montserrat, 19–22 March 2014,València). Universitat de València.

Ostrom, P. H., Schall, M., Gandhi, H., Shen, T.-L., Hauschka, P. V., Strahler, J. R., & Cage, D. A. (2000). New strategies for characterizing ancient proteins using matrix-assisted laser desorption ionization mass spectrometry. *Geochimica et Cosmochimica Acta, 64*(6), 1043–1050.

Pause, R., van derWerf, I. D., & van den Berg, K. J. (2021). Identification of pre-1950 synthetic organic pigments in artists' paints. A non-invasive approach using handheld Raman spectroscopy. *Heritage, 4*, 1348–1365.

Peets, P., Leito, I., Pelt, J., & Vahur, S. (2017). Identification and classification of textile fibres using ATR-FT-IR spectroscopy with chemometric methods. *Spectrochimica Acta – Part A Molecular and Biomolecular Spectroscopy, 173*, 175–181.

Peets, P., Kaupmees, K., Vahur, S., & Leito, I. (2019). Reflectance FT-IR spectroscopy as a viable option for textile fiber identification. *Heritage Science, 7*, 15–20.

Peruzzi, G., Cucci, C., Picollo, M., Quercioli, F., & Stefani, L. (2021). Non-invasive identification of dyed textiles by using Vis-NIR FORS and hyperspectral imaging techniques. *Color Culture and Science Journal, 13*, 61–69.

Peruzzi, G., Ciccola, A., Bosi, A., Serafini, I., Negozio, M., Hamza, N. M., Moricca, C., Sadori, L., Favero, G., Nigro, V., Postorino, P., & Curini, R. (2023). Applying gel-supported liquid extraction to Tutankhamun's textiles for the identification of ancient colorants: A case study. *Gels, 9*, 514. https://doi.org/10.3390/gels9070514

Pfister, R. (1936). Matériaux pour servir au classement des textiles égyptiens postérieurs à la conquête Arabe. *Revue des arts asiatiques, 10*(1), 1–16.

Picollo, M., Bacci, M., Magrini, D., Radicati, B., Trumpy, G., Tsukada, M., & Kunzelman, D. (2007) Modern white pigments: Their identification by means of noninvasive ultraviolet, visible, and infrared fiber optic reflectance spectroscopy. In T. J. S. Learner, P. Smithen, J. W. Krueger, & M. R. Schilling (eds) *Modern paints uncovered: Proceedings from the modern paints uncovered symposium* (May 16–19 2006, Tate Modern London) (pp. 129–139). Getty Conservation Institute. http://hdl.handle.net/10020/gci_pubs/paints_uncovered

Platania, E., Lombardi, J. R., Leona, M., Shibayama, N., Lofrumento, C., Ricci, M., Becucci, M., & Castellucci, E. (2014). Suitability of Ag-agar gel for the microextraction of organic dyes on different substrates: The case study of wool, silk, printed cotton and a panel painting mock-up. *Journal of Raman Spectroscopy, 45*, 1133–1139.

Platania, E., Lofrumento, C., Lottini, E., Azzaro, E., Ricci, M., & Becucci, M. (2015). Tailored micro-extraction method for Raman/SERS detection of indigoids in ancient textiles. *Analytical and Bioanalytical Chemistry, 407*, 6505–6514.

Plowman, J. E. (2007). The proteomics of keratin proteins. *Journal of Chromatography B, 849*, 181–189.

Plowman, J. E. (2018). Proteomics in wool and fibre research. In A. M. de Almeida, D. Eckersall, & I. Mille (Eds.), *Proteomics in domestic animals: from farm to systems biology* (pp. 281–296). Springer. https://doi.org/10.1007/978-3-319-69682-9_14

Pozzi, F., & Leona, M. (2016). Surface-enhanced Raman spectroscopy in art and archaeology. *Journal of Raman Spectroscopy, 47*, 67–77.

Puchalska, M., Połeć-Pawlak, K., Zadroz Pna, I., Hryszko, H., & Jarosz, M. (2004). Identification of indigoid dyes in natural organic pigments used in historical art objects by high-performance liquid chromatography coupled to electrospray ionization mass spectrometry. *Journal of Mass Spectrometery, 39*, 1441–1449.

Ribechini, E., Pérez-Arantegui, J., & Colombini, M. P. (2013). Positive and negative-mode laser desorption/ ionization-mass spectrometry (LDI-MS) for the detection of indigoids in archaeological purple. *Journal of Mass Spectrometry, 48*(3), 384–391.

Rosi, F., Paolantoni, M., Clementi, C., Doherty, B., Miliani, C., Brunetti, B. G., & Sgamellotti, A. (2010). Subtracted shifted Raman spectroscopy of organic dyes and lakes. *Journal of Raman Spectroscopy, 41*, 452–458.

Sabatini, F., Bacigalupo, M., Degano, I., Javér, A., & Hacke, M. (2020). Revealing the organic dye and mordant composition of Paracas textiles by a combined analytical approach. *Heritage Science, 8*(122). https://doi.org/10.1186/s40494-020-00461-5

Sanyova, J. (2008). Mild extraction of dyes by hydrofluoric acid in routine analysis of historical paint microsamples. *Microchimica Acta, 162*, 361–370.

Sanyova, J., & Reisse, J. (2006). Development of a mild method for the extraction of anthraquinones from their aluminum complexes in madder lakes prior to HPLC analysis. *Journal of Cultural Heritage, 7*, 229–235.

Sanz, E., Arteaga, A., García, M. A., Cámara, C., & Dietz, C. (2012). Chromatographic analysis of indigo from Maya Blue by LC–DAD–QTOF. *Journal of Archaeological Science, 39*, 3516–3523.

Schrader, B., Schulz, H., Andreev, G. N., Klump, H. H., & Sawatzki, J. (2000). Non-destructive NIR-FT-Raman spectroscopy of plant and animal tissues, of food and works of art. *Talanta, 53*, 35–45.

Selberg, S., Vanker, E., Peets, P., Wright, K., Tshepelevitsh, S., Pagano, T., Vahur, S., Herodes, K., & Leito, I. (2023). Non-invasive analysis of natural textile dyes using fluorescence excitation-emission matrices. *Talanta, 252*, 123805.

Serafini, I., Lombardi, L., Vannutelli, G., Montesano, C., Sciubba, F., Guiso, M., Curini, R., & Bianco, A. (2017). How the extraction method could be crucial in the characterization of natural dyes from dyed yarns and lake pigments: The case of American and Armenian cochineal dyes, extracted through the new ammonia-EDTA method. *Microchemical Journal, 134*, 237–245.

Serafini, I., McClure, K. R., Ciccola, A., Vincenti, F., Bosi, A., Peruzzi, G., Montesano, C., Sergi, M., Favero, G., & Curini, R. (2023). Inside the history of Italian Coloring industries: An investigation of ACNA dyes through a novel analytical protocol for synthetic dye extraction and characterization. *Molecules, 28*, 5331.

Serrano, A., Sousa, M. M., Hallett, J., Lopes, J. A., & Conceição Oliveira, M. (2011). Analysis of natural red dyes (cochineal) in textiles of historical importance using HPLC and multi- variate data analysis. *Analytical and Bioanalytical Chemistry, 401*, 735–743.

Serrano, A., Van den Doel, A., Van Bommel, M., Hallett, J., Joosten, I., & Van den Berg, K. J. (2015). Investigation of crimson-dyed fibres for a new approach on the characterization of cochineal and kermes dyes in historical textiles. *Analytica Chimica Acta, 897*, 116–127.

Shahid, M., Wertz, J., Degano, I., Aceto, M., Khan, M. I., & Quye, A. (2019). Analytical methods for determination of anthraquinone dyes in historical textiles: A review. *Analytica Chimica Acta, 1083*, 58–87.

Sionkowska, A., & Planecka, A. (2011). The influence of UV radiation on silk fibroin. *Polymer Degradation and Stability, 96*, 523–528.

Solazzo, C. (2019). Characterizing historical textiles and clothing with proteomics. *Conservar Património, 31*, 97–114. https://doi.org/10.14568/cp2018031

Solazzo, C., & Niepold, T. (2023). A simplified sample preparation for hair and skin proteins towards the application of archaeological fur and leather. *Journal of Proteomics, 274*, 104821.

Solazzo, C., Wadsley, M., Dyer, J. M., Clerens, S., Collins, M. J., & Plowman, J. (2013). Characterisation of novel α-keratin peptide markers for species identification in keratinous tissues using mass spectrometry. *Rapid Communication in Mass Spectrometry, 27*, 2685–2698.

Solazzo, C., Rogers, P. W., Weber, L., Beaubien, H. F., Wilson, J., & Collins, M. (2014a). Species identification by peptide mass fingerprinting (PMF) in fibre products preserved by association with copper-alloy artefacts. *Journal of Archaeological Science, 49*, 524–535.

Solazzo, C., Wilson, J., Dyer, J. M., Clerens, S., Plowman, J. E., von Holstein, I., Walton Rogers, P., Peacock, E. E., & Collins, M. J. (2014b). Modeling deamidation in sheep α-keratin peptides and application to archeological wool textiles. *Analytical Chemistry, 86*, 567–575.

Solazzo, C., Walton Rogers, P., Weber, L., Beaubien, H. F., Wilson, J., & Collins, M. J. (2014c). Species identification by peptide mass fingerprint (PMF) in fibre products preserved by association with copper-alloy artefacts. *Journal of Archaeological Science, 49*, 524–535.

Stathopoulou, K., Valianou, L., Skaltsounis, A. L., Karapanagiotis, I., & Magiatis, P. (2013). Structure elucidation and chromatographic identification of anthraquinone components of cochineal (Dactylopius coccus) detected in historical objects. *Analytica Chimica Acta, 804*, 264–272.

Szostak-Kotowa, J. (2004). Biodeterioration of textiles. *International Biodeterioration & Biodegradation, 53*, 165–170.

Szostek, B., Orska-Gawrys, J., Surowiec, I., & Trojanowicz, M. (2003). Investigation of natural dyes occurring in historical Coptic textiles by High-Performance Liquid Chromatography with UV–Vis and mass spectrometric detection. *Journal of Chromatography A, 1012*(2), 179–192.

Tamburini, D., & Dyer, J. (2019). Fibre optic reflectance spectroscopy and multispectral imaging for the non-invasive investigation of Asian colourants in Chinese textiles from Dunhuang (7th–10th century AD). *Dyes and Pigments, 162*, 494–511.

Tamburini, D., Cartwright, C. R., Melchiorre Di Crescenzo, M., & Rayner, G. (2019a). Scientific characterisation of the dyes, pigments, fibres and wood used in the production of barkcloth from Pacific islands. *Archaeological and Anthropological Sciences, 11*, 3121–3141.

Tamburini, D., Cartwright, C. R., Pullan, M., & Vickers, H. (2019b). An investigation of the dye palette in Chinese silk embroidery from Dunhuang (Tang dynasty). *Archaeological and Anthropological Sciences, 11*, 1221–1239.

Tamburini, D., Dyer, J., Davit, P., Aceto, M., Turina, V., Borla, M., Vandenbeusch, M., & Gulmini, M. (2019c). Compositional and micro-morphological characterisation of red colourants in archaeological textiles from pharaonic Egypt. *Molecules, 24*, 3761.

Tanaka, K., Kajiyama, N., Ishikura, K., Waga, S., Kikuchi, A., Ohtomo, K., Takagi, T., & Mizuno, S. (1999). Determination of the site of disulfide linkage between heavy and light chains of silk fibroin produced by Bombyx mori. *Biochimica et Biophysica Acta, 1432*, 92–103.

Taylor, G. W. (1983). Detection and identification of dyes on Anglo-Scandinavian textiles. *Studies in Conservation, 28*, 153–160.

Tiedemann, E. J., & Yang, Y. (1995). Fiber-safe extraction of red mordant dyes from hair fibers. *Journal of American Institute for Conservation, 34*, 195–206.

Valianou, L., Karapanagiotis, I., & Chryssoulakis, Y. (2009). Comparison of extraction methods for the analysis of natural dyes in historical textiles by High-Performance Liquid Chromatography. *Analytical and Bioanalytical Chemistry, 395*, 2175–2189.

van Doorn, N. L., Wilson, J., Hollund, H., Soressi, M., & Collins, M. J. (2012). Site-specific deamidation of glutamine: a new marker of bone collagen deterioration. *Rapid Communication in Mass Spectrometry, 26*(19), 2319–2327.

Van Elslande, E., Guérineau, V., Thirioux, V., Richard, G., Richardin, P., Laprévote, O., Hussler, G., & Walter, P. (2008). Analysis of ancient Greco–Roman cosmetic materials using laser desorption ionization and electrospray ionization mass spectrometry. *Analytical and Bioanalytical Chemistry, 390*, 1873–1879.

Vilaplana, F., Nilsson, J., Sommer, D. V. P., & Karlsson, S. (2015). Analytical markers for silk degradation: comparing historic silk and silk artificially aged in different environments. *Analytical and Bioanalytical Chemistry, 407*, 1433–1449.

Wallert, A. (1986). Fluorescent assay of quinone, lichen and redwood dyestuffs. *Studies in Conservation, 31*, 145–155.

Warinner, C., Korzow Richter, K., & Collins, M. J. (2022). Paleoproteomics. *Chemical Reviews, 122*, 13401–13446.

Wouters, J. (1985). High performance liquid chromatography of anthraquinones: Analysis of plant and insect extracts and dyed textiles. *Studies in Conservation, 30*(3), 119–128.

Wouters, J., & Rosario-Chirinos, N. (1992). Dye analysis of pre-Columbian Peruvian textiles with high-performance liquid chromatography and diode-array detection. *Journal of American Institute for Conservation, 31*, 237–255.

Wouters, J., & Verhecken, A. (1989). The coccid insect dyes: HPLC and computerized diode array analysis of dyed yarns. *Studies in Conservation, 34*(4), 189–200.

Wyplosz, N. (2003). *Laser desorption mass spectrometric studies of artists' organic pigments*. Molart. Available at: https://ir.amolf.nl/pub/987/9245F_wyplosz.pdf

Zhang, X., & Laursen, R. A. (2005). Development of mild extraction methods for the analysis of natural dyes in textiles of historical interest using LC–diode array detector–MS. *Analytical Chemistry, 77*, 2022–2025.

Zhang, X. M., & Wyeth, P. (2010). Using FTIR spectroscopy to detect sericin on historic silk. *SCIENCE CHINA Chemistry, 53*, 626–631.

Zhang, X., & Yuan, S. (2010). Measuring quantitatively the deterioration degree of ancient silk textiles by viscometry. *Chinese Journal of Chemistry, 58*(4), 656–662.

Zhang, X., Boytner, R., Cabrera, J. L., & Lauren, R. (2007). Identification of yellow dye types in pre-Columbian Andean textiles. *Analytical Chemistry, 79*, 1575–1582.

Zhang, X., Good, I., & Laursen, R. (2008). Characterization of dyestuffs in ancient textiles from Xinjiang. *Journal of Archaeological Science, 35*, 1095–1103.

Zhang, L., Tian, K., Wang, Y., Zou, J., & Du, Z. (2017). Characterization of Ancient Chinese Textiles by ultra-high performance liquid chromatography/quadrupole-time of flight mass spectrometry. *International Journal of Mass Spectrometry, 421*, 61–70.

Open Access This chapter is licensed under the terms of the Creative Commons Attribution 4.0 International License (http://creativecommons.org/licenses/by/4.0/), which permits use, sharing, adaptation, distribution and reproduction in any medium or format, as long as you give appropriate credit to the original author(s) and the source, provide a link to the Creative Commons license and indicate if changes were made.

The images or other third party material in this chapter are included in the chapter's Creative Commons license, unless indicated otherwise in a credit line to the material. If material is not included in the chapter's Creative Commons license and your intended use is not permitted by statutory regulation or exceeds the permitted use, you will need to obtain permission directly from the copyright holder.

Chapter 7
Radiocarbon for the Dating of Fibres and Textiles: The Case Study of a Silk Knitted Fabric from Pompeii

Mariaelena Fedi, Serena Barone, Francesca Coletti, and Lucia Liccioli

Abstract Radiocarbon (or ^{14}C) is a well-known long-living isotope, which is used as a natural chronometer to reconstruct the ages of organic materials and of some inorganic systems as well. In archaeological contexts, fibres and textiles, both of animal and vegetal origin, represent materials that are well suitable for the application of this dating method. Many important aspects have however to be considered while dating. As first, starting from the collection of the sample to be dated, the isolation of just the original carbon-based fraction is clearly mandatory. To achieve this and thus to remove all the possible contaminations, a proper sample preparation procedure is typically applied. Such a procedure must be tailored to the specific material to be treated and sometimes must be adapted to its preservation state. In this paper, we will show the case of the dating of an archaeological textile fragment found in Pompeii (Italy), discussing how much its degradation state had an impact on the overall preparation. Radiocarbon dating has been successfully performed on one silk-knitted textile found in Pompeii during excavations conducted in the nineteen century, carried out without a stratigraphical dig. However, the object has been included in the ancient textile collection of the Vesuvian area mainly composed of carbonized remains. The dating was performed to ascertain the actual age of the sample, demonstrating its later date between the fifteenth and the sixteenth centuries AD.

Keywords Radiocarbon dating · Pompeii · Textiles

M. Fedi · L. Liccioli
National Institute for Nuclear Physics – INFN, Florence, Italy

S. Barone
National Institute for Nuclear Physics – INFN, Florence, Italy
Department of Physics and Astronomy, University of Florence, Sesto Fiorentino, Italy

F. Coletti (✉)
Department of Science of Antiquities, Sapienza University of Rome, Rome, Italy
e-mail: francesca.coletti@uniroma1.it

© The Author(s), under exclusive license to Springer Nature Switzerland AG 2024
F. Coletti et al. (eds.), *Multidisciplinary Approaches for the Investigation of Textiles and Fibres in the Archaeological Field*, Interdisciplinary Contributions to Archaeology, https://doi.org/10.1007/978-3-031-73812-8_7

7.1 Introduction

Fibres of both animal and plant origins have been exploited by humans for most of their history to manufacture ropes and fabrics for several purposes. For instance, such items can be found as garments, accessories, soft furnishing, bandages to wrap mummies, and as other ancient artefacts, such as canvas and *incamottatura* in paintings (Fabiani et al., 2019; Gleba & Mannering, 2012; Jenkins, 2003; Good, 2001; Cardon & Feugère, 2000; Barber, 1991). Being originated from an organism, either an animal or a plant, that once has been alive, textiles fibres are good materials to be dated by radiocarbon, i.e. by the measurement of the residual concentration of this rare isotope. The growing academic interest in textile research demonstrates how much ancient fabrics can tell us about past societies' identity, social and economic factors, considering them as one of the early tangible expressions of human technology and culture. The recent methodological advance in textile archaeology, which includes the application of scientific diagnostic methods to textile materials, allows the in-depth investigation of these perishable and too-long underestimated artefacts. In the past, too often, textile materials were barely reported in excavation journals, stored separately from related objects found in the same context, and, thus, studied without considering their context of recovery. This all could cause to mislead the correct dating and interpretation of these artefacts from the technological and functional point of view, as well as their social and identity significance.

In this article, we will review the radiocarbon dating method and its possible application, choosing as a case study of a knitted silk fabric found in Pompeii during excavations conducted in the nineteen century. After introducing the basics of the dating method and which is the most suitable measuring technique to be used especially in cultural heritage frameworks, possible critical aspects will be discussed and the example of the application of radiocarbon dating to the mentioned sample recovered in an archaeological context will be given.

7.2 Basics of Radiocarbon Dating and Accelerator Mass Spectrometry (AMS)

Radiocarbon (^{14}C) is one of the natural isotopes of carbon (Libby, 1964). As its name itself suggests, radiocarbon is radioactive: it decays to ^{14}N with a half-life of 5700 ± 30 years. (Kutschera, 2013). It is present in the atmosphere, in the oceans, in rivers and lakes, and in all the living organisms of the biosphere that are in equilibrium with the atmosphere or the waters. Since the half-life is short with respect to the life of Earth, it would not be widespread in nature unless it were not continuously produced. In fact, ^{14}C is produced in the upper layers of atmosphere by interaction of neutrons from cosmic rays with ^{14}N nuclei (Gäggeler, 1995). Once produced, it rapidly oxidizes to $^{14}CO_2$ and eventually enters the natural carbon cycle. The balance that is established between the production mechanism, the times characteristics of the transitions from one carbon reservoir to another and the decay process is such that an equilibrium condition is established: as a first approximation, the radiocarbon concentration in atmosphere and, consequently, in all the living organisms that exchange carbon with the atmosphere, both in direct and in undirect ways, is constant and equal to about 1.2×10^{-12} (Choppin et al., 2002). When the living organism dies, or a certain inorganic system is isolated from its carbon reservoir, that exchange ceases. If the organism can afterwards be considered as a close system, since this moment, the ^{14}C concentration starts to decrease due to the radioactive decay, according to the well-known exponential law:

$$^{14}R(t) = {}^{14}R_0 e^{-\frac{t}{\tau}}$$

where $^{14}R(t)$ is the concentration after the time t since the death, $^{14}R_0$ is the concentration at the moment that can be identified as time 0, i.e. the moment of the death, and τ is the mean life, which is connected to the already mentioned half-life. By measuring the residual concentration $^{14}R(t)$, we can thus estimate the time t, provided that the initial concentration and the mean life are known:

$$t = \tau \ln\left(\frac{{}^{14}R_0}{{}^{14}R(t)}\right)$$

A detailed description of the dating method, including a comprehensive discussion of all the hypotheses which the method is based on, is beyond the scope of this paper (see e.g. Bronk Ramsey, 2008; Jull et al., 2013; Hajdas et al., 2021). Here, we just recall that, after measuring the residual radiocarbon concentration, the equation above allows us to estimate what we call the conventional radiocarbon age, typically expressed in years Before Present (BP), where present is 1950 CE.

To evaluate the conventional radiocarbon age, τ and $^{14}R_0$ are chosen as 8033 years, the so-called Libby mean life, and as the reference concentration in atmosphere in 1950, respectively.

Thus, the time scale of the conventional radiocarbon age does not actually correspond to our "normal" calendar scale and thus the dating measurement is not complete unless the process of calibration is performed. The most appropriate calibration curve must be chosen according to the carbon reservoir the organism had exchanged with and to the latitude where it lived: for instance, at present, IntCal20 is the curve to be used to calibrate[1] the radiocarbon ages measured for those terrestrial materials that lived in the northern hemisphere and are expected to be dated before 1950 (Reimer et al., 2020).

From the discussion above, a key issue of the dating method is clearly the choice of the technique used to measure the residual radiocarbon concentration. In principle, a mass spectrometric technique might be exploited to count the ^{14}C atoms in a

---

[1] The calibration curves are regularly revised and upgraded by the international radiocarbon community (Reimer, 2022); to look for the most recent ones, all the references and information can be found in the journal *Radiocarbon*, published by Cambridge University Press.

sample and then to evaluate its radiocarbon concentration. However, also in general but especially when dealing with archaeological and/or art contexts, several constraints must be considered (Boaretto, 2009; Wright, 2017).

The measurement of the radiocarbon concentration is invasive and the collection of at least one sample from the artwork or the stratigraphic layer to be dated is mandatory: a measurement technique that allows us to collect the smallest possible sample is thus clearly preferable to preserve the integrity of the original object or context, or—sometimes—to also give us the possibility to collect more than one sample so that the statistical significance of the measurement can be improved; the natural radiocarbon abundance in atmosphere and in the living systems is extremely low (see above) and it decreases along as time goes on after isolation of the system or its death: the measurement technique should be thus very efficient and sensitive (the higher is the sensitivity the older are the possible datable ages); in nature, there are elements and molecules, such as ^{14}N, ^{12}CH and $^{13}CH_2$ whose masses are remarkably similar to ^{14}C mass and that are much more abundant than radiocarbon itself, so that their signals can represent a strong interference in a mass spectrometry measurement, hiding the real signal we would be interested in: the measurement technique should suppress these interferences without decreasing the radiocarbon count rate.

At present, all these issues can be addressed by Accelerator Mass Spectrometry (AMS), which has so far become the most applied technique to count radiocarbon particles for dating purposes (Kutschera, 2016). In an AMS measurement, after a proper preparation, the sample, typically reduced to pure graphite or to gaseous CO_2, is inserted into the ion source of a tandem electrostatic accelerator. Ions from the sample are extracted, their characteristics, i.e. their charge, energy and mass, are analysed along the accelerator beam line to identify the ions we are interested in (^{14}C and the other natural carbon isotopes) and to reject all the others. Eventually, ions are accelerated and separately counted. The great advantage of AMS is the capability of suppress the elemental and molecular interferences of radiocarbon, just thanks to the mechanisms that are peculiar of a tandem accelerator. Remarkably high sensitivities can thus be reached: ^{14}C concentrations as low as about 10^{-15} can be measured, allowing us to date samples as old as about 50,000 years. In addition, in AMS, measurements are performed on samples whose carbon content[2] is well below 1 mg, even down to few tens of micrograms. This allows us to collect small samples from the artworks or the context to be dated, thus limiting the invasiveness of the method. Very good precision in quite short measuring times can be obtained: for a "modern" sample, just 30 min of measurement can be sufficient to get a precision on the measured ^{14}C concentration better than 0.5%, which corresponds to dating a sample with an experimental uncertainty better than 40 years.

---

[2] The mentioned masses correspond to the typical carbon mass of the graphite sample that is inserted in the accelerator ion source (or to the equivalent mass of the gaseous CO_2 flowing into the ion source as well); the masses to be collected are indeed larger, typically in the range from few tens to few hundreds of milligrams and depend on both the sample material (for instance, whether the sample is a charcoal or a bone) and on its state of preservation.

7.3 Radiocarbon Applied to Textiles

^{14}C allows us to get information about the age of materials, thus it supports us to solve the basic issue of "when". However, if talking about chronology, the first question to be addressed is: when did that event happen? Thus, when applying radiocarbon dating, the fundamental aspect is the relation between the event we are interested in and the age of the material we can determine. The age of a dated material can be either directly correlated to the event, or can be just indirectly associated, giving us a t*erminus post quem* information.

When we date a textile fragment, what we can estimate by radiocarbon is the age of the fibre (Turnbull et al., 2000; Hajdas, 2014): for instance, in case of an animal-origin material, we can date when the sheep were shaved (for wool), or, in the case of a plant-origin material, we can determine when the cotton or the linen plants were cut. Therefore, we can expect a time delay between the collection of the raw material and the preparation of the fibre and the thread, and, finally, the manufacturing of the work. Fortunately, when speaking about textiles, raw materials come from short-living organisms and, also considering that they can be fragile and highly degradable, we can expect just a minor delay between the cut or the collection and the manufacturing, well within the typical uncertainties we can obtain in radiocarbon dating. In addition, a textile can be teared up, or it can lose its mechanical properties, or it can be also easily subjected to strong wear: due to this, the possibility of re-using the same raw material for a different product after lot of time since the first use is not so likely. This characteristic makes textiles preferable for radiocarbon dating with respect to, for instance, wooden artifacts that are associated to the same temporal horizon, since wood may be affected by the so-called *old wood problem* (Schiffer, 1986).

Even though we can basically neglect the possible issue of a later re-use, the question of possible later mends and thus of the significance of sampling is worth to be mentioned. When working especially on a complex fabric object, the collection of the samples to be dated should be performed by the "scientist" and the archaeologist together with a textile expert, and a conservator. This is important to identify darns that may have been made after the original manufacturing, as well as possible distinct parts sewed together. In the latter case, one can suggest to—at least—collect a sample from each of the distinct sections to verify that any of the section is not a later addition.

To check the quality of the thread and whether more than one fibre have been used to produce the textile, high magnificence optical microscopy or electron microscopy (SEM) can be exploited (Goodway, 1987). Indeed, each of the fibre species has a very peculiar surface morphology. Wool shows overlapping scales called cuticle cells on the surface, cotton is characterised by twisted ribbon fibres or by collapsed and twisted tubes, silk surface is smooth with some possible fractures. Of course, if a same thread is composed of different natural species, this could not introduce any issue in the radiocarbon measurement, because one can expect that the different species, being natural, were produced and combined at the same time.

On the contrary, if some synthetic component is identified as mixed with the main natural fibre, it may introduce some old contamination, unless it is completely removed in the sample pre-treatment before the AMS measurement. Synthetic strands are originated from industrial processes exploiting petroleum-derived products and are thus expected to have a very low amount of ^{14}C, even close or below the limit of sensitivity of the measuring technique. Consequently, one can suggest verifying the quality and the species of the textile fibres by microscopy whenever one can suspect that modern or contemporary fibres have been added to the original materials, like, for example, in the case of mends or of possible fakes and forgeries.

The discussion just introduced above allows us to draw some other important considerations about the right carbon which must be identified and collected before the AMS measurement. As mentioned in Sect. 7.2, one of the fundamental hypotheses in radiocarbon dating is that the organism must have been a close system since the moment of its death. On the contrary, for example, if we suspect that a modern type of fibres may have been added to the original one, we know that the system has not been closed. The same can be applied to a textile which has been buried for centuries underneath the soil and that, just due to the prolonged contact with the external environment, has suffered degradation and carbon exchanges with the surroundings, thus altering its original radiocarbon content. Another situation that can occur is related to the treatments that textiles may have been subjected to in the moment of their use. For example, textile used for wrapping mummies in ancient Egypt were often soaked in natural carbon-containing materials, such as oils, gums and bitumen. While oils and gums are expected to be contemporary to the production of the fibres and then the textile, bitumen is expected to be depleted in radiocarbon content and thus it is expected to decrease the overall ^{14}C concentration, apparently ageing the dated sample (Quiles et al., 2014). Its complete removal before any AMS measurement is clearly mandatory. Other possible sources of contamination can be correlated to restoration processes. The possibility of mends has been already discussed above. In addition, conservative interventions may have been performed using glues or resins, which, if on one hand they have later contributed to make the restored textile more fragile, they have also introduced additional carbon characterized by a different radiocarbon content, thus possibly altering the original ^{14}C abundance and the apparent age that can be measured (Fedi et al., 2014).

All things considered, it is thus clear that no dating measurement can be performed without a first cleaning procedure that must remove all the possible contaminants and collect the carbon fraction, which is most appropriate for the measurement itself. This is mandatory and it is independent from the measurement technique we can choose, even different than AMS. The cleaning procedures, or the pre-treatment procedures, as they are typically referred to in the radiocarbon community, are based on either the use of acidic and basic aqueous solutions to get rid of possible natural exogenous substances or on the use of solvents, either exploiting Soxhlet extractions (Bruhn et al., 2001) or easier procedures based on magnetic stirring and only one solvent (Fedi et al., 2014; Liccioli et al., 2017), when anthropogenic contaminations are expected. The case study described in the present paper shows how all the just discussed issues can be applied to a "real" situation.

7.4 The Case of the Silk Fragment of the Textile Collection from Pompeii

The eruption of Mount Vesuvius in 79 AD sealed the city of Pompeii, causing exceptional micro-environmental conditions due to high temperature and fire occurrence in specific contexts, preserving a multitude of carbonised organic materials and textiles. These finds can be easily correlated to the eruption, giving them a *terminus ante quem* happened in 79 AD. However, few fragments, which are considered part of the large textile collection from the Vesuvian area, preserve part of their original organic properties without showing traces of carbonisation or mineralisation (Fig. 7.1). Due to the lack of information relating to the recovery and the specific context of discovery of these fabrics, six of them were selected for radiocarbon dating in order to verify their antiquity. Five samples showed manufacturing techniques and raw materials pertaining to the chronological period considered. The results of the investigations confirmed their antiquity, dating these samples between the I century BC and the I century AD (Coletti, 2020, forthcoming).

On the contrary, the case study selected for this paper, even though considered to be ancient (Schieck et al. 2014, fig. 12, Pl. VI), showed a technical construction never attested before for the Roman period and the textile raw material was likely to be imported and still poorly attested for the early imperial age. Therefore, the 79 AD *terminus ante quem* was called into question since this sample would have been unique in the Western world if dated to the first century AD.

The knitted fabric is now stored at the National Archaeological Museum in Naples and only a general provenance from Pompeii is known (Soler Villabella, 1937).

Fig. 7.1 The silk fabric. (Image: F. Coletti)

7.5 Description of the Sample

7.5.1 Technical Analysis

The find is highly fragmented, with an estimated minimum size of about 16×11 cm (Fig. 7.1). It also appeared very fragile, as can be noticed in Fig. 7.1. The surface is made with regular and tight loops and shiny reddish-brown threads. The fragment is realised with plain "two-needle knitting" made with silk fibres that are not spun and parallel to each other (Table 7.1). From a technical point of view, the fabric is formed with a single yarn that forms continuous rows with open loops. This is a weft knit, which means that the stitches run from left to right horizontally in the fabric. The fabric surface is characterised by a flat and uniform appearance. The only pattern is the interlocking 'v' shapes on the front and the crescent shapes on the back (Fig. 7.2). The fine loop size, about 1 mm, suggests the use of particularly small-diameter manufacturing tools.

7.5.2 Morphological Analysis

The fragmentary state of the fabric allowed us to take a small sample from already detached threads in order to perform microscopic investigations. The morphological investigation of the fibres was carried out combining optical and scanning electron (SEM) microscopy. Optical microscopy analyses were performed using a Nikon Eclipse transmitted light optical microscope (LM) with 10X aperture and 10x and 20x plan achromatic objectives with Digital Imaging Accessories. The scanning electron microscope—SEM Hitachi TM 3000, magnification 40x–2000x, was used in low vacuum with an acceleration voltage of 15 kV observation condition mode. In order to preserve and reuse the samples, the metallic film coating, generally required for SEM analysis, was not applied.

This high-power approach allowed us to identify the fibres used for the manufacturing of the fabric. The yarn is made with degummed silk fibres with a diameter of 10–13 µm, characterized by a smooth appearance and a general absence of surface morphology (see Figs. 7.2 and 7.3). Due to the state of degradation, the fibres tend to break into very short segments (see Fig. 7.3d).

7.5.3 Sample Preparation and AMS Measurement

As already discussed above, each sample to be dated must be carefully cleaned to remove all the possible contaminations due to the external environment where the sample had remained during past centuries. When we expect just possible natural contaminations, the typical pre-treatment and cleaning procedure that is applied is

Table 7.1 Technical details of the fabric

Object	Provenience	Museum	Material	Colour	Size (cm)	Yarn diameter in mm	Yarn twist	Wales (vertical loops) per 1 cm	Courses (horizontal loops) per 1 cm	Technique
Knitted fragments (30 pieces)	Pompeii	National Archaeological Museum of Naples. Italy	Silk	Reddish Brown (HPLC-DAD: absence of molecular markers characteristics of the indigo dyes)	Largest fragment 7 × 3.5	0.3	No twist	12	11	Undetermined, simple/plain knit

Image: F. Coletti

Fig. 7.2 Stereomicroscope images of the find: (**a**) low magnification image where the Stockinette manufacturing is evident (on the left side, reverse loops; on the right side, face loops); (**b**) details of the fabric construction and loops. (Image: F. Coletti)

based on baths in—alternatively—acidic and basic solutions. HCl solutions are usually used to get rid of possible secondary carbonates and NaOH solutions are used to remove humic substances that are expected especially in the case of archaeological samples. Molarity and quantity of the solutions, temperatures and duration of the treatments are chosen according to the material and its state of preservation. In fact, when the sample to be treated is not well preserved, losing it during one of the preparation steps can be highly probable.

In the present case, as already mentioned, the sample was very fragile and not well conserved. In such a condition, the treatment in NaOH could be very aggressive. In addition, the material was silk: silk contains the keratin protein, which is known to be partially soluble in alkaline solutions. Thus, we chose not to apply a basic pre-treatment, according to what explained above, but just a step in HCl. This bath was repeated twice. As expected, we obtained a large mass loss: a mass of 25 milligrams was treated, obtaining only 5 milligrams of cleaned sample, as measured after oven drying of the residual mass at the end of pre-treatment. That mass was anyway sufficient to independently prepare two separate graphite samples (laboratory codes Fi3191 and Fi3199). To this purpose, two fractions of the cleaned material were combusted using an elemental analyser (Thermo Flash 1112 in CN configuration), which also allowed us to separate the evolved CO_2 from the other combustion products. For each of the sample fractions, CO_2 was then transferred to the so-called graphitization line where it was converted to elemental carbon, i. e. to graphite, finally pressed in pellets to be inserted into the accelerator ion source for the following AMS measurement.

Measurement was performed at the AMS dedicated beam line of the 3 MV tandem accelerator installed in Florence, INFN-LABEC laboratory[3] (Fedi et al., 2007). The isotopic ratios $^{14}C/^{12}C$ measured in the unknown samples were corrected for

---

[3] INFN-Labec is part of CHNet, the network of laboratories of the National Institute of Nuclear Physics (INFN) that are involved in the development and the applications of techniques and technologies applied to Cultural Heritage.

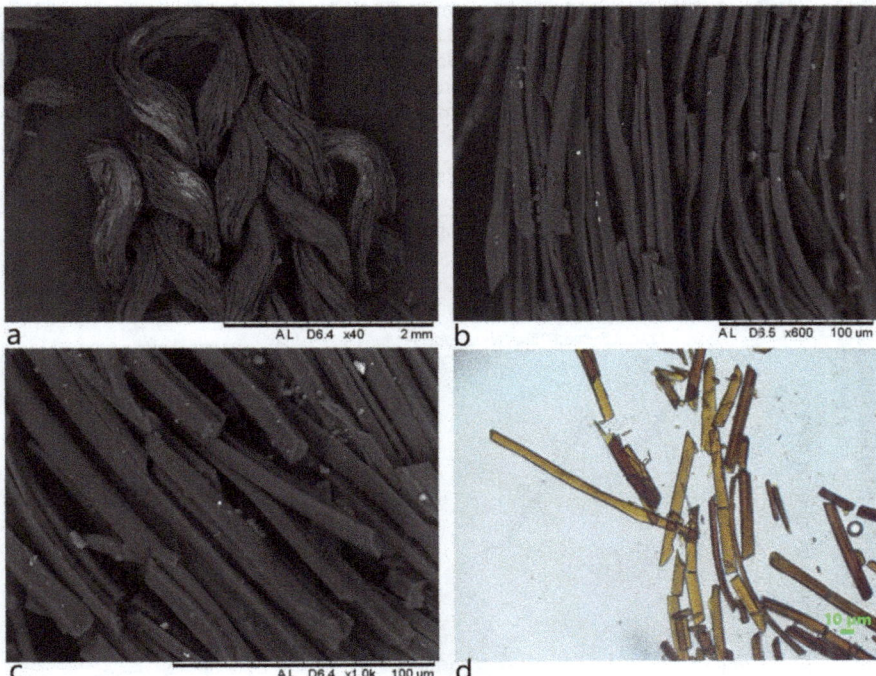

Fig. 7.3 Morphological analysis: (**a**) SEM micrograph of the mesh; (**b**) silk fibres, SEM longitudinal view; (**c**) silk fibres, SEM cross-sectional view; (**d**) LM image of the silk fibres, where their high fragmentation can be noticed. (Image: F. Coletti)

background counts and for isotopic fractionation ($^{13}C/^{12}C$ isotopic ratics were also measured in the accelerator beam line) and then normalized to the average ratios measured in a set of samples prepared from a standard reference material, namely NIST Oxalic Acid II (SRM4990C), whose radiocarbon concentration is known. Other secondary standard samples prepared from IAEA C7 were also measured to verify the accuracy of the overall procedure.

Calibration of the obtained conventional radiocarbon age was performed by using OxCal software, version 4.4 (Bronk Ramsey, 2009), and taking the IntCal20 calibration curve as reference (Reimer et al., 2020).

7.6 Results and Discussion

A summary of the dating results is presented in Table 7.2. After verifying that the two prepared graphite samples were statistically consistent one with the other, the best estimate of the ^{14}C concentration, and therefore of the conventional radiocarbon age, was evaluated as the weighted average of the two fractions Fi3191 and Fi3199.

Table 7.2 Results of the ^{14}C-AMS measurement. Both measured ^{14}C concentration and the correspondent conventional radiocarbon age are reported with 1-sigma experimental uncertainties; as for calibrated ages, the time intervals calculated at 68% and 95% levels of probability, respectively, are shown. In the case of the calibrated age at 68% level of confidence, two separate intervals have been obtained and are shown, also indicating in the brackets the level of probability for each of the intervals

	^{14}C conc. (pMC)	t_{RC} (years BP)	Cal age (CE) (68% level of probability)	Cal age (CE) (95% level of probability)
"Silk"	95.81 ± 0.46	345 ± 40	1485–1525 (24%) 1555–1635 (44%)	1460–1640

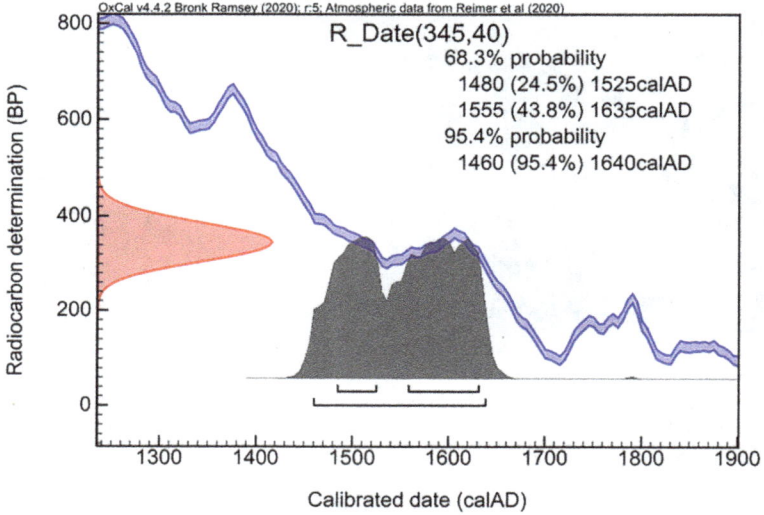

Fig. 7.4 Graphical representation of the calibration process for the measured radiocarbon age of 345±40 years BP. The portion of the IntCal20 calibration curve is drawn in blue, the measured conventional radiocarbon age, treated as a normally distributed random variable, is in red, and the distribution of probability for the calibrated age is in dark grey on the horizontal axis

The measured conventional radiocarbon age is 345 ± 40 years BP. The calibrated age probable time intervals are reported at 68% and 95% levels of probability, respectively. When two intervals are obtained, the level of probability for each of the intervals is indicated in brackets. Details of the calibration process are also shown in Fig. 7.4.

The silk knitted fabric from Pompeii has been dated to a period between the fifteenth and the seventeenth century AD, which is far more recent than the ancient remains of the Pompeian textile collection.

This result is in line with what is known about the history of the knitting technique, which was an innovation of the medieval and early modern periods originated in the Middle East (Malcom-Davies, 2018; Riley et al., 2013). This technique appears in scattered remains found in different geographic areas from the thirteenth to fifteenth centuries in Europe (Rutt, 1987; Wyss, 1973). However, the origin and spread of knitting are still unclear since it has received scant attention in scientific research, and little has been published so far (Black, 2012). The technique is frequently confused with the so-called 'nålbindning', realised with a single needle, dating back to the ninth millennium BC.

In this framework, the silk from Pompeii would have represented an unprecedented case in the history of textiles. On the contrary, the radiocarbon dating points to a Renaissance provenance, despite the inclusion of our sample in the ancient textile collection. To explain such a discrepancy, we can consider that the archaeological investigations in Pompeii had already started since 1748 and, thus, there is often a lack of recorded data regarding the recovery and find spots of the remains. At that time, the Vesuvian area was mainly a productive region. At the end of the fifteenth century AD, a canal for water supply between Torre Annunziata and the Sarno River was built, and this circumstance led to the early rediscovery of ancient Pompeii (Stefani & di Maio, 2011). Therefore, this item could either originate from a Renaissance period occupation of the site or could have been found elsewhere and erroneously included in the MANN Vesuvian collection.

To conclude, the work presented here contributes to evidence some interesting multidisciplinary points. As far as the radiocarbon dating method is concerned, it shows how much important is tailoring the sample preparation procedure to the material we are processing, and in particular to its preservation state. From the archaeological-historical point of view, the paper highlights the urgent need for a new and rigorous methodological approach to be applied in textile research. New projects, such as for example Knitting in Early Modern Europe (KEME) (Malcom-Davies, 2019), are for sure welcomed for the next. A common feature for all the expected new projects that we wish for is favouring the interdisciplinary collaboration between scientists, textile archaeologists, historians and conservators.

Acknowledgements The *Textile Culture at Pompeii* Project started in 2014 as a multidisciplinary project conducted in the framework of a research and cooperation agreement between the Archaeological Park of Pompeii, the Department of Science of Antiquity, Sapienza University of Rome, and the CEZA-Curt-Engelhorn-Centre of Archaeometry gGmbH, Mannheim. The research collaboration between Sapienza University and the Archaeological Park of Pompeii was renewed in 2019, integrating the Scientific Departments of Sapienza University. Currently the project is carried out in the framework of the Sapienza Research Center for "Archaeology and Archaeometry of Ancient Textile - A3Tex" (Director. Prof. M. Galli). We all are grateful to the Archaeological Park of Pompeii and the National Archaeological Museum of Naples (MANN), represented by the Director G. Zuchtriegel and the Director of the MANN, P. Giuglierini, as well as the General Director of the Italian Museums, Prof. M. Osanna for the kind permission to allow us to work on the textile remains. Our deepest thanks also go to Dr. S. Bracci, Dr. E. De Carolis, Prof. I. Degano, Dr. L. Melillo, Prof. E. Pernicka.

Authors' contributions Introduction: FC; Radiocarbon basics and dating: MF, SB. LL; Textile and fibre analysis: FC. All the authors equally contributed to the result and discussion.

References

Barber, E. J. W. (1991). *Prehistoric textiles: The development of cloth in the Neolithic and Bronze Ages with special reference to the Aegean*. Princeton University Press.
Black, S. (2012). *Knitting: Fashion industry craft*. Victoria and Albert Museum.
Boaretto, E. (2009). Dating materials in good archaeological contexts: The next challenge for radiocarbon analysis. *Radiocarbon, 51*(1), 275–281.
Bronk Ramsey, C. (2008). Radiocarbon dating: Revolutions in understanding. *Archaeometry, 50*(2), 249–275.
Bronk Ramsey, C. (2009). Bayesian analysis of radiocarbon dates. *Radiocarbon, 51*, 337–360.
Bruhn, F., Duhr, A., Grootes, P. M., & Mintrop, A. (2001). Chemical removal of conservation substances by 'Soxhlet'-type extraction. *Radiocarbon, 43*, 229–237.
Cardon, D., & Feugère, M. (Eds.). (2000). *Archéologie des textiles des origines au V siècle. Actes du colloque de Lattes, Octobre 1999* (Monographies Instrumentum 14). Éditions Mergoil.
Choppin, G. R., Liljenzin, J.-O., & Rydberg, J. (2002). *Radiochemistry and nuclear chemistry*. Elsevier.
Coletti, F. (2020). *I tessuti di Pompei: materiali, tecniche di lavorazione e contesti*. PhD thesis, Heidelberg-Rome.
Coletti, F. (forthcoming). *I reperti tessili di Pompei e d'area vesuviana*, Edizioni Quasar.
Fabiani, G., Fedi, M., Giuliani, M. R., Di Giulio, G., Galotta, G., Goli, G., Liccioli, L., Mazzanti, P., Signorini, G., & Togni, M. (2019). The discovery of "marouflage" on decorated structural timber in a villa of the XV century. *International Journal of Conservation Science, 10*(1), 59–68.
Fedi, M. E., Cartocci, A., Manetti, M., Taccetti, F., & Mandò, P. A. (2007). The ^{14}C AMS facility at LABEC, Florence. *Nuclear Instrument and Method in Physics Research B, 259*, 18–22.
Fedi, M. E., Caforio, L., Liccioli, L., Mandò, P. A., Salvini, A., & Tacceti, F. (2014). A simple and effective removal procedure of synthetic resins to obtain accurate radiocarbon dates of restored artworks. *Radiocarbon, 56*, 969–979.
Gäggeler, H. W. (1995). Radioactivity in the Atmosphere. *Radiochimica Acta, 70–71*, 345–353.
Gleba, M., & Mannering, U. (Eds.). (2012). *Textiles and textile production in Europe: From prehistory to AD 400*. Oxbow Books.
Good, I. (2001). Archaeological textiles: A review of current research. *Annual Review of Anthropology, 30*(1), 209–226.
Goodway, M. (1987). Fiber identification in practice. *Journal of the American Institute of Conservation, 26*, 27–44.
Hajdas, I. (2014). Textiles and radiocarbon dating. *Radiocarbon, 56*(2), 637–643.
Hajdas, I., Ascough, P., Garnett, M., & Fallon, S. J. (2021). Radiocarbon dating. *Nature Reviews Methods Primers, 1*(1), 1–26.
Jenkins, D. (Ed.). (2003). *The Cambridge history of western textiles*. Cambridge University Press.
Jull, T., Burr, G., & Hodgins, G. (2013). Radiocarbon dating, reservoir effects, and calibration. *Quaternary International, 299*, 64–71.
Kutschera, W. (2013). Applications of accelerator mass spectrometry. *International Journal of Mass Spectrometry, 349*, 203–218.
Kutschera, W. (2016). Accelerator mass spectrometry: State of the art and perspectives. *Advances in Physics: X, 1*(4), 570–595.
Libby, W. (1964). Radiocarbon dating. In *Nobel lectures, chemistry 1942–1962*. Elsevier.
Liccioli, A., Fedi, M., Carraresi, L., & Mandò, P. A. (2017). Characterization of the chloroform-based pre-treatment method for 14C dating of restored wooden samples. *Radiocarbon, 59*, 757–764.
Malcom-Davies, J. (2018). Knitting virtual tribes together: New audiences for cultural objects. *IOP Conference Series: Materials Science and Engineering, 364*(1), 012031. https://doi.org/10.1088/1757-899X/364/1/012031

Malcom-Davies, J. (2019). Knitting comes of age: The development of a scientific approach to the study of knitwork. In A. Serrano, M. J. Ferreira, & E. C. de Groot (Eds.), *Estudos sobre têxteis históricos. Studies in historical textiles. Conservar Património* 31, 133–143.

Quiles, A., Delqué-Količ, E., Bellot-Gurlet, L., Comby-Zerbino, C., Ménager, M., Paris, C., Souprayen, C., Vieillescazes, C., Andreu-Lanoë, G., & Madrigal, K. (2014). Embalming as a source of contamination for radiocarbon dating of Egyptian mummies: On a new chemical protocol to extract bitumen. *ArcheoSciences, revue d'archéométrie, 38*, 135–149

Reimer, P. J. (2022). Evolution of radiocarbon calibration. *Radiocarbon, 64*, 523–539.

Reimer, P. J., Austin, W. E. N., Bard, E., Bayliss, A., Blackwell, P. G., Bronk Ramsey, C., Butzin, M., Cheng, H., Edwards, R. L., Friedrich, M., Grootes, P. M., Guilderson, T. P., Hajdas, I., Heaton, T. J., Hogg, A. G., Hughen, K. A., Kromer, B., Manning, S. W., Muscheler, R., Palmer, J. G., Pearson, C., van der Plicht, J., Reimer, R. W., Richards, D. A., Scott, E. M., Southon, J. R., Turney, C. S. M., Wacker, L., Adolphi, F., Büntgen, U., Capano, M., Fahrni, S. M., Fogtmann-Schulz, A., Friedrich, R., Köhler, P., Kudsk, S., Miyake, F., Olsen, J., Reinig, F., Sakamoto, M., Sookdeo, A., & Talamo, S. (2020). The IntCal20 Northern Hemisphere radiocarbon age calibration curve (0–55 cal kBP). *Radiocarbon, 62*(4), 725–757.

Riley, J., Corkhill, B., & Morris, C. (2013). The benefits of knitting for personal and social wellbeing in adulthood: Findings from an international survey. *British Journal of Occupational Therapy, 76*(2), 50–57.

Rutt, R. (1987). *A history of hand knitting*. Batsford.

Schieck, A., Mitschke, S., & Melillo, L. (2014). Purpur, Gold und Seide. Textile Vielfalt aus der Asche des Vesuvs. *Antike Welt, 45*, 15–21.

Schiffer, M. B. (1986). Radiocarbon dating and the "old wood" problem: The case of the Hohokam chronology. *Journal of Archaeological Science, 13*(1), 13–30.

Soler Villabella, R. N. (1937). Una stoffa romana bimillenaria: la "mappa" dell'antiquarium del governatorato di Roma. *Bullettino della Commissione archeologica Comunale di Roma, 65*, 73–82.

Stefani, G., & di Maio, G. (2011). Il Canale Conte di Sarno. In G. Curcio, N. Navone, & S. Villari (Eds.), *Studi su Domenico Fontana 1543–1607* (pp. 213–228). Mendrisio.

Turnbull, J., Sparks, R., & Prior, C. A. (2000). Testing the effectiveness of AMS radiocarbon pre-treatment and preparation on archaeological textiles. *Nuclear Instruments and Methods in Physics Research Section B: Beam Interactions with Materials and Atoms, 172*(1), 469–472.

Wright, D. K. (2017). Accuracy vs. precision: Understanding potential errors from radiocarbon dating on African landscapes. *African Archaeological Review, 34*(3), 303–319.

Wyss, R. (1973). *Die Handarbeiten der Maria: Eine ikonographische Studie unter Berücksichtigung der Textilen Techniken Artes Minores*. Verlag Stämpfli.

Chapter 8
Which Tool for Which Fiber? Experimental Spinning Tests Using Bone, Glass and Amber Instruments

Maria Stella Busana, Denis Francisci, and Agnese Lena

Abstract The TEXPA Project (Textile EXperimental Archaeology), carried out by the Department of Cultural Heritage of the University of Padua within the research on Roman textile in North-Eastern Italy, focused on the link between fibres, especially wool and flax, and textile tools through experimental tests. Combining 3D scanning and traditional craftsmanship, instruments for spinning (spindles, spindle whorls, distaffs) and weaving (loom weights) were reproduced. The paper focuses on the spinning tools and experimental tests. The context in which they were found (burials) and their features (precious and/or fragile materials) have led scholars to hypothesise that these tools only had a symbolic purpose. Our experiments however showed that these instruments could actually be functional: they were suitable for specific types of fibres (especially wool) and the bone spindle with the connected spindle whorl could be used to make a very thin yarn. Furthermore, by analysing the yarns produced using different sets of tools, the experimental tests have highlighted the determining role of fiber and spinner's skill in the characteristics of the resulting yarns. Experimental archaeology applied to textile production has once again proved to be a useful method to understand the function and effectiveness of textile tools and to verify the correspondence between fibres, textiles and instruments.

Keywords Experimental archaeology · Roman age · North-Eastern Italy · Spinning tools · Fiber · Textile

---

M. S. Busana (✉) · A. Lena
Department of Cultural Heritage, University of Padua, Padua, Italy
e-mail: mariastella.busana@unipd.it

D. Francisci
Regional Directorate of Museum – Padua, Padua, Italy

© The Author(s), under exclusive license to Springer Nature Switzerland AG 2024
F. Coletti et al. (eds.), *Multidisciplinary Approaches for the Investigation of Textiles and Fibres in the Archaeological Field*, Interdisciplinary Contributions to Archaeology, https://doi.org/10.1007/978-3-031-73812-8_8

8.1 Introduction

As shown by literary and epigraphic sources, the Roman Venetia (North-Eastern Italy) was very famous for wool and textile production (Basso et al., 2004). The Department of Cultural Heritage of the University of Padua has been developing research projects related to the archaeological textile evidence of the area for several years, analyzing different aspects of the topic. The Pondera project (2009–2014) focused on textile craftsmanship with an innovative approach, based on the systematic census of textile tools discovered in the Veneto Region and the province of Brescia (Lombardy), which resulted in recording 2866 textile tools (Busana et al., 2012; Busana & Tricomi, 2016; Tricomi, 2018). The TRAMA project (Textile in Roman Archeology: Methods and Analysis) (2015–2017) aimed at the census and study of Roman mineralized and organic fabrics, recording 27 samples and offering, for the first time, a picture of textiles produced in the Veneto Region (Busana & Gleba, 2018, 2021). The Lanifica project (2016–2019), as a development of the previous projects, has focused on the study of the textile tools found in burials, extending it to all of Northern Italy and some adjacent provinces, in order to reconstruct the role of women in the productive, social and ideological landscape of the Roman world, with particular attention to textile manufacturing (Rossi, 2018; Busana & Rossi, 2020, 2021; Rossi & Francisci, 2021).

At the same time, the TEXPA project (Textile EXPerimental Archaeology) started to investigate the functionality of some Roman textile tools through their reproduction, made possible by combining innovative 3D technologies and traditional crafts, and experimental archeology (Lena, 2019–2020; Lena et al., 2021). The project focused on both spinning tools (spindles, spindle whorls and distaffs) and weaving tools (loom weights) from the Veneto Region, with the additional aim of understanding the effectiveness of textile tools and reconstructing the characteristics of the yarns and fabrics that could be made using these instruments.

This paper focuses on the preliminary results of the experimental spinning tests carried out using reproductions of some instruments, which were selected for the study because they: (i) were found in Roman graves (first to third century AD); (ii) were intact; (iii) were made of precious materials (amber, bone, glass); (iv) had particular morphometric and weight characteristics.

The four chosen tools are: a bone spindle with an arrow-shaped end, buried with its very light (7 g), discoidal, bone spindle whorl still in situ (Montebelluna, first century AD) (Gambacurta & Manessi, 2000, 34–37; Casagrande et al., 2012, 219); a glass finger distaff (Montebelluna, first century AD) (Gambacurta & Manessi, 2000, 50–53; Casagrande et al., 2012, 164); an amber hand distaff (Verona, second to third century AD) (Bolla, 2004, 207) (Fig. 8.1).

Our experimental tests aimed to answer the following questions: Were they usable working tools? Before being placed in a burial, were they actually used by their owner or were they made specifically for the funerary context? What kind of yarn could they be used to produce? (M.S.B.)

Fig. 8.1 The three original instruments: bone spindle and spindle whorl (Museum of Natural History and Archeology of Montebelluna, Inv. No. 222893; photo: A.M. Lena); glass finger distaff (Museum of Natural History and Archeology of Montebelluna, Inv. No. 241218; photo: C. Rossi) and amber hand distaff (Archaeological Museum of the Roman Theater of Verona; photo: A.M. Lena)

8.2 The Faithful Replicas

Among the guiding principles of the experimental method there is the use of faithful reproductions of the original tools during experimentations (Olofsson et al., 2015, 77): in order to achieve this objective, it was decided to take advantage of new 3D technologies. The ancient textile tools were scanned in 3D using a structured light scanner, a detection technique which consists in projecting on the object a luminous pattern, whose dysfunction read by vision systems allow to calculate the relative depth of the different points of the affected object and get a point cloud with further information concerning the surface (Fig. 8.2).

The planning phase of the scans involved an evaluation of the material and geometric characteristics of the object to be acquired. In particular, due to the physical characteristics of the fossil resin, it was not possible to produce by scanner the 3D model of the amber distaff: in this case, the model was obtained by digital modeling, starting from the archaeological drawing.[1]

---

[1] The design of the amber distaff was provided by Margherita Bolla (Archaeological Museum at the Roman Theatre—Verona).

Fig. 8.2 Phases of digital scanning of the glass finger distaff. (Photo: A.M. Lena)

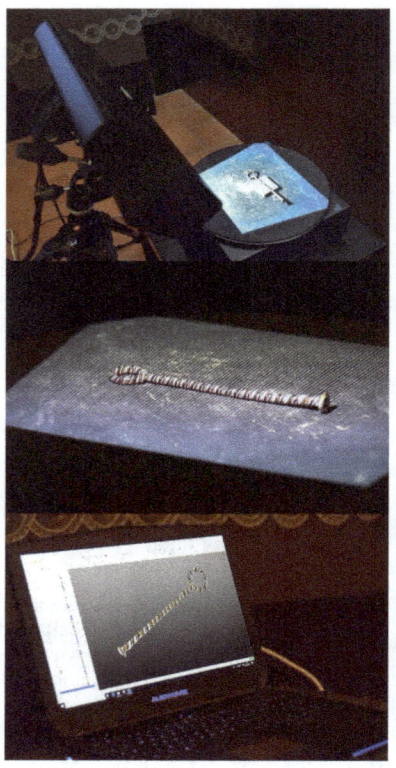

The objects' point clouds were then processed by an appropriate software (RevEng Pro) and the models produced were later converted to .stl format to be finally printed in 3D.[2]

Thanks to this process, three-dimensional prints of the textile tools were obtained which would morphometrically perfectly correspond to the original tools (Fig. 8.3). In contrast, they differ in the weight, which obviously depends on the material of the reproduction.[3]

---

[2] Spinning tools were scanned by Emanuela Faresin (dBC) and printed at the laboratory Te.Si (University of Padua) in Rovigo (printer ConneX3 PolyJet Technology).

[3] The 3D prints have been realized in photopolymer material Vero White Plus for the reproduction of the spindle and the hand distaff, and Digital ABS for the ring distaff.

8 Which Tool for Which Fiber? Experimental Spinning Tests Using Bone, Glass...

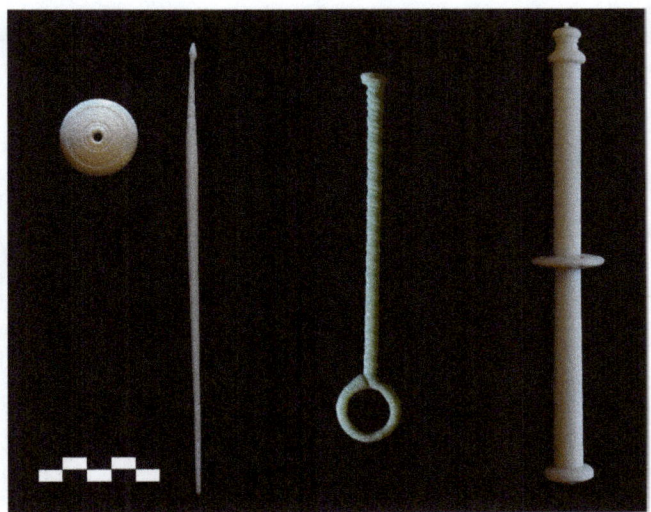

Fig. 8.3 3D prints of the textile tools. (Photo: A.M. Lena)

The printed samples were then handed over to expert artisans[4] who, based on the 3D replicas, tool drawing and photographs, created faithful copies of the originals reproducing all parameters and materials of the originals[5] (Fig. 8.4). (A.M.L.)

8.3 The Spinning Tests

A total of 13 tests, each of them lasting 1 h, were performed[6]: in seven tests were used the bone spindle and spindle whorl, weighing respectively 4.5 and 7 g (Set 1), and for the other six tests was used another set, consisting of a wooden spindle weighing 5 g and a spherical clay spindle whorl of 30 g (Set 2) (Fig. 8.5). The second set was chosen to compare the yarns produced using bone tools with those

---

[4] The glass distaff was made by glass-maker Cesarina Mantoan (Le perle di Mauro S.r.l., Murano, Venezia); the amber distaff was made by the goldsmith Francesco Pavan (4 Nove Gicielli, Mestre, Venezia) and by the restorer Sara Garbellini; the bone spindle and spindle whorl were reproduced by the archaeologist Alberto Rossi (Abaco Cooperative Society, Fermo).

[5] The reconstructions of the objects were made using modern techniques and machinery, because it was estimated that the method of realization did not affect the final performance and functionality of the instrument.

[6] The experimental spinning tests were performed by the archaeologist and expert spinner Elena Ciccarelli (Società Cooperativa Abaco, Fermo), who conducted also the experimental spinning tests for the TexSEt Project with the artisan Assunta Perilli (Ciccarelli & Perilli, 2017).

Fig. 8.4 Replicas of the tools produced by the craftspeople: bone spindle and spindle whorl (photo: A. Rossi); glass finger distaff (photo: A.M. Lena); amber hand distaff (photo: F. Pavan)

made by using a spindle whorl, whose weight value was comparable to the average Roman spindle whorls surveyed in Veneto Region by the Pondera project.[7]

The two sets were designed for use in a suspended drop-spindle position: in the first set, the spindle whorl was placed at the top of the spindle (high-whorl spindle), while in the second set it was placed in the lower part of the wooden spindle shaft (low-whorl spindle).

The textile fibers used were merino wool and flax,[8] which were organized during spinning on the glass or amber distaff in order to compare the functionality of the two types of distaff, of the two different ways of gripping the distaff (by finger and by hand), and of the two different materials they were made of.

Furthermore, spinning for both sets was performed in clockwise (producing a z twist) and counterclockwise direction (producing an s twist).

A questionnaire, submitted to the spinner at the end of the 13 spinning sessions, collected her observations on the functionality, efficiency and comfort of the tools used.

Regarding the distaffs, the spinner was able to compare the different handgrip positions of the two types of distaffs: the glass finger distaff was found to be more comfortable than the amber one.[9] In fact, the finger distaff was perceived as sturdy

---

[7] The weight range of the spindle whorls recorded by the Pondera project is from 1 g to 56, with most falling within the ranges of 21–25 g and 26–30 g (Tricomi, 2018, 308).

[8] Both fibers have been purchased already combed so that they could be easily processed.

[9] Same impressions in Caufield, 2018.

Fig. 8.5 The two sets used in the experiments. Set 1: bone spindle (4.5 g) and bone spindle whorl (7 g) in high position (left); Set 2: wooden spindle (5 g) and clay spindle whorl (30 g) in low position (right). (Photo: E. Ciccarelli)

and stable despite being made of a material considered fragile: the ring provided a secure anchorage to the finger, allowing it to be held firmly in the hand during the spinning procedure. The finger used by the spinner was the index finger as it was found to be the most comfortable for free hand movement and tension-free hands. Nevertheless, the amber hand distaff was also found to be fully usable, disproving the often voiced opinion that electrostatic properties of amber would make spinning difficult: no effect produced by these properties was recorded on the textile fibers used.

Both distaffs resulted to be more comfortable in holding wool fibres rather than flax ones, confirming that, in the case of long and not very elastic plant fibres, larger distaffs possibly equipped with prongs were used as documented by more recent ethnographic examples.

With regard to the spindle and spindle-whorls, the spinner confirmed that she had no problem spinning with tools made of bone: their light weight does not compromise their efficiency, but rather increases the speed of rotation,[10] while the combination with the glass distaff amplifies their efficiency. Set 1 resulted in successful spinning. However, Set 2, which used a spindle of greater weight in the lower part, was found to offer greater stability during the spinning process.

---

[10] Other tests have shown that lighter spindles perform a greater number of rotations per unit of time than heavier ones (Grömer, 2005, 112).

It was possible to spin both wool and flax using both sets, even though both were found to be more efficient with wool fibres. In fact, the tool tends to end the rotational movement quicker with the plant than with the animal fiber, requiring a more frequent action of the spinner to restart the rotation. The arrow-shaped base of the bone spindle was considered useful for fixing the thread that would otherwise tend to slip off the smooth tool surface.

Finally, the (right-handed) spinner confirmed what is already known in the literature about the direction of rotation (Gleba 2008; Andersson Strand, 2012b): the high-whorl spindle is instinctively turned counterclockwise producing an s-twist, while the low-whorl spindle makes it more natural for the spinner to rotate it clockwise, producing a thread with a z-twist. (A.M.L.)

8.4 Analysis of the Yarns: Methods and Results

At the completion of the spinning tests, the 13 resulting yarns were analyzed with a Dino-Lite digital microscope (Edge AM4515ZTL Series, zoom 100x) extracting precise metric measurements. In order to obtain numerous and uniformly distributed measurement points along the entire yarn, a photograph was made with the microscope approximately every 10 cm: this made the subsequent statistical analyzes much more reliable than a sampling based on few measures of yarns that sometimes exceed 40 m in length.[11] To speed up the image acquisition process, a manual tool for unwinding and rewinding the yarns has been specially created (Fig. 8.6), a tool that allows a single operator to take, on average, 450 photos per hour.

A total of 4552 microscope shots were made, which were subsequently processed by means of an image processing software (Image J) from which a total of 4552 diameter measurements and 4404 twist angle measurements were obtained. The data were statistically processed using the R software.

For each yarn produced, different dimensional parameters were considered: the *total length*; the *total weight*; the *linear density*; the *diameter*; the *twist angle*. For the last two parameters the following statistical indices were calculated: *Minimum value; Maximum value; Mean; Median; Standard deviation; Evenness index* (only for diameter), that is the relative ratio between standard deviation and average (Kania, 2015, 124), revealing the degree of uniformity of the yarn. All these indices were calculated by eliminating from the total of the measurements of diameter and twist of each yarn those relating to the initial and final 2 m and those representing extreme values (outliers).[12] The anomalous values must still be taken into

---

[11] The number of measurements used in other experimental tests is 20 (Andersson Strand, 2012a, 208; Möller-Wiering, 2015, 102).

[12] Following a common approach in statistics, all values greater than or less than one and a half times the interquartile range were considered outliers.

Fig. 8.6 Tool for unwinding and rewinding the yarns to be measured. (Concept and realization: D. Francisci)

consideration to evaluate the overall quality of the yarn, because the greater their number, the lower the quality and uniformity of the product (Tables 8.1 and 8.2).

Regarding the *length*, it was observed that, with the same initial fiber quantity, 25 g, and with the same spinning time, 1 h each test, both sets produced much longer wool yarns than linen yarns (Fig. 8.7).

The reason could lie in the greater dexterity and speed of the spinner in drafting the wool fibers from the distaff. Moreover, during the spinning of flax fiber, the rotation speed quickly slows down, requiring a greater number of reactivations and therefore a greater use of time. Furthermore, the two sets produced wool and linen yarns of very similar length. Among the linen yarns, the one produced by the Set 2 is slightly longer: this difference is probably due to the greater efficiency of the heavier spindle for spinning plant fibers, as also confirmed by the testimony of the spinner.

Linear density, sometimes called *grist, yardage* (Kania) or *yarn numbers* (Andersson), is a way for evaluating different types and qualities of yarn. Measured in TEX, it represents the weight of yarn per 1000 m: the thinner the yarn, the lower the number (Fig. 8.8).

Table 8.1 Results of the analysis on the yarns produced by Set 1: bone spindle (4.5 g) and bone spindle whorl (7 g) in high-whorl position

Test	Fibre	Twist	Length (m)	Weight (g)	Lin.d. (TEX)	Diameter (mm)		Twist angle (°)	
1	Wool	z	41.90	4	95.47	Min	0.13	Min	14
						Max	0.63	Max	47
						Mean	0.38	Mean	29.6
						Median	0.37	Median	29
						St. deviation	0.09	St. deviation	6.9
						Outliers (%)	3.12	Outliers (%)	1.30
						Evenness index	0.24		
2	Wool	s	36.20	5	138.12	Min	0.25	Min	10
						Max	0.76	Max	42
						Mean	0.48	Mean	25.4
						Median	0.47	Median	25
						St. deviation	0.10	St. deviation	6.4
						Outliers (%)	1.02	Outliers (%)	1.71
						Evenness index	0.21		
3	Wool	z	42.70	5	117.10	Min	0.23	Min	9
						Max	0.79	Max	41
						Mean	0.48	Mean	24.7
						Median	0.46	Median	25
						St. deviation	0.11	St. deviation	6.1
						Outliers (%)	1.64	Outliers (%)	2.46
						Evenness index	0.23		
4	Wool	s	45.80	5	109.17	Min	0.23	Min	12
						Max	0.76	Max	39
						Mean	0.47	Mean	25.5
						Median	0.45	Median	26
						St. deviation	0.11	St. deviation	5.7
						Outliers (%)	1.25	Outliers (%)	4.75
						Evenness index	0.23		

(continued)

Table 8.1 (continued)

Test	Fibre	Twist	Length (m)	Weight (g)	Lin.d. (TEX)	Diameter (mm)		Twist angle (°)	
5	Wool	z	42	3	71.43	Min	0.26	Min	12
						Max	0.80	Max	43
						Mean	0.48	Mean	27
						Median	0.47	Median	27
						St. deviation	0.11	St. deviation	6.1
						Outliers (%)	2.46	Outliers (%)	0.82
						Evenness index	0.23		
6	Linen	s	23.50	3	127.66	Min	0.23	Min	14
						Max	0.62	Max	40
						Mean	0.41	Mean	25.1
						Median	0.41	Median	25
						St. deviation	0.09	St. deviation	5.3
						Outliers (%)	4.10	Outliers (%)	3.59
						Evenness index	0.21		
7	Linen	z	24.40	3.5	143.44	Min	0.22	Min	13
						Max	0.69	Max	42
						Mean	0.44	Mean	25.9
						Median	0.43	Median	25
						St. deviation	0.09	St. deviation	5.6
						Outliers (%)	2.58	Outliers (%)	3.61
						Evenness index	0.21		

Regarding the wool threads, there are few differences in the individual tests of the two sets: beyond the greater variability of the density of the yarns produced with bone tools (which is paired with the lesser uniformity found in subsequent analyses of diameters), in fact, the medians are almost identical. Furthermore, the calculation of the total meters of wool yarn produced with the light bone Set 1 (170.2 m) and with the heavier clay spindle whorl of Set 2 (208.6 m) produce similar TEX values, respectively 109 and 111. Again, it is very similar, but with the bone tools a slightly lighter yarn is produced. On the other hand, the values for linen yarns are different, with a median equal to 136 for Set 1 and 99.5 TEX for Set 2. Even considering that

Table 8.2 Results of the analysis on the yarns produced by Set 2: wooden spindle (5 g) and clay spindle whorl (30 g) in low-whorl position

Test	Fiber	Twist	Length (m)	Weight (g)	Lin.d. (TEX)	Diameter (mm)		Twist angle (°)	
1	Wool	s	43.70	5	114.42	Min	0.21	Min	9
						Max	0.70	Max	39
						Mean	0.45	Mean	23
						Median	0.44	Median	23
						St. deviation	0.09	St. deviation	5.7
						Outliers (%)	5.10	Outliers (%)	1.02
						Evenness index	0.20		
2	Wool	z	45.60	5	109.65	Min	0.25	Min	12
						Max	0.72	Max	44
						Mean	0.47	Mean	27.9
						Median	0.46	Median	28
						St. deviation	0.09	St. deviation	6.3
						Outliers (%)	2.53	Outliers (%)	1.77
						Evenness index	0.20		
3	Wool	z	44.20	5	113.12	Min	0.26	Min	10
						Max	0.83	Max	42
						Mean	0.51	Mean	25.8
						Median	0.50	Median	25
						St. deviation	0.12	St. deviation	6.1
						Outliers (%)	1.33	Outliers (%)	0.53
						Evenness index	0.23		
4	Wool	s	36.70	4	108.99	Min	0.25	Min	10
						Max	0.73	Max	36
						Mean	0.45	Mean	22.8
						Median	0.45	Median	23
						St. deviation	0.10	St. deviation	4.5
						Outliers (%)	1.25	Outliers (%)	0.63
						Evenness index	0,22		

(continued)

Table 8.2 (continued)

Test	Fiber	Twist	Length (m)	Weight (g)	Lin.d. (TEX)	Diameter (mm)		Twist angle (°)	
5	Linen	s	26.10	3	114.94	Min	0.22	Min	12
						Max	0.64	Max	40
						Mean	0.39	Mean	24.2
						Median	0.39	Median	23
						St. deviation	0.09	St. deviation	5.8
						Outliers (%)	0.95	Outliers (%)	0.47
						Evenness index	0.22		
6	Linen	z	33.15	3	90.50	Min	0.19	Min	16
						Max	0.62	Max	40
						Mean	0.38	Mean	25.3
						Median	0.37	Median	25
						St. deviation	0.09	St. deviation	5.3
						Outliers (%)	1.81	Outliers (%)	1.44
						Evenness index	0.23		

the tests with linen are few to consider the statistics reliable, apparently the heavier Set 2 produces a linen yarn that tends to be finer than the one produced by the lighter Set 1, an effect also confirmed by the analysis of the thread diameters.

With regard to the *diameters of the yarns* produced, there are no significant differences (Fig. 8.9 top). The wool yarns and the linen yarns made with both sets have similar values: for wool around 0.5 mm and for linen around 0.4 mm (in this case, the yarns of Set 2 are slightly lower than those of Set 1). When looking at the *evenness index* (Fig. 8.9 bottom), closely related to the thread diameter, it was noted that the wool yarns produced with the Set 2 show a greater homogeneity (lower value) than the wool yarns produced with the Set 1 (higher value): this difference is probably due to the lesser experience of the spinner in using very light tools (a 4.5 g spindle associated with a 7 g spindle whorl) and a high-whorl spindle. Between the first and last tests, however, there is a slight improvement in the yield of the yarn as a consequence, probably, of the practice in the new tools and spinning technique. The linen yarns show instead inverted averages: 0.21 for the yarns produced using the bone set, 0.23 for the yarns produced using the wood and clay set.

There are no substantial differences in the *twist angle* between the yarns produced by the two sets (Fig. 8.10): for wool the mean values are around 22.8° and 29.6°, for linen between 24.2° and 25.9°.

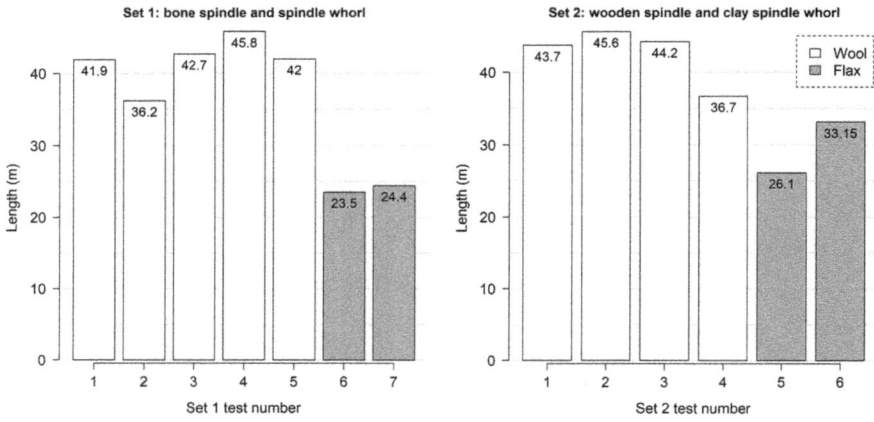

Fig. 8.7 Length of the wool and linen yarns produced by bone Set 1 (left) and wooden and clay Set 2 (right). (Elaboration: D. Francisci)

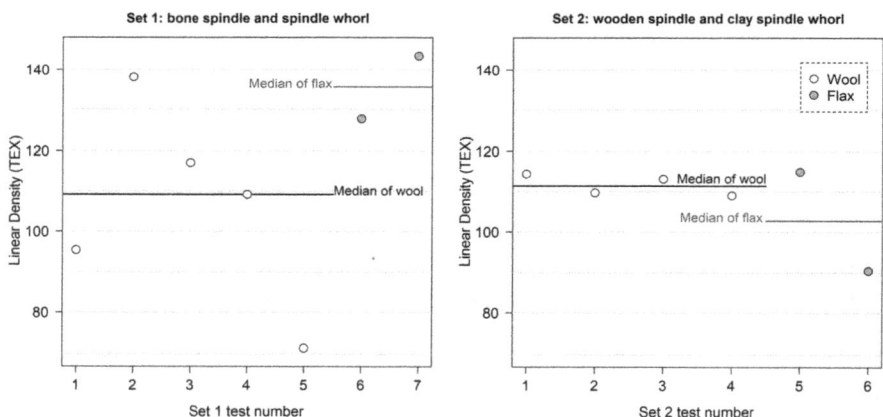

Fig. 8.8 Linear density of wool and linen yarns produced by Set 1 (left) and Set 2 (right), with indication of the median values. (Elaboration: D. Francisci)

Values that identify a medium or medium/weak twist. The greater twist of wool compared to linen is due to different fiber characteristics: wool fibers are shorter and more elastic than flax ones. For both fibers, a slight tendency to more twisting should be noted for yarns produced with Set 1 in bone: the higher rotation speed of the lightweight Set 1 may be the cause of the increased twisting of the fibers spun with it. The *direction of rotation* of the spindle did not produce any differentiation on the resulting yarn: this could be due to the spinner's ability in changing twist direction. (D.F.)

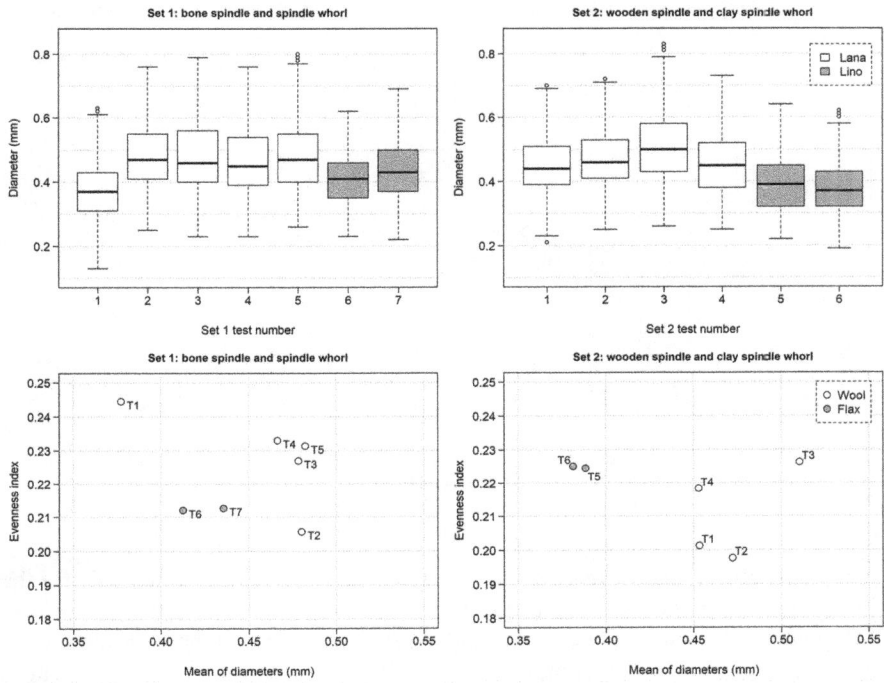

Fig. 8.9 Top: distribution of the diameter values of the wool and linen yarns produced by Set 1 (left) and by Set 2 (right). Bottom: scatter diagram of the mean of the diameters (on the abscissa) and of the evenness index (on the ordinate) of the wool and linen yarns produced by Set 1 (left) and by Set 2 (right). Each point represents the yarn produced by a single test. (Elaboration D. Francisci)

8.5 Comparison with Other Experimental Tests

In order to better understand the significance of the metric data obtained from the spinning tests of the TEXPA project, a comparison with some of the other experimental archeology projects carried out in Europe in the last two decades is useful. However, the comparison is not always straightforward due to the numerous differences that characterize the various projects, which manifest themselves in the types of fibers and tools used, in the spinning methods, in the parameters considered, in the methods of measurement and data recording, etc.

The *length* of the yarns produced in one hour with the 7 g bone spindle, on average 42 m for wool and 24 m for linen, is in line with the lengths achieved in the same period of time using an 8 g spindle whorl in the tests conducted by the CTR (Center for Textile Research) in Copenhagen: for wool between about 40 and 41 m, for linen between about 24 and 33 m (Mårtensson et al., 2006b, 8, fig. 7; Mårtensson et al., 2006a, 8, fig. 6). The tests of the Danish researchers, however, showed a close correlation between the weight of the spindle and the length of the yarn (the increase of

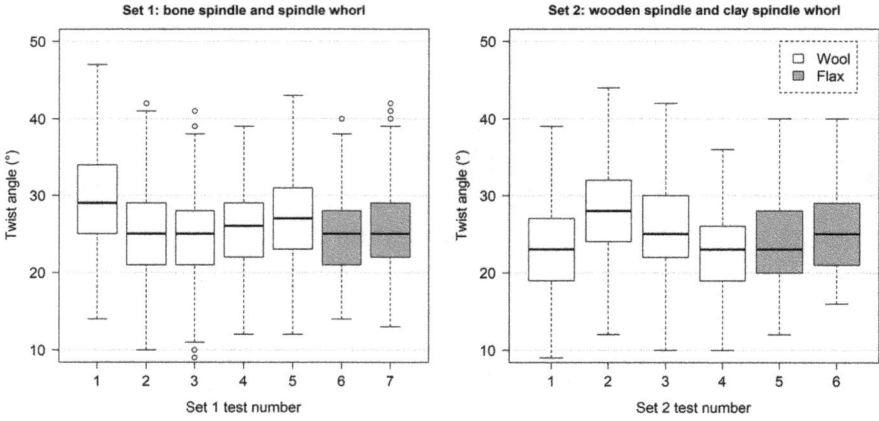

Fig. 8.10 Distribution of the angular torsion values of the wool and linen yarns produced by Set 1 (left) and by Set 2 (right). (Elaboration: D. Francisci)

one corresponds to the increase of the other); in our tests this happened only for the linen yarns, while the two sets produced wool yarns of similar length.

Regarding the *linear density*, our results differ from those of the CTR tests, from which it appears that with spindle whorls of different weight the density changes significantly: the yarns produced using an 18 g spindle whorl had a 39.5% higher density than that of the yarns produced with an 8 g spindle whorl (Andersson Strand, 2015, 140–141), while we do not find that at all.

Looking at the *diameter* values, our results again differ from the CTR tests (and other tests, including TexSET), which noted a direct and proportional relationship between the weight of the spindle whorl and the thickness of the yarn: using a heavier spindle whorl a thicker yarn is obtained (Andersson & Nosch, 2003, 198; Grömer, 2005, 109–111; Bazzanella & Mayr, 2009, 149–150; Olofsson et al., 2015, 82, 87; Ciccarelli & Perilli, 2017, 161). In our tests, the diameters of the yarns produced are distinguished by the fiber (slightly thinner wool than the linen ones), but not by the set used. It is true, however, that in many of these experiments the possibility of producing fine yarn also with medium or medium-heavy spindles is not excluded (Grömer, 2005, 110; Andersson Strand, 2012a, 208) and common to many of these tests is the conclusion that, with a spindle of medium weight (30–50 g), yarns of a wide range of thicknesses can be produced (Grömer, 2005, 111; Bazzanella & Mayr, 2009, 150; Olofsson et al., 2015, 86). Also K. Kania, while rejecting a "direct connection" between the weight of the spindle and the yarn thickness, admits a tendency to prefer a light set for fine yarns and a heavy set for thicker yarns (Kania, 2015, 119–120).

The substantial similarity of the thicknesses is also reflected in the *eveness index* which does not present major differences between the two sets. These results correspond to those of Kania, who notes: "The evenness of the yarns spun […] seems to depend on the individual spinner and their preference for a spindle-fiber combination" (Kania, 2015, 129).

Our values of the twist angles once again differ from the CTR tests, in which heavier and larger spindle whorls seem to produce more twist than the light and smaller ones (Möller-Wiering, 2015, 106, 114–115), and agree with Kania's test that did not find significant effect of the different moment of inertia (provided by weight and diameter) on the type of yarn produced (Kania, 2015, 121). In contrast, no differences were observed regarding the direction of spinning: the alternation between s-twist (counterclockwise) and z-twist (clockwise) did not produce significant differentiations between the 13 yarns produced. (M.S.B.)

8.6 Conclusion

At the end of our experiments, an attempt was made to answer the initial research questions.

Regarding the function of the tools, the tests revealed that the precious material does not compromise their functionality. The traces of wear on the bone spindle and on the handle of the amber distaff used as prototypes for our experimental tools confirm that the tools have actually been used (Bolla, 2004, 207). However, it is assumed that they have not been used daily, but exclusively on certain occasions, given their fragility (in particular the bone spindle and the glass distaff) and preciousness.

With regard to the functionality, the bone Set 1 was effective in spinning both wool and flax, even if it performed better with wool, confirming that such light tools were used for short fibers such as sheep's wool.

The yarn produced with these textile tools can be classified as a relatively fine thread (between 0.4 and 0.7 mm) and medium twisted (25–30°), comparable in all respects to yarns made with the more common 30 g clay spindle whorl.

These tests showed that the most relevant factors affecting the type of yarn are not (or not only) the morphometric features of the tools, but the quality and preparation of the fibers (Olofsson et al., 2015, 86–87) and the experience, skill and cultural background of the spinner (Kania, 2015). It is difficult to say what type of yarn could be produced using different type of instruments and the question in the title of this contribution (Which tool for which fiber?) must remain (partially) unanswered.

It will be necessary to expand the experimentation on spinning of the TEXPA project, reproducing more instruments with different morphometric and weight characteristics; involving more spinners; planning further spinning sessions; extending the tests also to the weaving phase; comparing our results with those achieved by other textile experimental researches.

In order to make the experimental approach effective, it is above all necessary to develop a shared protocol of experiments and measurements: *parameters*, which instead vary in the different projects (spindle whorl weight, spindle weight and spindle whorl weight, spindle diameter, moment of inertia, quantity and type of initial fiber, spinning time, etc.); *number of measurements along the yarns*; *measurement acquisition method* (optical microscope, calculation from the number of threads out of a cm, image analysis software); *data publication methods* (raw and not only summary data).

The work stands at the beginning of a still long and unexplored journey, overall when it comes to the Roman period, that is little considered by the experimental textile research, which until now has focused on earlier eras. It is however a promising field and future research will allow to increase the knowledge related to the Roman textile production. (M.S.B., D.F., A.M.L.)

References

Andersson, E., & Nosch, M.-L. (2003). With a little help from my friends: Investigating Mycenaean textiles with help from Scandinavian experimental archaeology. In K. P. Foster & R. Laffineur (Eds.), *Metron. Measuring the Aegean Bronze Age. Proceedings of the 9th international aegean conference (New Haven, 18–21 April 2002)* (pp. 197-206). Peeters Publishers & Booksellers.

Andersson Strand, E. (2012a). From spindle whorls and loom weights to fabrics in the Bronze Age Aegean and Eastern Mediterranean. In M.-L. Nosch & R. Laffineur (Eds.), *KOSMOS. Jewellery, adornment and textiles in the Aegean Bronze Age. Proceedings of the 13th international Aegean conference (Copenhagen, 21–26 April 2010)* (pp. 207–213). Peeters Press.

Andersson Strand, E. (2012b). The textile chaîne opératoire: Using a multidisciplinary approach to textile archaeology with a focus on the Ancient Near East. *Paléorient, 38*(1–2), 21–40.

Andersson Strand, E. (2015). From tools to textiles, concluding remarks. In E. Andersson Strand & M. L. Nosch (Eds.), *Tools, textiles and contexts: Investigating textile production in the Aegean and Eastern Mediterranean Bronze Age* (pp. 139–144). Oxbow Books.

Basso, P., Bonetto, J., & Ghiotto, A. R. (2004). Produzione, lavorazione e commercio della lana nella Venetia romana: le testimonianze letterarie, epigrafiche e archeologiche. In G. L. Fontana & G. Gayot (Eds.), *Wool: Products and markets (13th–20th century). Proceedings of the Euroconference (Verviers, 5–7 April 2001 and Schio, Valdagno, Follina, Biella, 24–27 October 2001)* (pp. 49–78). Cleup.

Bazzanella, M., & Mayr, A. (2009). *I reperti tessili, le fusaiole e i pesi da telaio dalla palafitta di Molina di Ledro*. Provincia autonoma di Trento.

Bolla, M. (2004). La "Tomba del medico" di Verona. *Aquileia Nostra, LXXV*, 194–264.

Busana, M. S., & Gleba, M. (2018). Textile production and consumption in Roman Venetia (Italy): Preliminary results of the study of mineralised fibres and textiles. In M. S. Busana, M. Gleba, F. Meo, & A. R. Tricomi (Eds.), *Textiles and dyes in the Mediterranean Economy and Society. Purpureae Vestes VI. Proceedings of the VIth international symposium on textiles and dyes in the Ancient Mediterranean World (Padova – Este – Altino, Italy 17–20 October 2016)* (pp. 333–349). Libros Portico.

Busana, M. S., & Gleba, M. (2021). L'uso del tessuto nei rituali funerari del Veneto antico: continuità in età romana di una tradizione preromana. In M. Gamba, G. Gambacurta, F. Gonzato, E. Pettenò, & F. Veronese (Eds.), *Metalli, creta, una piuma d'uccello. Studi di archeologia per Angela Ruta Serafini* (pp. 186–195). SAP.

Busana, M. S., & Rossi, C. (2020). Textile tools in funerary contexts of Roman Venetia (Italy). In M. Bustamante Álvarez, E. H. Sánchez López, & J. Jiménez Ávila (Eds.), *Purpureae Vestes VII, redefining ancient textile handcraft. structures, tools and production processes. Proceedings of the VIIth international symposium on textiles and dyes in the Ancient Mediterranean World (Granada, Spain 2–4 October 2019)* (pp. 295–310). EUG Editorial Universidad de Granada.

Busana, M. S., & Rossi, C. (2021). Strumenti tessili in sepolture romane dell'Italia nord-orientale (Regio X). In M. S. Busana, D. Francisci, & C. Rossi (Eds.), Lanifica. *Il ruolo della donna nella produzione tessile attraverso le evidenze funerarie* (pp. 53–89). Padova University Press.

Busana, M. S., & Tricomi, A. R. (2016). Textile archaeology in Roman Venetia (Italy). In J. Ortiz, C. Alfaro, L. Turell, M. J. & Martinez (Eds.), *Purpureae Vestes V, textiles, basketry and dyes in the Ancient Mediterranean World. Proceedings of the Vth international symposium on textiles and dyes in the Ancient Mediterranean World (Montserrat, 19–22 March 2014)* (pp. 111–118). Universidad de València.

Busana, M. S., Cottica, D., & Basso, P. (2012). La lavorazione della lana nella Venetia. In M. S. Busana & P. Basso (Eds.), *La lana nella Cisalpina romana: economia e società. Studi in onore di Stefania Pesavento Mattioli. Proccedings of the conference in Padova-Verona, 18–20 May 2011* (Antenor Quaderni 27) (pp. 383–433). Padova University Press.

Casagrande, C., Cresci Marrone, G., Larese, A., & Marinetti, A. (2012). L'età romana. In *Carta geomorfologica e archeologica del Comune di Montebelluna. Il progetto Archeogeo* (pp. 147–232). Museo di Storia naturale e Archeologia di Montebelluna (Treviso).

Caufield, K. (2018). The hand-held distaff: Also known as the underestimated stick. In M. S. Busana, M. Gleba, F. Meo, & A. R. Tricomi (Eds.), *Textiles and dyes in the Mediterranean Economy and Society. Purpureae Vestes VI. Proceedings of the VIth international symposium on textiles and dyes in the Ancient Mediterranean World (Padova – Este – Altino, Italy 17–20 October 2016)* (pp. 517–524). Libros Portico.

Ciccarelli, E., & Perilli, A. (2017). Tracing the thread. Spinning experiments with Etruscan spindle whorl replicas. In M. Gleba & R. Laurito (Eds.), *Contextualising textile production in Italy in the 1st Millennium BC. Origini, XL* (pp. 155–164).

Gambacurta, G., & Manessi, P. (2000). Necropoli in località Caonada, fondo Sernaglia: catalogo delle tombe. In P. Manessi (Ed.), *Pusilai. Corredi funerari da due necropoli romane di Montebelluna* (pp. 17–43). Museo di Storia naturale e Archeologia di Montebelluna (Treviso).

Gleba, M. (2008). *Textile production in pre-Roman Italy (Ancient Textile Series 4)*. Oxbow Books.

Grömer, K. (2005). Efficiency and technique – Experiments with original spindle whorls. In P. Bichler, K. Grömer, R. H.-d. Keijzer, A. Kern, & H. Reschreiter (Eds.), *Hallstatt textiles. Technical analysis, scientific investigation and experiment on iron age textiles* (pp. 107–116). Archaeopress.

Kania, K. (2015). Soft yarns, hard facts? Evaluating the results of a large-scale hand-spinning experiment. *Archaeological and Anthropological Sciences, 7*, 113–130.

Lena, A. M. (2019–2020). *Archeologia sperimentale e filatura: studio preliminare di strumenti integri per l'attività di filatura provenienti da contesti funerari della Venetia romana*. Masters Thesis, (Supervisor Prof. M. S. Busana, co-supervisor Dr. D. Francisci). University of Padova.

Lena, A. M., Francisci, D., Busana, M. S. (2021). Tra simbolo e realtà. I test sperimentali su strumenti per filatura in osso, vetro e ambra da sepolture romane della Venetia. In M. S. Busana, D. Francisci, C. Rossi (Eds.), Lanifica. *Il ruolo della donna nella produzione tessile attraverso le evidenze funerarie* (pp. 163–180). Padova University Press.

Mårtensson, L., Andersson, E., Nosch, M.-L., & Batzer, A. (2006a). *Technical report, experimental archaeology part 2:1 flax*. Danish National Research Foundation's Centre for Textile Research (CTR), University of Copenhagen: Centre for Textile Research, Tools and Textiles – Texts and Contexts Research Programme. https://ctr.hum.ku.dk/research-programmes-and-projects/previous-programmes-and-projects/tools/technical_report_2-1_experimental_archaeology.pdf (04/02/2021).

Mårtensson, L., Andersson, E., Nosch, M.-L. & Batzer, A. (2006b). *Technical report, experimental archaeology part 2:2 whorl or bead?* Danish National Research Foundation's Centre for Textile Research (CTR), University of Copenhagen: Centre for Textile Research, Tools and Textiles – Texts and Contexts Research Programme. https://ctr.hum.ku.dk/research-programmes-and-projects/previous-programmes-and-projects/tools/technical_report_22__experimental_arcaheology.pdf (04/02/2021).

Möller-Wiering, S. (2015). External examination of spinning and weaving samples. In E. Andersson Strand & M. L. Nosch (Eds.), *Tools, textiles and contexts* (pp. 101–118). Oxbow Books.

Olofsson, L., Andersson Strand, E., & Nosch, M.-L. (2015). Experimental testing of Bronze Age textile tools. In E. Andersson Strand & M. L. Nosch (Eds.), *Tools, textiles and contexts: Investigating textile production in the Aegean and Eastern Mediterranean Bronze Age* (pp. 75–100). Oxbow Books.

Rossi, C. (2018). The *Lanifica* project: The feminine ideal and textile crafts in Roman burial practices. In M. S. Busana, M. Gleba, F. Meo, & A. R. Tricomi (Eds.), *Textiles and dyes in the Mediterranean Economy and Society. Purpureae Vestes VI. Proceedings of the VIth international symposium on textiles and dyes in the Ancient Mediterranean World (Padova – Este – Altino, Italy 17–20 October 2016)* (pp. 381–393). Libros Portico.

Rossi, C., & Francisci, D. (2021). Strumenti tessili in sepolture romane dell'Italia nord-occidentale (Regio IX e Regio XI) e della Gallia Narbonensis. In M. S. Busana, D. Francisci, & C. Rossi (Eds.), *Lanifica. Il ruolo della donna nella produzione tessile attraverso le evidenze funerarie* (pp. 91–146). Padova University Press.

Tricomi, A. R. (2018). Instrumenta textilia *nella* Venetia romana: il progetto Pondera (2009–2015). In M. S. Busana, M. Gleba, F. Meo, & A. R. Tricomi (Eds.), *Textiles and dyes in the Mediterranean Economy and Society. Purpureae Vestes VI. Proceedings of the VIth International Symposium on Textiles and Dyes in the Ancient Mediterranean World (Padova – Este – Altino, Italy 17–20 October 2016)* (pp. 305–316). Libros Portico.

Chapter 9
Residues of Activities: Towards an Analytical Protocol for Studying Residues on Textile Tools

Vanessa Forte, Francesca Coletti, Carlo Virili, Alessandro M. Jaia, and Cristina Lemorini

Abstract Textiles are relatively rare in archaeological contexts. Specific environmental conditions and post-depositional processes can favour their preservation, providing evidence of their production and consumption. Spinning and weaving are commonly testified by tools and, according to experimental studies, evidence of textile activities can preserve even in the form of organic residues (e.g. fibre and wood) on tool surfaces along with modifications of the original tools in the form of wear. On this basis, the present contribution proposes a research protocol for studying the use of textile tools through the analysis of residues of spinning, highlighting the potential and limits of this approach. Although some scholars have applied use-wear analysis, residue analysis still needs to be explored to investigate textile tools actual use and the development of dedicated protocols for extraction and analysis is needed. The method of analysing textile tools presented here integrates observation techniques at different magnifications applied to experimental replicas and archaeological spindle-whorls to assess the state of residue preservation and identify the type of preserved fibres.

Keywords Analytical protocol · Textile residues · Textile tools

9.1 Introduction

Textiles are relatively rare finds in archaeological contexts since organic fibres can be affected by degradation processes. Conversely, ceramic, bone and metal tools used in spinning and weaving constitute most of the material evidence of textile craft activities. The study of this category of artefacts plays a key role primarily in

---

V. Forte (✉) · F. Coletti · C. Virili · A. M. Jaia · C. Lemorini
Department of Science of Antiquities, Sapienza University of Rome, Rome, Italy
e-mail: vanessa.forte@uniroma1.it

© The Author(s), under exclusive license to Springer Nature Switzerland AG 2024
F. Coletti et al. (eds.), *Multidisciplinary Approaches for the Investigation of Textiles and Fibres in the Archaeological Field*, Interdisciplinary Contributions to Archaeology, https://doi.org/10.1007/978-3-031-73812-8_9

prehistoric periods when iconographic and written sources are almost absent. Spindle whorls and loom weights have been mostly analysed and documented according to their morphometrical features. Nevertheless, mostly over the last fifteen years, textile studies benefited from the application of experimental approaches to spinning and weaving. Replicating fibres processing in controlled conditions was a significant occasion for scholars to directly experience the diverse kind of textile activities and the techniques used to spin and weave; mostly, experiments allowed exploring the functionality and performance of the tools. Some examples include the studies carried out on the relationship between the size/weight of the tool and the quality of the final product or the spinning technique employed (Andersson Strand, 2012a, b and references therein; Grömer, 2016 and references therein; Ciccarelli & Perilli, 2017). Several questions regarding the actual use of textile tools remain open and only partially answered through contextual information. For example, according to the chronological period, textile tools, and mostly spindle whorls, were used as grave goods in burials. Doubts could raise about their actual use: the deposition in tombs could have been the last phase of a textile tool life cycle, or these objects could have been produced as grave goods, or small-sized tools interpreted as spindle-whorls could have been actually used as ornaments (e.g. clothes clips). The investigation of the actual use of a tool is possible through the study of use wear and residue analysis which aims to identify and interpret modifications due to the activities performed. Research on stone tools, ceramic vessels and bone artefacts recently advanced in this perspective. Huge steps forward were made in this direction, supported by sophisticated equipment, such as microscopes at low and high magnifications, and scientific analyses developed by chemical and bioarchaeological research regarding organic and inorganic residues (Marreiros et al., 2015 and references therein; Evershed, 2008; Roffet-Salque et al., 2015; Drieu et al., 2020). Textile remains benefited from these advancements (Coletti et al., 2021; Ciccola et al., 2020; Galli et al., 2020; Gleba & Harris, 2018; Gleba, 2021; Bergfjord et al., 2012; Serafini et al. in this volume). Conversely, textile tools are only partially affected by this approach (Forte & Lemorini, 2017; Forte et al., 2019; Żebrowska, 2020; Cheval, 2021; Spinazzi-Lucchesi, 2022). Tools used by contemporary artisans as well as traditional textile collections or experimental replicas used in spinning and weaving, frequently show use alterations. The original surfaces impair leaving space to altered areas characterised by striations or irregular depressions due to detachments of material by mechanical stress (Forte & Lemorini, 2017). Use alterations consist not only in removing surficial particles but also causing deposits of organic or inorganic residues of surfaces the tool interacted with. Observing an archaeological artefact, it is not rare to identify use alterations, yet surface modifications could have been associated with post-depositional processes. Experimental archaeology played a pivotal role in suggesting how and which kind of use alterations can modify a textile tool and how to distinguish these alterations by post-depositional modifications. Experiments allow also to define where use-alterations can mostly be found along an artefact suggesting adequate sampling strategies for applying scientific analyses (Forte & Lemorini, 2017, fig. 7).

In this contribution, we use spindle-whorls as a representative case to discuss frequent use traces along textile surfaces with a focus on residues left behind these activities. An archaeological spindle-whorl from the late prehistoric site of Paduli (Central Italy) was selected to present a replicable protocol for the identification, analysis and interpretation of residues on archaeological textile tools.

9.2 Experimental Collections, Use Wear and Residue Analysis in Textile Tools Research

Textile tools production and use offer a wide range of information regarding craftsmanship in past societies (Gleba, 2008). The *chaîne opératoire* of spindle whorls and loom weights can provide key information on the complexity of the productive systems from household to workshop. Studying how textile tools were used is a way to gather data about craft systems and provide a glimpse into ancient daily life and cultural-behavioural complexity. Morphometrical and stylistic features of textile tools only partially provide information about production and use, and experiencing and mimicking spinning and weaving currently remains one of the most powerful means to study craft figures and assess the complexity of personal or mass productions (Ciccarelli & Perilli, 2017). Experimental archaeology allows us to replicate techniques and gestures in controlled conditions imitating past productive contexts and experiencing the activity to assess the performance of the tools used (Coles, 1979; Godino et al., 2020). Yet this approach has a more powerful potential if integrated with scientific analyses such as use wear and residues study (Forte & Lemorini, 2017; Żebrowska, 2020). The experiments carried out over the last years show that textile activities directly modify tool surfaces, causing not only a surface impairment due to a mechanical detachment of material, but even organic residues can be found (Forte et al., 2019, fig. 5–8). For this reason, we suggest that integrating residue investigation and use-wear analysis on textile tools represent the necessary step in this methodological framework. Building a collection of textile tools replicas produced and used according to ancient contexts provides a solid reference for interpreting traces preserved along archaeological artefacts. Traces of use can certainly be observed by analysing toolkits of contemporary artisans, spinners or weavers who perform textile activities in a traditional way. The difference between such a certainly informative approach and dedicated experimental protocols consists of the reliability and completeness of the research data. Observing use wear on a craftsperson toolkit can provide a general view of alterations caused by their work, and often is also difficult to gather precise information by the artisan regarding the time of use or activities performed. Moreover, use wear on these toolkits comprises overlapping traces that are often difficult to be isolated. Experimental archaeology fills this gap, allowing us to document and measure any single step of the performed activity. In designing experiments, it is possible to select how many variables we need in relation to the aim of the study; moreover, variables can be implemented over time, obtaining more complex experiments reproducing a variety of use wear adequately documented over their formation process. To exploit the potential of experimental archaeology and the experience of craftspeople, we designed and carried out dedicated experimental protocols of spinning using replicas of archaeological spindle-whorls and in collaboration with artisans with long experience in textile activities (Ciccarelli & Perilli, 2017; Forte & Lemorini, 2017; Forte et al., 2019). This allowed us to use spindle-whorls mimicking ancient spinning techniques performed by skilled spinners and document in detail the experimental samples before and after the activity. In this way was possible to isolate traces directly produced by spinning and alterations due to unintentional events such as falls of the tools, and alterations due to non-use phases (e.g. storage of the tools). On the other hand, this led us to infer the variety and features of traces we could find on archaeological textile tools, paying particular attention to distinguishing use traces, which include both use wear and residues, from post-depositional modifications and contaminations.

Over the last years, some contributions regarded residues on ceramic spindle-whorls (Belgiorno & Lentini, 2011; Forte et al., 2019) and bone textile artefacts (Cheval, 2021), showing the potential of studying tools through surface alterations and micro remains left by textile activities. Yet, they are still limited to being widely applied, especially due to contamination risks potentially affecting the sample. Taking into consideration these limits, and the former studies on use wear, we present here an analytical protocol of spinning residue analysis applied to archaeological objects with the aim to provide a novel approach in the textile field and contribute to improve the methodology used so far.

9.2.1 Use Wear and Their Localisation

According to former experimental studies, the prolonged use of a textile tool leave use wear along its surfaces visible as localised detach of ceramic material. This group of traces comprises: (1) use wear localised along the internal hole, due to abrasive processes involving ceramic surfaces and wooden spindle and the contact of the yarn with the spindle-whorl. (2) fatigue wear as small spall detachments recurring along the hole edge caused by the repeated assembling of the spindle-whorl on the spindle, and (3) spall detachment and fractures following accidental drops (Forte & Lemorini, 2017) (Fig. 9.1).

In some cases, it is also possible to observe a connection between morphology/localisation of use wear and the spinning technique adopted. Drop-spindle technique affects mainly the hole's edge and its internal surfaces causing rounding and spall detachments along the edge and polishing over the edge and/or along the internal surface of the hole (Forte et al., 2019). Usually, the external protruding parts of the tool are free from alterations. Moreover, unintentional drops of the spindle whorls during spinning, independently by the technique performed, can cause spall detachments localised along the protruding parts of the tools since they

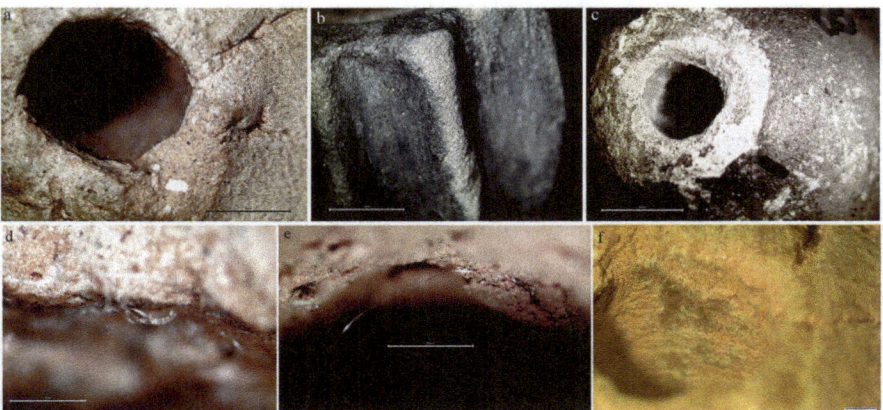

Fig. 9.1 Use wear and residues at low magnifications deposited on experimental spindle-whorls after controlled spinning activities. (**a**) small detachments along the central hole; (**b**) extended abrasive wear along protruding parts due to spinning performed with a spinning bowl; (**c**) abrasive wear along the hole's edge due to repeated contact of the yarn with the spindle-whorl; (**d–e**) residues of fibres deposited along the upper part of the central hole, f. residues of wood left by the repeated contact with the wooden spindle. (Picture modified after Forte et al., 2019)

mostly are exposed to mechanical shocks (Fig. 9.1a). According to the experimental spinning test, use wear due to spinning performed with a spinning bowl modify extensively the surfaces of the tool due to the prolonged mechanical stress following to the repeated contact of the tool surfaces with the internal bowl's walls (Forte & Lemorini, 2017) (Fig. 9.1b). Modifications of spindle 'whorls can be caused even by the distribution of the yarn along the spindle. Based on experimental use wear collections (Forte et al., 2019), the direct contact of the yarn with the central hole's edge of the spindle whorl produces modifications difficult to identify to a fresh eye: on the experiments in which the yarn repeatedly touches the spindle-whorls is possible to observe localised abrasions leading to the rounding of the hole's edge. In case of no contact, the edge appears more preserved. Duration of the spinning activity and hardness of the tool, usually related to the firing temperature, play a role in the development of use wear along a surface and further experiments can provide more precise data over their diversification in relationship to the gestures performed and the kind of fibres spun.

9.2.2 *Beyond Use Wear: Experimental Organic Residues on Spindle-Whorls Replicas*

The analysis of experimental replicas involved in dedicated protocols of spinning provided general criteria for applying residues analysis to this category of artefacts. The preliminary analysis applied to the experimental spindle-whorls using an optical light microscope (magnification range 0.75X–7.5X) allows to assess the distribution of traces along the tool surfaces. Based on low magnifications is possible to localise preliminarily the presence of residues and their relationship to use wear. Usually, at this phase of the analysis, residues of fibres from yarn or wood detached by the spindle are visible. Deposits are primarily spotted along the tool and then analysed in detail at high magnification using a SEM microscope (magnifications 50X–2000X). At higher magnification is possible to identify specific features suggesting the kind of residues and distinguish ancient fibres (often degraded) from post-depositional materials (roots or deposits of modern fibres as man-made and dyed fibres).

Experimental trials suggest that the most common kind of residue depositing during textile activity consists of variably sized fragments of yarn (Fig. 9.1). The deposition of residue coincides with the edge and the internal surface of the central hole, starting from the area immediately lower the hole's edge or inside. Fibres fragments (Fig. 9.1d) or wood residues (Fig. 9.1f) deposit in this area during spinning and any time the spindle whorl is assembled or pulled off the spindle. The repetition of these gestures pushes fibres deposits deeper along the hole's edge and contribute to fibre degradation over time. For this reason, yarn is often found in fragments. The side of the tool interested by residue deposition corresponds with the side in contact with the yarn. Granulometry of the clay paste of the tool can affect residue deposition since yarn fibres remain embedded on the rough surface.

The critical point of residue analysis applied to spindle whorls is the identification of the type of fibres and their distinction from roots developing within or on top of the sediment layer inside the central hole. Roots degradation often leaves organic tissues misinterpreted as fibres. This latter case could occur in absence of a specialist able to distinguish degraded fibres from degraded roots tissues. The size of the fibres detached by the yarn and mechanical stress due to friction among spindle and spindle-whorls frequently alter the residue making the morphological characterisation of the fibre sometimes difficult or impossible in the absence of specific features. Nevertheless, testing diverse kinds of yarn during experiments allowed us to define if and which features can survive mechanical degradation after spinning. Based on experimental trials, cotton fibres maintained their helix structure. At the same time, wool, in some cases, appeared to be damaged by the friction among spindle and spindle-whorls and partially losing the typical scales. Bast fibres, even fragmented and damaged, frequently show their surface characteristics with transversal nodes (Fig. 9.2).

An important point to consider is that experimental fibres lack post-depositional alteration that conversely affects archaeological items. Moreover, cleaning activity carried on during or after excavations can alter use wear and residues as well as contaminate residue deposits. Use trace visible on experimental spindle-whorls are fresh deposits free from alterations. In this case, indeed, contamination of the sample with fibre is reduced by controlled atmospheres in the laboratory during the analysis. Moreover, modern fibres are easily distinguishable since they are randomly scattered on the tool surface and rarely localised in precise spots depending

9 Residues of Activities: Towards an Analytical Protocol for Studying Residues...   165

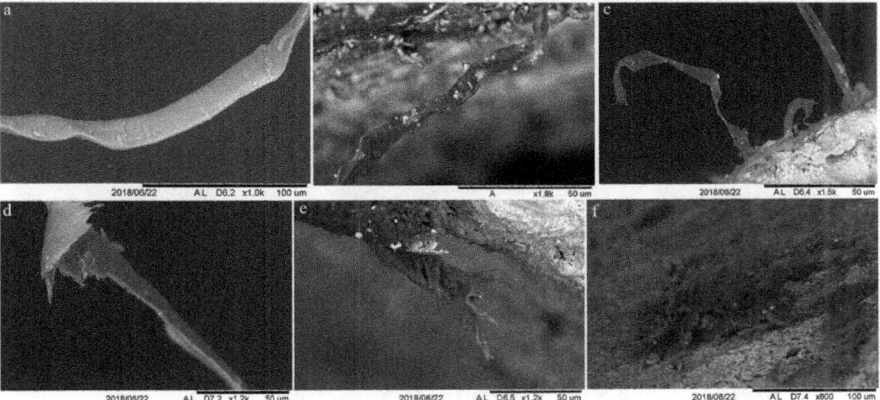

Fig. 9.2 Residues at high magnifications deposited along the spindle whorls surfaces after experimental spinning. (**a–c**) fibers; (**d–f**) wood. (Picture modified after Forte et al., 2019)

on the use activity performed or embedded on the surface roughness as experimental fibres show. These critical points played a key role in guiding the development of a correct approach for understanding how to apply residue analysis on textile tools, which contamination processes could interest a residue deposit and how to design a residue analysis or a sample extraction to avoid contamination and fibres degradation.

9.3 Developing an Analytical Protocol for Extraction and Analysis of Organic Residues on Textile Tools

Traces analysis and experimental archaeology showed that the study of residues is applicable even to textile tools providing further evidence helpful to interpretate their actual use. Nevertheless, the critical points in the application of residue analysis to textile tools comprises: (1) the degree of preservation of residues, and (2) the identification of micro-remains. Using experimental archaeology as first step of such a kind of approach allows to establish what kind of residue develop on textile tool, how and where. Addressing the study of residues on archaeological tools requires to be more cautious and consider several aspects that could compromise the final interpretation. Archaeological tools could indeed have been used in more than one spinning or weaving technique, leading to an overlapping of use wear. Moreover, the use traces could have been amplified by post-depositional processes. The following paragraph will address the main analytical steps of our protocol from the sample selection to the residue interpretation.

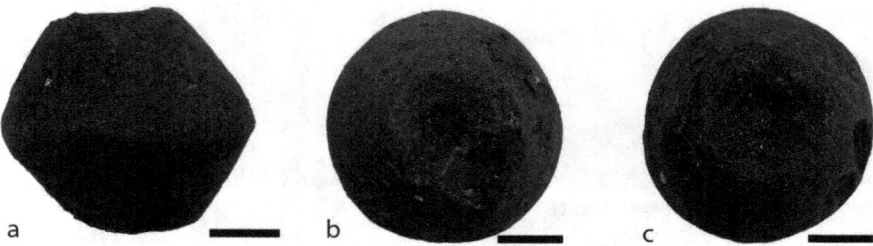

Fig. 9.3 Archaeological spindle whorl from the site of Paduli selected for the residues extraction and analysis (black bar is 1 cm). (Picture V. Forte)

9.3.1 Step 1: Case Study, Artefacts Selection and Documentation

To explore the potentials of residues analysis applied to archaeological textile tools we selected a spindle whorl from the site of Paduli (Central Italy).

Since 2011 the Sapienza-University of Rome has started a territorial research project in the area of the conca velina and in the Piediluco Lake aimed at the diachronic reconstruction of the human population. Part of the research was devoted to the excavation of the lakeshore settlement of Paduli (Colli sul Velino, RI). Survey and digs highlighted a continuity of the site's life from the middle Bronze Age to the early Iron Age. Between late Bronze Age and early Iron Age (XI-X sec. B.C.) an open area developed on stratified drainage (Jaia et al., 2020; Virili et al., 2022).

The case study of Paduli was selected due to the availability of textile tools recently dug and still not cleaned as a necessary condition to test residues analysis. This allowed to work on an object keeping the sediment with the central hole and along the surfaces reducing the risk of contamination.

The spindle whorl selected has a biconical shape (3.2 cm height and 3.5 cm length) and was found from the top layers upset by plowing, this suggest the tool was in a secondary position. Nevertheless, it is possible to associate the spindle whorl to an early phase of the Iron age since the reworked layers contain ceramics dated to this chronological phase (Fig. 9.3).

9.3.2 Step 2: Residues Extraction and Analysis

The extraction was made in a laboratory of use wear and residue analysis. The environment was cleaned before the extraction, the working station also was carefully cleaned, and plastic suits (latex gloves and plastic covers) were used to cover clothes that potentially could have contaminated the sample. Moreover, were selected clothes of synthetic fibres to easily distinguish fibres residues from contamination (Fig. 9.4). Soil residues were gently removed from the spindle whorls' hole with a

9 Residues of Activities: Towards an Analytical Protocol for Studying Residues... 167

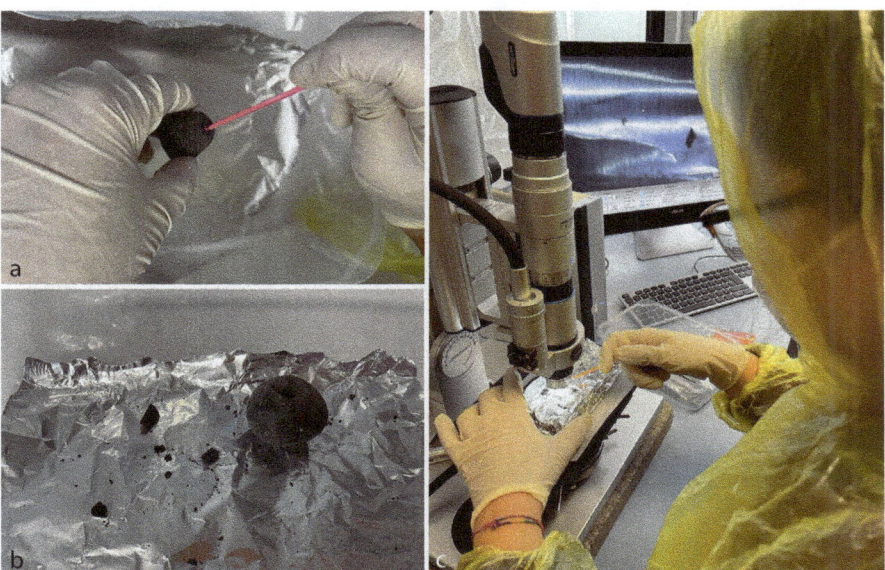

Fig. 9.4 Extraction and analysis of fibres. (**a–b**) extraction of the sediment embedded within the central hole of the spindle-whorl using a plastic stick and a plastic box, (**c**) Analysis at Hirox of the sample extracted. (Picture V. Forte)

plastic stick avoiding contact with the internal hole's edge to preserve possible use wear traces. The soil has been dropped on an aluminium foil to prevent contamination (e.g., by paper fibres). Soil residue was preserved in aluminium foil labelled with the ID of the archaeological item.

9.3.3 Step 3: Fibres Analysis

Once extracted the residue, three samples (T1, T2 and T3) were separately analysed at Hirox and SEM to localise eventual fibres embedded along the internal hole of the tool or isolate fibres within the soil extracted. No fibres embedded along the surfaces of the hole were identified and the analysis focused on the soil samples.

The soil extracted from the central hole was first observed using a Hirox. The more promising soil clusters were selected for SEM analysis (TM 3000, magnifications 50X–2000X), pictures were made at low vacuum 15 kv (Fig. 9.5a, b). The samples observed at high magnification show the presence of at least three fibres. These residues are preserved in the form of short segments, preserving their original cross-section intact. The fibre diameters range between 12–16 μm. Transversal nodes are relatively flat but well recognisable, allowing us to identify these residues as remains of bast fibres (T1 and T2, Fig. 9.5c, d). In addition to the distinctive nods, the fibre diameters are consistent with that of bast fibres as well.

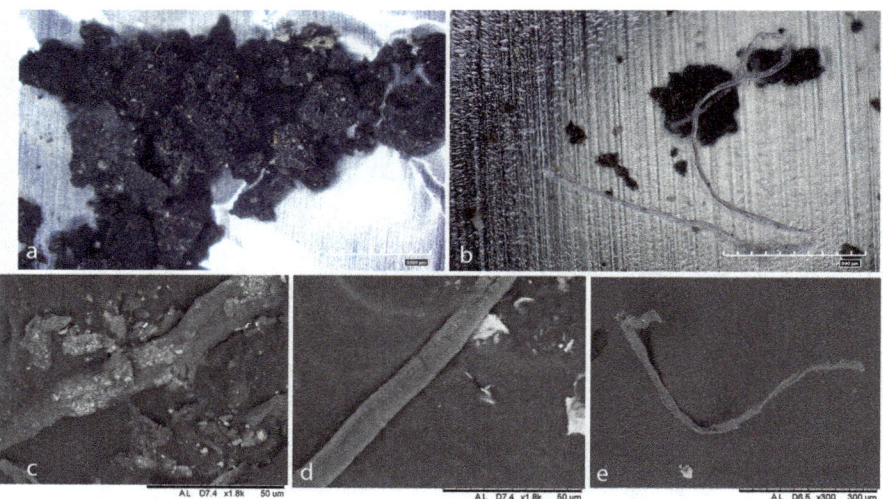

Fig. 9.5 Archaeological fibres analysed at high magnification: (**a**) soil extracted from the archaeological tool, (**b**) fibre identified at Hirox, (**c–e**). residues of bast fibres preserved on archaeological spindle whorl from Paduli. (Picture F. Coletti)

Remarkably, T3 presents partially curled with flattened ends, which can attribute to the spinning activity (Fig. 9.5e). Flattened ends were already noticed on the fibres residues inside the experimental spindle-whorls (Forte et al., 2019).

9.4 Conclusion

Experimental archaeology plays a key role in answering research questions regarding behaviours and processes which left no direct evidence. Its application in textile field improves our knowledge regarding the actual use of specific tools as spindle whorls and loom weights employed in specific economic contexts. In particular, tracing and investigating the relationship among some groups of objects to specific stages of the fibre's processing (e.g. spinning) can improve our comprehension of what actually was done in a specific archaeological context. Combining experimental archaeology with scientific analyses and laboratory investigation consistently improve the potentials of such a kind of empirical approach, providing more data to the theoretical reconstruction. As discussed in this contribution, use wear and residues analysis integrated with experimental protocols suggested that the analysis of an apparently simple tool can provide diversified information helpful to improve our knowledge about the object life-cycle and the archaeological context it was used. According to former experimental studies, textile tools modify during their use in spinning and weaving and the localisation of use traces suggest their actual use allowing to assess if they were actually used or if their life cycle was short.

Moreover, organic traces of textile activities can preserve over time and in case of favourable post depositional condition it is possible to identify, extract and characterise them. The results of this study prove that, as hypothesised by the experimental study, fibres can be left by textile activity, and they can be extracted from deposits along spindle-whorls surfaces and analysed applying the replicable protocol presented here. This kind of approach can be applied also to other kind of textile tools looking for residues suggesting the actual use of the objects analysed. The main required condition to identify this fragile kind of evidence is to grant access to material directly from the excavation to reduce the contamination of the residues and ensure the preservation of the evidence. The protocol proposed aims to ensure conditions to maximise the possibility to find residues and identify which fibres were processed in specific archaeological contexts and if there was a connection among kind of tool and nature of fibres processed.

Aknowledgements The extraction protocol was developed at LTFAPA Laboratory of Sapienza University of Rome.

Authors' Contributions Introduction: VF; Use wear paragraphs: VF; residue paragraphs: VF, FC; archaeological contextualisation of the data: CV, AJ; Use wear analysis: VF, CL; sampling: VF, FC; fibers analysis: FC. All the author equally contributed to the discussion and conclusion.

References

Andersson Strand, E. (2012a). The textile chaîne opératoire: Using a multidisciplinary approach to textile archaeology with a focus on the Ancient Near East. *Paléorient, 38*(1), 21–40.

Andersson Strand, E. (2012b). From spindle whorls and loom weights to fabric in the Bronze age Aegean and eastern Mediterranean. In M. L. Nosch & R. Laffineur (Eds.), *KOSMOS. Jewellery, adornment and textiles in the Aegean Bronze age. Proceedings of the 13th International Aegean Conference/ 13e Rencontre égéenne internationale*. University of Copenhagen, Danish National Research Foundation's Centre for Textile Research, 21–26 April 2010. Aegaeum 33. Liège (pp. 207–2012).

Belgiorno, M., & Lentini, A. (2011). Origini e sviluppo dell'industria tessile a Pyrgos-Mavrorachi (Cipro), durante il II millennio a. C. In M. P. Riccardi & E. Basso (Eds.), *Patron Editore. Atti del VI Congresso Nazionale di Archeometria "Scienza e Beni Culturali"*, Pavia 15–18 February 2010. Bologna (pp. 1–13).

Bergfjord, C., Mannering, U., Frei, K. M., Gleba, M., Scharff, A. B., Skals, I., Heinemeier, J., Nosch, M. L., & Holst, B. (2012). Nettle as a distinct Bronze Age textile plant. *Nature, Scientific Reports, 2*(664), 661–664. https://doi.org/10.1038/srepsrep00664

Cheval, C. (2021). The loom weight, the spindle whorl, and the sword beater–Evidence of textile activity in the Early Neolithic? Open Archaeology 7(1), 1458–1472.

Ciccarelli, E., & Perilli, A. (2017). Tracing the thread: Spinning experiments with Etruscan spindle whorl replicas. *Origini* n. XL. Gangemi Editore spa, 155–164.

Ciccola, A., Serafini, I., Ripanti, E., Coletti, F., Vincenti, F., Bianco, A., Galli, M., Curini, R., & Postorino, P. (2020). Dyes from the ashes: discovering and characterizing natural dyes from mineralized textiles. *Molecules, 25*(6), 1417. https://doi.org/10.3390/molecules25061417

Coles, J. (1979). *Experimental archaeology*. Academic.

Coletti, F., Cestelli Guidi, M., Romani, M., Ceres, G., & Zammit, U. (2021). Evaluation of microscopy techniques and ATR-FTIR spectroscopy on textile fibres from the Vesuvian area: A pilot study on degradation processes that prevent the characterization of bast fibres. *Journal of Archaeological Science Reports, 36*, 102794. https://doi.org/10.1016/j.jasrep.2021.102794

Drieu, L., Lepère, C., & Regert, M. (2020). The missing step of pottery chaîne opératoire: considering post-firing treatments on ceramic vessels using macro-and microscopic observation and molecular analysis. *Journal of Archaeological Method and Theory, 27*(2), 302–326.

Evershed, R. P. (2008). Organic residue analysis in archaeology: the archaeological biomarker revolution. *Archaeometry, 50*(6), 895–924.

Forte, V., & Lemorini, C. (2017). Traceological analysis applied to textile implements: An assessment of the method through the case study of the 1st millennium BCE ceramic tools in Central Italy. In *Origini* n. XL. Gangemi Editore spa, 165–182.

Forte, V., Coletti, F., Ciccarelli, E., & Lemorini, C. (2019). The contribution of experimental archaeology in addressing the analysis of residues on spindle-whorls. *EXARC Journal* 2019/4. https://exarc.net/ark:/88735/10456

Galli, M., Coletti, F., Ciccola, A., & Serafini, I. (2020). Archeologia e archeometria del tessuto antico: un gruppo di manufatti aurei dall'area vesuviana (Pompei, Ercolano, Oplontis). *Scienze dell'Antichità, 26*(1), 205–223.

Gleba, M. (2008). *Textile production in pre-Roman Italy*. Oxbow Books.

Gleba, M. (2021). From textiles to sheep: Investigating wool fibre development in pre-Roman Italy using scanning electron microscopy (SEM). *Journal of Archaeological Science, 39*, 3643–2661.

Gleba, M., & Harris, S. (2018). The first plant bast fibre technology: Identifying splicing in archaeological textiles. *Archaeological and Anthropological Sciences, 10*. https://doi.org/10.1007/s12520-018-0677-8

Godino, Y., Lebole, C., & Di Gangi, G. (2020). "Fornire la pratica che sostiene la teoria": una riflessione sull'Archeologia Sperimentale. *Archeologie sperimentali. Temi, metodi, ricerche, 1*, 1–27.

Grömer, K. (2016). *The art of prehistoric textile making. The development of crafts traditions and clothing in Central Europe*. Naturhistorisches Museum Wien.

Jaia, A. M., Virili, C., Curci, A., Fiori, F., Di Pasquale, G., & D'Auria, A. (2020). Il sito perilacustre di epoca protostorica di loc. Paduli (Colli sul Velino, RI). Indagini di superficie 2011–2013 e saggio di scavo 2015. In *Preistoria e Protostoria in Etruria*. Atti del XIV Incontro di Studi. Milano (pp. 415–444).

Marreiros, J. M., Bao, J. F. G., & Bicho, N. F. (Eds.). (2015). *Use-wear and residue analysis in archaeology*. Springer.

Roffet-Salque, M., Regert, M., Evershed, R. P., Outram, A. K., Cramp, L. J., Decavallas, O., et al. (2015). Widespread exploitation of the honeybee by early Neolithic farmers. *Nature, 527*(7577), 226–230.

Spinazzi-Lucchesi, C. (2022). Preliminary remarks on some wear traces on Egyptian and Levantine textile tools. In A. Dickey, M. Gleba, S. Hitchens, & G. Longhitano (Eds.), *Exploring ancient textiles. Pushing the boundaries of established methodologies*. Oxbow Books.

Virili, C., Jaia, A.M., Zanini, A., Cantisani, E., Vettori, S., Vanacore, L., & D'Auria, A. (2022) Il sito perilacustre di epoca protostorica di loc. Paduli (Colli sul Velino, RI). Indagini radiometriche, archeometriche e paleobotaniche. In *Preistoria e Protostoria in Etruria*. Atti del XV Incontro di Studi. Milano (pp. 779–814).

Żebrowska, K. (2020). The application of use-wear analysis to the study of function of prehistoric Sicilian textile tools. *Quaternary International, 569*, 128–134.

Chapter 10
Resolving the Mystery of the 2000-Year-Old Net Found in the "Cave of Letters"

Reuven Yosef, Lee Perry-Gal, and Naama Sukenik

Abstract Since ancient times, humans have used nets for a variety of purposes, including catching prey. Here we consider the likely uses of a large net unearthed by Yadin (1963) in the Cave of Letters in Nahal Hever, in the Judean Desert. Like all finds in the cave, the net dates from the time of the Bar Kokhba Revolt (132–135/6 CE). It was brought into the cave towards the end of the revolt by Jewish rebels, who apparently fled from the Ein Gedi area. At the time, Yadin opposed the use of the net for fishing suggesting that it was used either for fowling (i.e., catching of waterfowl) or that of a gladiator. In this article, after a thorough and in-depth study of all the possible uses of the net, we propose that it is a bird net. We study the function of the net from different angles including archaeology, anthropology, ornithology, and archaeozoology to elucidate the true function of the net. In addition, we suspect that the net was used to trap indigenous avian, desert species (Rock Pigeon *Columba livia*, Chukar partridge *Alectoris chukar*, Sand Partridge *Ammeperdix heyi*) or migrants (Quail *Coturnix coturnix*, Turtle Dove *Streptopelia turtur*). Based on the features of the net and the zooarchaeological findings from the Judean Desert, we suspect that this appears to be a walk-in trap for avian species that prefer to walk on the ground while foraging or fleeing potential predators. It may also have been used to capture Rock Pigeons, which also nest in the caves where the rebels took refuge.

Keywords Net · Bird · Flowing · Roman period

R. Yosef
Ben Gurion University of the Negev, Eilat Campus, Eilat, Israel

L. Perry-Gal
Israel Antiquities Authority, Jerusalem, Israel

Leon Recanati Institute for Maritime Studies, University of Haifa, Haifa, Israel

N. Sukenik (✉)
National Treasures Department, Israel Antiquities Authority, Jerusalem, Israel
e-mail: naamas@israntique.org.il

© The Author(s), under exclusive license to Springer Nature Switzerland AG 2024
F. Coletti et al. (eds.), *Multidisciplinary Approaches for the Investigation of Textiles and Fibres in the Archaeological Field*, Interdisciplinary Contributions to Archaeology, https://doi.org/10.1007/978-3-031-73812-8_10

10.1 Introduction

Nets have been developed to capture prey such as fish, birds, and other mammals since prehistoric times when humans were hunter-gatherers (Bekker-Nielsen & Bernal Casasola, 2010; Lupo & Schmidtt, 2002; Slingenberg, 2016). However, the available information on this activity is limited and the scientific literature contains few references. In most cases, the information on nets is largely based on iconographic representations or literary texts, if available, due to the fact that the nets were made of perishable organic material and in most cases have not survived in the archaeological context (Armott, 2007; Bailleul-LeSuer, 2012; Houlihan, 1986; Slingenberg, 2016). In most cases, only fragments of nets have been found in archaeological excavations, making it difficult to identify their function (*e.g.* Wendrich, 1989, 183). Furthermore, it has to be considered that the technique of weaving mesh nets was also used for other activities, such as carrier nets for holding pots (Veldmeijer, 2009; Veldmeijer & van Roode, 2004; Wendrich, 1989, 182–185), bags or as hairnets (Crowfoot, 1961, 62; Sheffer & Granger-Taylor, 1994, 216–220). The latter is easier to recognize by the size of the net and by the remains of human hair, but still in most cases it is very difficult to see the function of the net from the small fragments.

Here we deal with the use of a fully intact net, one of the unique objects unearthed by Yadin in the Cave of Letters (henceforth CoL net) located at Nahal Hever in the Judean Desert (Yadin, 1963, 267–268). Like most of the finds in the cave, the CoL net was archaeologically dated to the time of the Bar Kokhba Revolt (AD 132–135/6). It was probably brought into the cave by Jewish rebels who apparently fled to the cave from the Ein Gedi area towards the end of the uprising (Yadin, 1963). The CoL net (find no. 98–64.3, IAA no. 1999–9010) was found folded and tied at locus 64 in the cave and, like all other organic objects in the cave, was well preserved due to the xeric environment of the Judean desert (Yadin, 1963). The rare CoL net (Fig. 10.1) allows us to examine a lay tool and provide essential data to draw historical and technological conclusions. The net was described in detail by Yadin in the final report (Yadin, 1963, 267–268), but the function of the net was not fully clarified. Yadin ruled out the possibility that this was a fishing net since its owner lived on the shores of the Dead Sea and suggested that the net was intended either for fowling or for a gladiator (Yadin, 1963, 268, 1971, 196). The hypotheses put forward by Yadin have never been tested and the actual use of the net has not been established. The function of the net will be discussed from various angles including archaeology, anthropology, zooarchaeology, and ornithology to clarify the true function of the net. A number of parameters can help us to determine the function of the net, including the technical data of the CoL net, such as the shape of the net, the material of the threads, the diameter of the strands of mesh and the size of the mesh, and the archaeological context. The research includes comparisons with various nets in the visual arts, as reflected and represented in mosaic floors or iconographic evidence, to elucidate the net's true function.

Fig. 10.1 Part of the open net during research

10.2 Description of the Net and Material

The net was tied and wrapped with two different ropes, the anchor rope and a lighter one from the outside. When opened, the net formed a triangular shape resembling the letter Y in English, with one end being broad and tapering towards the other end in a triangular fashion (Fig. 10.2). The open net measured approximately 6 × 9.5–10 m.

A re-examination of the raw materials of the CoL net using a microscope (Dino light and optical microscope) confirmed Yadin's identification that the net is composed of linen, while the anchor rope is made of palm fibers. The linen fiber was characterized by multiple segments of equal length separated by deep linear grooves and with very narrow lumina (Sukenik & Tepper, 2019 204; Fig. 10.3a). Linen is a plant fiber obtained from the stalks of the flax plant (*Linum usitatissimum* L.) and is characterized by a strong, flexible fiber that is over 120 cm long. The choice of linen fiber to make the net is not surprising; Linen is characterized by strong, long and smooth fibers, making it suitable for many functional products. Flax was a common agricultural crop in ancient Israel and was an important raw material in the weaving industry up until the Islamic period (Zohary et al., 2013, 103–106). According to archaeological finds, linen textiles were mainly used for functional purposes such as sacks (Yadin, 1963, 61); shrouds (Shamir, 2015, 21.); clothes and ribbons for various purposes (Yadin, 1963, 261–67).

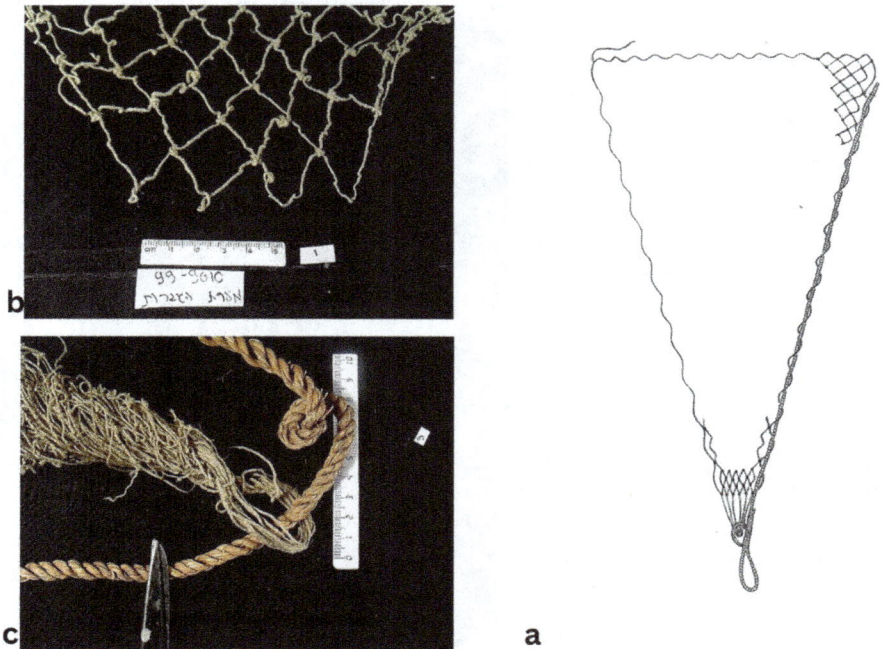

Fig. 10.2 (**a**) schematic drawing of the net (Yadin, 1963: Fig. 89, Israel Exploration Society); (**b**) The bottom rhomboids of the net; (**c**) The end of the flax net attached to the rope. (Photos: Clara Amit, courtesy of the Israel Antiquities Authority)

Most of the linen cords in the net consisted of three-plyed yarns (3sZ; see Fig. 10.3b) with a diameter of 1 mm, while the diameter of the cord increases to 1.2 mm at the edge, i.e., two strings twisted to 2 (2sZ)S, probably to strengthen the edge. These ply cords also made the entire surface more elastic and stronger. The use of palm fronds (*Phoenix dactylifera* L.) to make rope was common in the cordage industry during the Roman period. Date palms were common in Israel from the fourth century B.C. an intensively cultivated agricultural crop (Safrai, 1994, 140). For example, many ropes found in the Cave of Letters (Yadin, 1963, 61), Ein Rahel (Shamir, 1999, 105), and Mo'a (Shamir, 2005, 108) was made from palm fronds. The palm rope in the net has a diameter of 7.5 mm and consists of three two-part strands twisted together (3sZ; Fig. 10.2c). The rope is 6 meters long and has been threaded at various points around the edge of the net to create a large loop and is tied to the net at the end (Fig. 10.1c).

A mesh knot can be made in several ways, but in our case, it is a flat sheet-bend knot forming rhombuses of different sizes (Fig. 10.4a). Most rhomboids in the central area are about 4 cm long, the rhomboids at the edge are larger, measuring 8 cm, while the diamonds at the lower edge are 15 cm long (see also Yadin, 1963, 268).

There are 120 meshes along the open side of the net, while there are 73 meshes along the side of the rope (Yadin, 1963, 268). Sheet-bend knots are

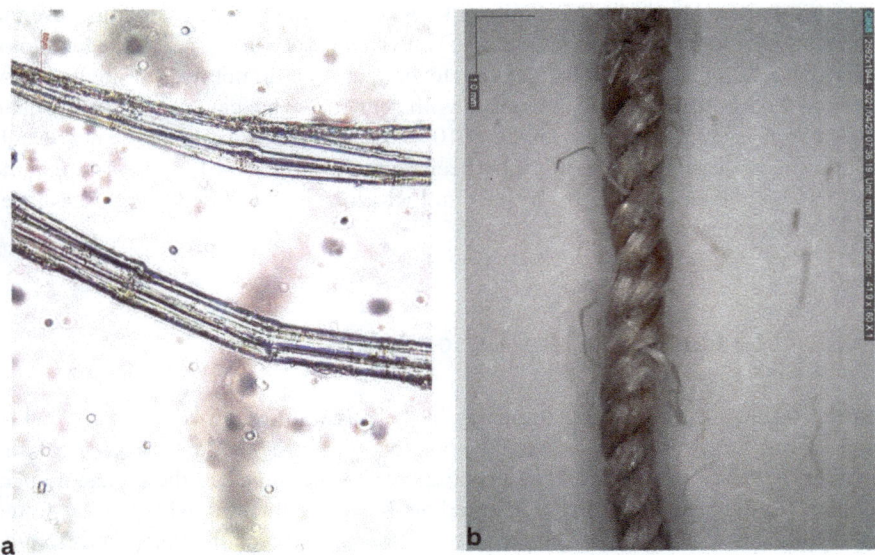

Fig. 10.3 (**a**) The net fiber is seen in a Microscope; (**b**) Part of the linen string under Dino Lite. (Photos: Naama Sukenik)

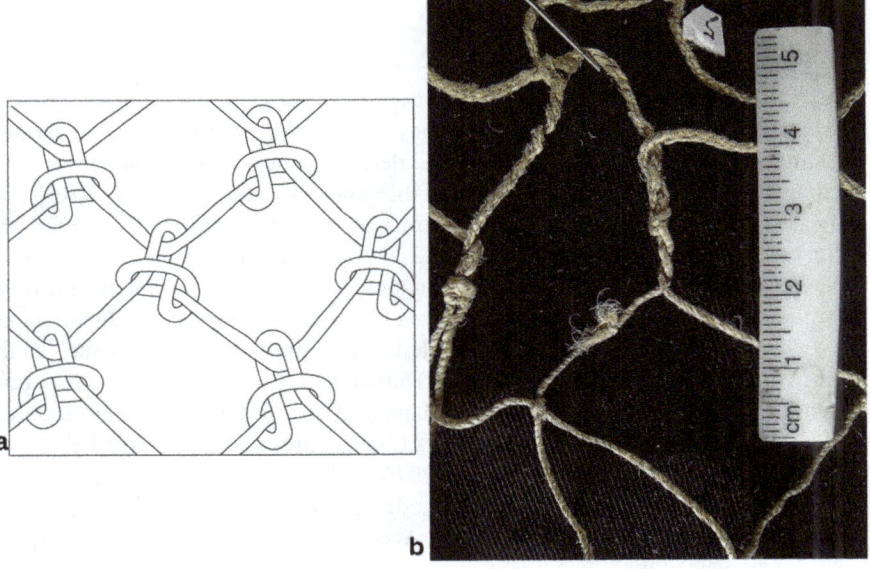

Fig. 10.4 (**a**) Diagram of the flat sheet bend knot (Drawn by Mrs. A. Pundik); (**b**) A repair knot showing wear and tear in the CoL net mesh. (Photo: Naama Sukenik by Dino lite)

generally proven to be the predominant knot type, followed by square knots used in the manufacture of nets (Levy, 2020, 163). Both methods are very simple technologies that belong to the manual weaving techniques that do not require great skill or special tools and are usually only made with net needles but can also be tied by hand (Wendrich, 1989, 179; Alfaro Giner, 2010, 57). Close examination of the net reveals that some of the string and cords have been repaired (Fig. 10.4b), suggesting that the net has seen extensive use in the past and was torn and repaired in several places before it was brought to the cave.

10.3 The Question of the Use of the CoL Net

In the following lines, we examine again the possibilities of using a large net as found in the cave from an archaeological, zooarchaeological, anthropological and ornithological point of view. The proposal is also examined in the archaeological context, with reasonable use being based on the environment in which it was found (cf. Mithen et al., 2022) and the political realities that forced the inhabitants to hide in the cliff-side caves. Unfortunately, this investigation does not include residue analysis as the net was cleaned for restoration purposes in the mid 1970s and all residue, if any, was removed.

10.3.1 Gladiator Net

The retiarius was one of the different types of gladiators that made up the Roman gladiator games (Manas, 2018). The name derives from rete (net), one of his main weapons, which distinguishes him from the other gladiators (Manas, 2016, 704, 2018). The retiarius gladiator's equipment was influenced by the fisherman and included a trident (or harpoon; fascina) and a net (Manas, 2016; Junkelmann, 2000). Since no nets survive, only minimal information is available on the net that the retiarius gladiator fended off, or entrapped, his opponents in the arena (Junkelmann, 2000). The information currently available is based only on visual arts such as the Madrid mosaics (third century AD; Fig. 10.5a) depicting a retiarius named Kalendio fighting a secutor named Astyanax (Manas, 2016) and ancient literature (e.g B. Satires II). Manas estimated the net to be circular in shape and likely to be between 3 and 4 m in diameter (Manas, 2016, 704). Weights like those attached to fishing nets were probably attached to the edge of the net to tie up the opponent and overcome his defenses (Wisdom, 2003). According to experimental mock-ups, it has been suggested that the cords of the nets were 0.7–1 cm in diameter and made of hemp (*Cannabis sativa*) to maintain the defenses of the captured opponent, who was armed with edged weapons (cf. Manas, 2016). Hemp is taller and stronger than flax and its fibers are coarser. It was not generally used for clothing but rather for sails, rope and nets (Alfaro Giner, 2010, 66). Therefore, despite the methodological

Fig. 10.5 (**a**) Part of the Madrid mosaics. The retiarius Kalendio captures the secutor Astyanax in his net. Late third century. National Archaeological Museum (Image taken from this website., Public domain, via Wikimedia Commons); (**b**) Roman mosaic (third century) showing fishmen at work, villa Nile (Leptis Magna) Libya (Marco Prins, CC0, via Wikimedia Commons); (**c**) Netting Birds, Tomb of Khnumhotep, (Nina de Garis Davies Nina M. Davies, CC0, via Wikimedia Commons)

problems with this determination, since it is not based on archaeological finds, we hold the view that a net made of relatively thin linen yarn, such as the CoL net with a cord diameter of 1–1.2 mm made of flax, could not withstand the onslaught of sharp metal weapons. In addition, the large surface area of the net would be too cumbersome for a retiarius to deploy. In addition, gladiator combat gear, such as the net, was not typically found in civilian homes; instead, it was given to them just before gladiator fights (Stibel, pers. comm.). Therefore, we think it unlikely that a retiarius net would be found in the cave or private home of a Jewish citizen at Ein Gedi in the Judean Desert. Therefore, we can safely assume that this particular net cannot be considered a gladiator net.

10.3.2 Fishing Net

One of the important functions of net use in antiquity was fishing, which has been extensively described in other studies (Alfaro Giner, 2010; Bekker-Nielsen, 2010; Veldmeijer, 2004; Soria-Trastoy, 2022; Brewer & Friedman, 1989). Although Yadin ruled out this possibility due to the fact that its owner lived on the shores of the Dead

Sea, a few other parameters confirm the fact that it is not a fishing net: the shape of the CoL net, which is characterized by a triangular structure is not typical for fishing nets. According to fine arts in Roman times and ethnographic studies, two main fishing nets were used—the earlier cast net or vertical net (Bekker-Nielsen, 2010). The most common fishing method in Roman times was casting a net, also called a cast-net (Soria-Trastoy, 2022, 247, 249). This is a circular net with small weights distributed around the edge that sinks into the water and envelops the fish before the net is closed (Bekker-Nielsen, 2010, 191; Soria-Trastoy, 2022). It is important to note that archeological cast nets from Egypt were also made of linen fibers but were found with small lead weights still knotted to the net (Soria-Trastoy, 2022, 263). Other methods included purse-seine fishing, which was rectangular in shape and hung vertically in the water, with floats at the top and weights at the bottom to enclose the fish, or casting a round net. Furthermore, the CoL net lacks weights (Alfaro Giner, 2010, 76–79) as well as other fishing gear typical for the fisheries context (Veldmeijer, 2004, 103–104; *e.g.* Fig. 10.5b).

10.3.3 Bird Net

Similar to the Retiarius net, information on bird nets is also limited and few ancient nets have been found in archaeological contexts. On the other hand, the practice of trapping birds was well known in the literature (see for example: Homer, Odyssey 22.468; Aristophanes, The Birds 528, 1083, 1036; Bub, 1991, 12572) and in the visual arts, including Egyptian murals (Bailleul-LeSuer, 2012), hunting scenes in Aegean iconography (Papageorgiou, 2014) and various Roman mosaics (see for example: López Monteagudo, 2010, fig. 8; Ben Abed, 2006, 9, fig. 5.10). These important sources describe different methods of fowling and trapping birds, which were probably chosen by the hunters according to local hunting traditions, but also the biology of the bird. In order to develop the simplest and least expensive methods of trapping birds, bird trapping methods depend on understanding specific bird behaviors (MacPherson, 1897). Besides hunting methods with bows, dogs (Bailleul-LeSuer, 2012, 26) or sticks coated with glue (lime sticks; MacPherson 1897, 29–32; Pliny, NH XVI, 94), there are several methods of hunting birds, aided by the use of nets. The net, which is similar to fishing nets, increases the success of the catch enormously compared to other methods (Alfaro Giner, 2010, 56). Although the evidence is independent and from different sources and periods, it is possible to outline several types of bird nets that were used in antiquity and are still used today (cf. Bub, 1991). The net is sometimes combined with other stimuli, mainly food or other food substrates, or devices to attract birds to the trap (vocals), dogs, etc. (MacPherson, 1897).

A clap net is usually combined with other incentives or devices to lure the birds into the trap (Sebastian, 2005, 371) and is an extremely effective technique for catching large numbers of waterfowl, as detailed in Pharaonic art, Activity associated with bird hunting aimed at making food offerings to the dead in the Egyptian tomb, such as the scene from the Middle Kingdom tomb of Khnumhotep (1897–1878 BC; Fig. 10.5c) or the tomb of Nakht (c. 1400–1390 BC; Bailleul-LeSuer, 2012). This net is held in the coiled position by a spring-loaded clasp. When a flock of birds moves into the trapping zone, the net is released using a drawstring and thrown over the birds. The clap nets depicted in ancient Egypt are hexagonal in shape, set up horizontally and held open by men with ropes (MacPherson, 1897, 271). In some cases, a decoy (Judas bird) was placed near the pond with its leg tied to a post to encourage conspecifics to land in its immediate vicinity (Bailleul-LeSuer, 2012, 24). The clap nets are made of heavy material and have large areas (MacPherson, 1897, 270–277; Slingenberg, 2016) and can even be purchased commercially to this day. This method was suitable for bird hunting along the Nile with various bird species such as ducks and geese (Fig. 10.5c). Another type of clap-net is the traditional clap-net trap, which was also depicted in Egyptian murals (2125–1985 BC; Slingenberg, 2016, 4) but is small and usually intended for hunting a single bird using mechanical methods.

Another method, often depicted in fine art, is a vertical net, suitable for trapping native wildlife and migrants, with cords threaded through the vertical sides, and carried by people, as in hieroglyphs (Houlihan, 1986). A sixth-dynasty relief carving from the mastaba of Mereruka at Saqqara shows four peasants catching a flock of quail (*Coturnix coturnix*) with a (mist?) net. The net pictured is rectangular in shape and two men grab a rope attached to one corner of the net. Catching migrating quail with long nets along the Mediterranean coast was first reported by Diodorus (mid-first century BC); probably described by Homer in the Odyssey. And as if long-winged thrushes or doves fall into a snare set up in a thicket (Homer Odyssey 22.468), and this practice continues to this day (Abd Rabou, 2021). Unlike the clap-net, this net does not have to be very strong (Yosef, personal experience).

As depicted on a mural in Egypt, tree netting is another method used to trap large numbers of birds, especially songbirds, which are usually perched in trees. This is depicted in the fourth Dynasty mural painting in the tomb of Hesi at Saqqara, where a net is thrown over one of the trees to catch small birds (Slingenberg, 2016, 4, fig. 1.1).

Another method was found in the hunting scene mosaic from the House of Laberii at Uthina (Oudhna) in Tunisia, which depicts country life and includes a scene of birds being nudged toward a net trap. This type of net is suitable for catching partridges and other small land prey and is very similar in design to a walk-in trap (Ben Abed, 2006, 98, Fig. 5.10). This net is suitable for birds walking on the ground. It has a triangular shape, increasing the volume with the help of pins, and in shape resembles the CoL net. It is of interest that the triangular shape of the net, with the central section supported by a stick or bush, allows for a narrowing at the end and the handle at the end to be pulled once the birds have entered the hopper, and are weighted and entangled in the net (Bub, 1991, 76, 83). Foraging groups are tricked into entering these funnel traps by laying a trail of grain/maize mash on the ground (for a modern version see Senar et al., 1997). Larger versions of these funnel traps are used at bird migration research stations such as Heligoland in Germany, Kaliningrad in Russia, Chokpak in Kazakhstan, and Eilat in southern Israel (Yosef

& Markovets, 2009). This triangle trap concept has also been used to capture other species such as gazelles (Holzer et al., 2010).

The study area, present-day Israel, is known to be an important migration route for migratory birds in spring and autumn (*e.g.* Yosef & Markovets, 2009). This fact was also recognized by the ancients. The Bible mentions that: Yea, even the stork in the heaven knoweth her appointed times; and the turtledove, and the crane, and the swift observe the time of their coming (Jeremiah 8:7). The capture and consumption of migratory birds, particularly the quail (also known as Pharaoh's quail) was recorded during the Exodus of the Israelites from Egypt under the leadership of the prophet Moses—a wind went out from the Lord and drove quail in from the sea (Numbers 11:31). This suggests that this was a spring migration, just as the birds had just completed their northward crossing of the Sahara Desert and the Red Sea (Zduniak & Yosef, 2008). In addition, quail are known to migrate at night, coinciding with "the time God specified" for their arrival (Numbers 11:32). Each person caught a large number of quail while the migratory flocks flew in from the sea all night, exhausted and were easily collected from the ground. The explicit mention that the quails were two cubits (roughly 3 feet) deep around the camp has led scientists to believe that the quails were flying about three feet off the ground, so with proper equipment, possibly nets, they could easily be caught. In addition to the species caught during the migratory season, rock pigeons (*C. livia*), which breed on ledges and in rock crevices, are local species that are still found in the wild and could support families in the Judean Desert during the Roman siege and were extremely common (Tristram, 1898), Chukar partridge (*Alectoris chukar*) and Sand Partridge (*Ammoperdix heyi*) on the flat plains above them (1 Samuel 26:20; Tristram, 1898). In the Bible, the chukar and the partridge were both grouped under the title kore (Rufer; Wood, 1869, 625; France, 1986, 166; Goodfellow, 2013, 160). The merging of chukars and partridges is also known in ancient times from Greece (Kakkabe) and Turkey (Keklik; Armott, 2007).

10.3.4 Archaeozoology Aspect

In the archaeological record, bird remains (chickens, partridges, pigeons/doves, ducks and geese) are known from Late Bronze and Iron Age sites in the Levant (for a full list of sites see: Perry-Gal et al., 2015; Spiciarich, 2020; Dirrigl et al., 2020). Spiciarich (2020) attributes their presence at sites to some level of environmental stress (such as a drought or the specific inability to obtain meat from large mammals), leading them to resort to alternative wild taxa, mainly fish or poultry. Nonetheless, poultry also appears to be a culinary preference that often appeals to Jewish and Samaritan populations (Fulton et al., 2015; Tamar et al., 2015; Spiciarich et al., 2017). In the case of the Cave of Letters residents, we hypothesize that the two main factors that influenced their subsistance strategy were, first and foremost the dietary stress, and second, the cultural factor.

Unfortunately, the bones in the Cave of Letters were not collected during excavation in the 1960s, preventing archeozoological research in the cave. However, archeozoological finds from other recently excavated sites in the immediate vicinity support the case for the importance of birds (particularly chickens, partridges and pigeons) in the local diet during Roman times. For example, remains of partridges have been found at various sites in Jerusalem (Bouchnick et al., 2010, 122–123, 128–130) and at the Herodium (dated to the time of the Bar Kokhba revolt, Bouchnick, 2016, 483). Rock dove and turtledove (*Streptopelia turtur*) were also important parts of the Jewish diet, and in particular served as portable/compact offerings for pilgrims to the Jewish temple (Hartman et al., 2013; Spiciarich et al., 2017). A study of more than 50 caves in the Judean Desert also found significant numbers of bird and fowl remains (Kolska Horwitz, 2002, Table 1).

The presence of bird remains in the zooarchaeological assemblages of the Judean Desert is well documented in two caves which, like the Cave of Letters, are also located in Nahal Hever: the Cave of Horrors and the Cave of Duba (Perry-Gal, 2023). Although both caves share a similar area and climate, each cave has a very different ratio of bird bones: in the Cave of Horrors (500 m from the Cave of Letters), 60% of the fauna have been identified as birds, particularly rock pigeon (19%) and Chukar partridge (7%). However, birds made up only 5% of the fauna in Duba Cave. It is worth noting that the topographical conditions of the caves are very different: the Cave of Horrors is high in the cliff, a few meters below the Roman siege point, and offers an overview of the cave where the fugitives were hiding and is not easy accessible. In addition, the rock pigeon bones in Cave of Horrors contained little bone other than the humerus (wing bone), mainly concentrated in one location (L.112) and associated with Bar Kokhba period material. This context also included two metal needles and numerous remnants of thin rope and line threads. If these people ate meat at all, catching rock pigeons and other birds (natural residents of the caves) was probably their only option, as was the case for the Cave of Letters dwellers after the Romans set up camp on the plateau above the three caves, erected to prevent their escape.

10.4 Discussion and Conclusion

Nets as a technique for capturing wildlife were a widespread practice in ancient times, often using similar methods and materials, and making the identification and function of net fragments in archaeological contexts all but impossible. In addition, like fishermen and fowlers, the retiarius gladiators apparently had similar instruments and nets at their disposal, which in most cases made their identification difficult. However, in the case of the CoL net, we have the rare opportunity to examine a complete net in an archaeological and geographic context and to determine its potential use. Analysis of the technical aspects of the net, including the raw material, the form and shape of the net, the dimensions of the meshes and threads, the ethnographic comparisons, the archaeological context, and the ornithological perspectives show that the net was used for the purpose of bird hunting. Obviously, given the political nature of the time, bird trapping was not a recreational activity, but to improve the food supply of the refugees who had fled to the caves on the cliffs at the edge of the Dead Sea. This may explain why the net is made of fine, thin-diameter linen cord rather than hemp or thicker cord. Furthermore, based on the archaeozoological background and neighboring faunal assemblages and other biological aspects, we suggest that the rock pigeon was one of the main target species of the cave dwellers.

According to the important information from the letters found in the cave, the cave dwellers were devout Jews (Yadin, 1963; Safrai, 2005). As such, it is a crucial indicator in the list of birds suitable for kosher consumption and allows them to include these birds in their diets in accordance with Jewish dietary laws. In particular, chukars/partridges found in the Judean Desert region were considered kosher and were commonly eaten by the Jewish population.

Archaeological finds in the Cave of Letters, including documents and correspondence, indicate that the inhabitants, who had fled the Roman army, were from the Ein Gedi area (Yadin, 1963, 1971). Therefore, we can assume that the net found in the cave probably came from around Ein Gedi, which is on the shore of the Dead Sea. However, because the Dead Sea is a hypersaline body of water, it is not home to any wildlife, and no birds rest or forage on it (Censi et al., 2017). Therefore, the net could not be used for fowling as there are no places in the Dead Sea where waterfowl would concentrate. Additionally, there are no natural, long-term, or seasonal freshwater reservoirs in the Judean Desert for waterfowl to congregate, whether native breeding species or migratory. We also argue that when Ein Gedi residents fled to the caves with their families, they carried only items that were either valuable to them, such as house keys, important documents, expensive glassware and metal utensils, etc. (Yadin, 1963) or would help to survive during the long siege they endured and hoped to survive. Therefore, carrying a net into the mountains would make sense only if the net was a useful means of catching local wildlife, a practice that would help them survive. Especially in the Judean Desert, where vegetation is limited, pigeons and other local game species were probably an important source of protein necessary for survival.

We compared the CoL net with that of a modern mist net. Although modern nets are now made from synthetic materials, the underlying principles remain the same. The border/rope surrounding the net, currently made of synthetic cord, was formerly made of a heavier material such as date palm. In both nets, the flat sheet-bend is used to create square meshes (rhomboid-shaped; see Fig. 10.4) which are attached to a thin rope (now called trammel lines) that is connected in a ring to the edge rope. The mesh size is 4 cm, similar to the mist nets used today to catch wild birds.

In summary, our argument based on the absence of waterfowl in the Dead Sea or Judean Desert leads us to rule out the possibility of using the CoL net for fowling. We can safely conclude that this net was used to trap local game species such as pigeons/rock pigeons, chukars and sand partridges, probably as a food source for the last remaining members of the Ein Gedi community during the Bar Kokhba uprising.

The CoL net provides evidence of another way people used to diversify their diets and incorporate wild bird species from the region.

References

Abd Rabou, A. F. N. (2021). On the hunting of Common Quail (*Coturnix coturnix*) along the Mediterranean coast of the Gaza Strip, Palestine. *Journal of Natural Studies, 29*, 1–19.

Alfaro Giner, C. (2010). Fishing nets in the ancient world: The historical and archaeological evidence. In T. Bekker-Nielsen & D. B. Casasola (Eds.), *Ancient nets and fishing gear. Proceedings of the international workshop on Nets and fishing gear in Classical antiquity: A first approach* (pp. 55–82). Servicio de Publicaciones de la Universidad de Cadiz/Aarhus University Press.

Armott, W. G. (2007). *Birds in the ancient world: From A to Z*. Routledge.

Bailleul-LeSuer, R. (2012). From kitchen to temple: The practical role of birds in ancient Egypt. In R. Bailleul-Lesuer (Ed.), *Between heaven and earth: Birds in Ancient Egypt* (pp. 23–32). Oriental Institute of Chicago.

Bekker-Nielsen, T. (2010). Fishing in the Roman world. In T. Bekker-Nielsen & D. B. Casasola (Eds.), *Ancient nets and fishing gear. Proceedings of the international workshop on Nets and fishing gear in Classical antiquity: A first approach* (pp. 187–203). Servicio de Publicaciones de la Universidad de Cadiz/Aarhus University Press.

Bekker-Nielsen, T., Casasola, D. B. (2010). *Ancient Nets and Fishing Gears*. Proceedings of the International Workshop on Nets and Fishing Gear in Classical Antiquity: A First Approach. Servicio de Publicaciones de la Universidad de Cadiz/Aarhus University Press

Ben Abed, A. (2006). *Tunisian mosaics: Treasures from Roman Africa (Sharon Greve tran)*. Getty Conservation Institute.

Bouchnick, R. (2016). Finds of animal remains from the excavation on the Northern slope of Herodium. In R. Porat, R. Chachy, & Y. Kalman (Eds.), *Herodium: Final reports of the 1972–2010 excavations directed by Ehud Netzer. Volume I: Herod's tomb Precinct (Herodium)* (pp. 476–503). Israel Exploration Society.

Bouchnick, R., Bar-Oz, G., & Reich, R. (2010). On the importance of poultry in the animal economy of Judea in the Late Second Temple period. In E. A. Baruch, A. Levy-Reifer, & A. Faust (Eds.), *New studies on Jerusalem 16* (pp. 119–140). (Hebrew).

Brewer, J. D., & Friedman, F. R. (1989). *Fish and fishing in ancient Egypt*. Aris and Phillips.

Bub, H. (1991). *Bird trapping and bird banding: A handbook for trapping methods*. Cornell University Press.

Censi, P., Raso, M., Yechieli, Y., Ginat, H., Saiano, F., Zuddas, P., Brusca, L., & D'Alessandro Winguaggato, C. (2017). Geochemistry of Zr, Hf, and REE in a wide spectrum of Eh and water Composition: The case of Dead Sea fault system (Israel). *Geochemistry, Geophysics, Geosystems, 18*, 844–857. https://doi.org/10.1002/2016GC006704

Crowfoot, G. M. (1961). The textiles and basketry. In P. Benoit, J. T. Milik, & R. de Vaux (Eds.), *Discoveries in the Judaean Desert II: Les Grottes De Murabbaʿāt* (pp. 51–63). Clarendon.

Dirrigl, J. F., Brush, T., Morales-Muniz, A., & Bartosiewica, L. (2020). Prehistoric and historical insights in avian zooarchaeology, taphonomy and ancient bird use. *Archaeological and Anthropological Studies, 12*, 57. https://doi.org/10.1007/s12520-020-01016-2

France, P. (1986). *An encyclopedia of Bible animals*. Croom Hel.

Fulton, D. N., Gadot, Y., Kleiman, A., Freud, L., Lernau, O., & Lipschits, O. (2015). Feasting in Paradise: Feast remains from the Iron Age palace of Ramat Raḥel and their implications. *Bulletin of the American Schools of Oriental Research, 374*(1), 29–48.

Goodfellow, P. (2013). *Birds of the Bible*. John Beaufoy Publishing.

Hartman, G., Bar-Oz, G., Bouchnick, R., & Reich, R. (2013). The pilgrimage economy of Early Roman Jerusalem (1st century BCE–70 CE) Reconstructed from the δ15N and δ13C values of goat and sheep remains. *Journal of Archaeological Science, 40*(12), 4369–4376.

Holzer, A., Avner, U., Porat, N., & Horowitz, L. K. (2010). Desert kites in the Negev Desert and Northeast Sinai: Their function, chronology and ecology. *Journal of Arid Environments, 74*, 806–817. https://doi.org/10.1016/j.jaridenv.2009.12.001

Houlihan, P. F. (1986). *The Birds of ancient Egypt*. Aris and Phillips.

Junkelmann, M. (2000). Familia gladiatoria: The heroes of the Amphitheatre. In E. Köhne & C. Ewigleben (Eds.), *Gladiators and Caesars: The power of spectacle in ancient Rome* (pp. 31–74). British Museum Press.

Kolska Horwitz, L. (2002). The fauna from caves in the northern Judean Desert. *Atiqot, 41*(2), 257–280.

Levy, J. (2020). *The genesis of the textile industry from adorned nudity to ritual regalia*. Archaepress Publishing.

López Monteagudo, G. (2010). Nets and fishing gear in Roman mosaics from Spain. In T. Bekker-Nielsen & D. B. Casasola (Eds.), *Ancient nets and fishing gear. Proceedings of the international workshop on Nets and fishing gear in Classical antiquity: A first approach* (pp. 161–185). Servicio de Publicaciones de la Universidad de Cadiz/Aarhus University Press.

Lupo, K. D., & Schmidtt, D. N. (2002). Upper Paleolithic net-hunting, small prey exploitation, and women's work effort: A view from the ethnographic and ethnoarchaeological record of the Congo Basin. *Journal of Archaeological Method and Theory, 9*(2), 147–179.

MacPherson, H. A. (1897). *A History of Fowling*. Edinburgh. David Douglas.

Manas, A. (2016). Evolution of the *Retiarius* fighting technique: Abandoning the net? *International Journal of the History of Sport, 33*, 704–733.

Manas, A. (2018). Was Pontarii fighting the origin of the gladiator-type Retiarius? An analysis of the evidence. *International Journal of the History of Sport*. https://doi.org/10.1080/09523367.2017.1402760

Mithen, S., White, J., Finlayson, B., Greet, B., & Khoury, F. (2022). Birds as indicators of early Holocene biodiversity and the seasonal nature of human activity at WF16, an early Neolithic site in Faynan, Southern Jordan. *Journal of Quaternary Science, 37*(6), 1148–1163. https://doi.org/10.1002/jqs.3429

Papageorgiou, I. (2014). The Practice of bird hunting in the Aegean of the Second Millennium BC: An investigation. *Annual of the British School at Athens, 109*, 111–128.

Perry-Gal, L. (2023). Two caves, two Stories? Reconstructing environmental and anthropogenic activities in Judean Desert Caves: A Zooarchaeological view. In O. Sion, J. Uziel, A. Ganor, E. Klein, New Studies in the Archaeology of the Judean Desert: Collected Papers (pp. 359–386). The Israel Antiquities Authority.

Perry-Gal, L., Erlich, A., Gilboa, A., & Bar-Oz, G. (2015). Earliest economic exploitation of chicken outside East Asia: Evidence from the Hellenistic Southern Levant. *Proceedings of the National Academy of Sciences, 112*(32), 9849–9854.

Safrai, Z. (1994). *The economy of Roman Palestine*. Routledge.

Safrai, Z. (2005). Halakhic observance in the Judaean Desert documents. In R. Katzoff & D. Schaps (Eds.), *Law in the documents of the Judaean Desert* (pp. 205–236). Leiden.

Sebastian, A. (2005). Papageno down the ages: *A study in fowling methods, with particular reference to the Palaeolithic of Western Europe*. Munibe Anthropology - Archeology 57, 369–397.

Senar, J. C., Domenech, J., Carrascal, L. M., & Moreno, E. (1997). A funnel trap for the capture of tits. *Bulletin GCA, 14*, 17–24.

Shamir, O. (1999). Textiles, basketry and cordage from 'En Raḥel. *Atiqot, 38*, 99–124.

Shamir, O. (2005). Textiles, Basketry, Cordage and Whorls from Mo'a (Moje Awad). *Atiqot 50*, 99–152.

Shamir, O. (2015). Textiles from the Chalcolithic period, Early and Middle Bronze Age in the southern Levant. *Archaeological Textiles Review, 57*, 12–25.

Sheffer, A., & Granger-Taylor, H. (1994). Textiles From Masada—A preliminary selection. In J. Aviram, G. Foerster, & E. Netzer (Eds.), *Masada IV* (pp. 153–256). Israel Exploration Society and The Hebrew University of Jerusalem.

Slingenberg, M. J. (2016). *'Catch me if you can'—Bird trapping with a hexagonal net in the 'daily life' scenes in the Old Kingdom elite tombs of the Memphite Area.* Master thesis in Classics and Ancient Civilizations, track Egyptology. Leiden University.

Soria-Trastoy, M.T. (2022). Fishing with Cast Nets in Ancient Egypt. *Journal of Maritime Archaeology 17*, 245–326.

Spiciarich, A., Gadot, Y., & Sapir-Hen, L. (2017). The faunal evidence from Early Roman Jerusalem: The people behind the Garbage. *Tel Aviv, 44*(1), 98–117.

Spiciarich, A. (2020). Birds in Transition: Bird Exploitation in the Southern Levant During the Late Bronze Age, *Iron Age I, and Iron Age II. Bulletin of the American Schools of Oriental Research, 383*, 61–78.

Sukenik, N., & Tepper, Y. (2019). A linen wick from the northern church at Shivta, Israel. In I. Motsianos & K. S. Garnett (Eds.), *Glass, wax and metal: Lighting technologies in late antique, Byzantine and Medieval Times* (pp. 203–209). Archaepress Publishing.

Tamar, K., Bar-Oz, G., Bunimovitz, S., Lederman, Z., & Dayan, T. (2015). Geography and economic preferences as cultural markers in a border town: The faunal remains from Tel Beth-Shemesh. *Israel. International Journal of Osteoarchaeology, 25*(4), 414–425.

Tristram, H. B. (1898). *The natural history of the Bible: A review of the physical geography, geology, and meteorology of the Holy Land; with a description of every animal and plant mentioned in the Holy Scripture.* Society for the Promotion of Christian Knowledge, Adamant Media Corporation.

Veldmeijer, A. J. (2004). Fishing nets from Berenike (Egyptian Red Sea coast). *Papers on Ancient Egypt, 3*, 99–110.

Veldmeijer, A. J. (2009). Cordage production. In W. Wendrich (Ed.), *UCLA encyclopedia of egyptology.* http://digital2.library.ucla.edu/viewItem.do?ark=21198/zz001ndr4n

Veldmeijer, A. J., & van Roode, S. M. (2004). Carrier netting from the Ptolemaic Roman harbour town of Berenike (Egyptian Red Sea coast). *Antiguo Oriente, 2*, 9–25.

Wendrich, W. (1989). Preliminary report on the Amarna basketry and cordage. In B. J. Kamp (Ed.), *Amarna Report V* (pp. 169–201). Egypt Exploration Society.

Wisdom, S. (2003). *Gladiators 100 BC–AD 200* (Warrior Series no. 39). Osprey Publishing.

Wood, J. G. (1869). *Bible animals.* Guelph. J.W. Lyon and Company Publishers.

Yadin, Y. (1963). *The finds from the Bar Kokhba period in the Cave of Letters.* The Israel Exploration Society.

Yadin, Y. (1971). *Bar Kokhba—The rediscovery of the legendary hero of the second Jewish revolt against Rome.* Weidenfeld and Nicolson (Hebrew).

Yosef, R., & Markovets, M. (2009). Spring bird migration phenology at Eilat. *Israel ZooKeys, 31*, 193–210.

Zduniak, P., & Yosef, R. (2008). Age and sex determine the phenology and biometrics of migratory Common Quail (*Coturnix coturnix*) at Eilat, Israel. *Ornis Fennica, 85*, 37–45.

Zohary, D., Hopf, M., & Weiss, E. (2013). *Domestication of plants in the old world* (4th ed.). Oxford University Press.

Index

A
Abdel-Kareem, O., 75
Abrasive wear, 163
Accelerator mass spectrometry (AMS), 6, 124–126, 128, 130–133
Aceto, M., 75
Actual use, 6–8, 160, 165, 168, 169, 172
Amber, 7
Analytical protocols, 3, 7, 73, 111, 162, 165–168
Armitage, R.A., 94
Artisans, 160–162
Asbestos, 4, 5, 57–67
Azémard, C., 104, 105, 108, 109

B
Barone, S., 123–135
Bast fibres, 4, 14, 29, 30, 33, 38, 47, 49, 51, 164, 167, 168
Birds, 172, 177–183
Bones, 7, 13, 26, 39, 102, 126, 159, 160, 162, 181
Bosi, A., 81
Bruni, S., 78
Burials, 4, 7, 12, 13, 18, 26, 28, 38–40, 60, 72, 84, 105, 109, 110, 160
Busana, M.S., 4, 15, 143
Buttons, 26–40

C
Campos Ayala, J., 93
Carbonisation, 44–53, 129
Chaîne opératoire, 3, 161
Ciccola, A., 57–67, 72–114
Ciccola, I., 5
Cleland, T.P., 72–114
Clementi, C., 75
Clothing, 28, 38, 39, 176
Coletti, F., 2–8, 44–53, 57–67, 124–135, 166
Cotton, 4, 29, 30, 33, 37, 39, 40, 46, 49, 50, 78, 80, 81, 85, 95, 127, 164
Crafts, 2, 3, 7, 161

D
Degano, I., 78
Degradation, 12, 47, 49, 51, 72, 85, 86, 88, 89, 91, 94, 102, 105, 109–111, 128, 130, 159, 164, 165
de Palaminy, L., 98, 99
Dinolite, 13
Dong Su, I., 49
Dyer, J., 75, 87
Dyes, 2, 72

E
Excavations, 6, 28, 30, 31, 39, 40, 44–46, 51, 52, 58, 60, 61, 105, 124, 164, 166, 169, 172, 181
Experimental archaeology, 7, 8, 140, 160–162, 165, 168

F
Fatigue wear, 162
Favero, G., 71–114

Fedi, M., 129
Fibre identification, 12–14, 16
Fibre processing, 7
Fibres, 3, 11, 44, 57, 72, 124, 144, 159, 173
Finland, 4, 26–40
Flax, 4, 7, 14–16, 27–31, 39, 40, 46, 49–51, 173, 174, 176, 177
Fonseca, B., 74
Forte, V., 2–8, 159–169
Fourier-transform infrared spectroscopy (FTIR), 5, 78, 82, 95–101, 104
Francisci, D., 148
Funerary rituals, 4, 12, 60, 140

G
Gabra-Sanders, T., 17
Germinario, G., 81, 95
Glass, 7, 29, 62, 65
Gleba, M., 4, 14

H
Hailuoto Island, 26
Hemp, 28, 30, 35, 40, 46, 49–51, 88, 176, 182
Hooks, 26–40

I
Iron age, 166, 180
Iron age period, 166, 180
Israel, 8, 173, 174, 179, 180
Italian peninsula, 58, 59
Italy, 4, 12, 18, 59, 60, 161, 166

J
Jaia, A.M., 7, 159–169
Judean desert, 8, 172, 177, 180–182

K
Kania, K., 154
Kavich, G.M., 71–114
Kramell, A.E., 92–94, 96

L
Laursen, R.A., 89
Lee, B., 113
Lemorini, C., 7, 167

Lena, A., 140–156
Leona, M., 80, 91
Liccioli, L., 132
Life-cycle, 160, 168
Linens, 26, 28, 29, 38, 127, 173–175, 177, 178, 182
Lipkin, S., 4, 26–40
Lofrumento, C., 80
Loom weights, 7, 160, 161, 168

M
Margariti, C., 2–8, 44–53
McGregor, B.A., 96, 97
Microscopy, 3–5, 8, 13, 29, 32–38, 45, 61–63, 96, 103, 127, 128, 130
Mineralisation, 4, 11, 12, 15, 17, 18, 129
Mineralised textiles, 11, 12, 15, 17, 18
Modified Herzog test, 4, 29, 31, 35, 38, 39
Morphological analyses, 4, 5, 59, 61, 63, 66, 96, 130, 133
Moulhérat, C., 17
Multi-technical approach, 6, 72–114

N
Nakamura, R., 76
Net, 8, 59, 172
Nettle, 4, 30, 37, 39, 46, 49–51
North eastern Italy, 7, 18, 140

O
Optical microscopy, 4, 59, 61, 104, 127, 130
Organic residues, 161, 163–168

P
Paduli, 161, 166, 168
Peets, P., 100
Perry-Gal, L., 8, 172–182
Peruzzi, G., 74
Plant fibres, 4, 14–16, 26–40, 50
Pompeii, 4, 44–53, 59, 60, 67, 110, 124, 129, 134, 135
Post-depositional, 44, 160, 162, 164, 165, 169
Postorino, P., 5, 57–67
Proteins, 6, 12, 72–114, 132, 182
Proteomics, 6, 104, 105, 109, 110, 112–113
Protocols, 2, 4, 5, 7, 82, 85, 89, 92, 95, 111, 114, 161–163, 165, 168, 169

R

Radiocarbon dating, 6, 124–129, 135
Raman, 5, 6, 59, 60, 62, 65–67, 77–81, 101
Rast-Eicher, A., 17, 18
Raw materials, 2, 12, 16–18, 58, 78, 88, 114, 127, 129, 173, 181
Replicas, 7, 160–165
Residues, 3, 5, 7–8, 35, 37, 40, 83, 84, 86, 90, 103, 104, 110, 111, 160–169, 176
Roman age, 12, 13, 58, 140, 178, 181
Roman Empire, 2, 18, 111
Roman period, 12, 129, 174
Roman *Venetia*, 14
Rosi, F., 79
Ryder, M.L., 17, 18

S

Saiful Islam Khan, M., 63
Scanning electron microscopy (SEM), 4, 11–18, 46, 49, 61, 63, 88, 90, 127, 130, 133, 164, 167
Selberg, S., 76, 77
Serafini, I., 72–114
Sheep wool, 16, 46
Silks, 4, 6, 28, 45, 46, 51, 61, 78, 80, 83, 84, 88, 90–93, 95, 97–99, 101–105, 110, 111, 124, 127, 129, 130, 132–135
Skłodowska-Curie, M., 6
Solazzo, C., 72–114
Spantidaki, S., 2–8
Spectroscopic techniques, 5, 73–82, 101
Spindle-whorls, 7, 145, 160–169
Spinning techniques, 151, 160, 162
Spinning tools, 140, 142
Sukenik, N., 8, 175
Suomela, J.A., 4, 26–40
Szostek, B., 94

T

Tamburini, D., 74, 75
Textile crafts, 12, 159

Textile fibres, 44–53, 59, 128
Textile production, 2, 12, 66, 67, 86, 140, 156
Textile residue, 5, 7, 161, 165–169
Textiles, 2, 11, 44, 57, 72, 124, 140, 159, 173
Textile tools, 2, 3, 7, 160–169
Thermal degradation, 4, 46–48, 50–53

U

Use wear, 7, 160–165, 168
Use wear analysis, 161, 169
Use wear and residue analysis, 166

V

Van Elslande, E., 92
Vesuvian area, 6, 18, 51, 129, 135
Virili, C., 7, 163
Volcanic eruptions, 18, 45, 53, 72

W

Wallert, A., 75, 76
Weaving techniques, 165, 176
Wood, 39, 45, 76, 127, 163–165, 180
Wool, 4, 16, 45, 76, 127, 140, 164
Wyeth, P., 98
Wyplosz, N., 92

Y

Yadin, Y., 172, 173, 177
Yarns, 7, 12, 26, 30, 31, 33, 35, 37, 39, 44, 46, 58, 61, 76, 81, 83, 85, 86, 88, 89, 94, 95, 97, 98, 130, 162–164, 174, 177
Yosef, R., 8, 177

Z

Zhang, L., 91
Zhang, X., 89
Zhang, X.M., 98